macromedia®
freehand®mx
training from the source

patti schulze

macromedia®
PRESS

Macromedia FreeHand MX: Training from the Source

 Published by Macromedia Press, in association with Peachpit Press, a division of Pearson Education.

Macromedia Press
1249 Eighth Street
Berkeley, CA 94710
510/524-2178
510/524-2221 (fax)
Find us on the World Wide Web at:
http://www.peachpit.com
http://www.macromedia.com

Printed and bound in the United States of America

ISBN 0-321-17916-1

9 8 7 6 5 4 3 2

CREDITS

Author
Patti Schulze

Editor
Wendy Sharp

Copy Editor
Judy Ziajka

Production Coordinator
Myrna Vladic

Compositor
Patti Schulze

Indexer
Julie Bess

Technical Review
David W Gangwisch

Cover Production
George Mattingly, GMD

This edition is based upon materials developed by:
Digital Training & Designs, Inc.

Many thanks to everyone who helped me with this book: Joan Hilbert, Digital Training & Designs, who patiently read through many iterations of this book, and all the staff at Digital Training & Designs, who took over as I wrote this book.

This book is dedicated to my Mom and Dad; Dad gave me my strength, Mom gave me my vision.

table of contents

introduction

FreeHand MX is a powerful illustration tool that enables designers and web developers to create rich graphics for print, the Internet, and Macromedia Flash projects. With FreeHand MX, you can start with a concept for a project, create the graphics, and then publish your work, all while working within a single document. Not only can you create multipage documents, but each page can be a different size, making file management an easier task. Your documents can also be multipurposed: you can create illustrations or logos for print, and then add animation and interactivity for use online.

This Macromedia Training from the Source guide introduces you to the major features of FreeHand MX by taking you step by step through the process of creating several types of illustrations. The book assumes that you are new to FreeHand, and thus you begin by creating a simple logo for a company using the basic drawing tools: the Rectangle tool, the Ellipse tool, and the Line tool. As you get more proficient with the drawing tools, you will learn to use layers to help you manage your illustrations, and then you will learn to use the Bezigon tool and the Pen tool, FreeHand's main drawing instruments. The last two lessons in this book show you how to create Macromedia Flash animations and movies and how to export your pages as SWF, PDF, or HTML files.

The curriculum of this course should take you 20 to 24 hours to complete and includes the following lessons:

Lesson 1: FreeHand Basics

Lesson 2: Adding Pages and Text

Lesson 3: Colors, Gradients, and Styles

Lesson 4: Using Layers

Lesson 5: Using Points and Paths

Lesson 6: Adding Special Effects

Lesson 7: Page Layout and Printing

Lesson 8: Symbols, Brushes, and Hoses

Lesson 9: Creating Animations and Movies

Lesson 10: Creating Web Pages

SETTING UP THE LESSON FILES

All of the files you need to complete this course are included on the accompanying CD. Copy the Lessons folder to your hard drive before you start the lessons. Each lesson has its own folder, with three additional folders inside: Start, Media, and Completed. Start files are those you use as you begin and work through each lesson. The Completed files show how the files should appear at the end of the lesson. The Media folder contains additional graphics you may need to complete the lesson.

As you work through the lessons, you will open files within the Lessons folder on your hard drive. If you are working on a Windows machine, the files you copy from the Lessons folder on the CD may be locked. If you do not unlock the files, you may get a warning message when you open them.

In Lesson 1, you will create the camera as a logo for a fictitious company. In Lesson 3, you will draw the film canister and then add the film strip in Lesson 4.

In Lesson 5, you will draw a bicycle using the Bezigon tool and draw the rider and the background with the Pen tool.

ACTION PHOTOS

USING THIS BOOK

Each lesson begins with an overview of its contents and what you can expect to learn. Lessons are divided into focused, bite-size tasks to build your FreeHand skills. Each lesson builds on what you've learned in previous lessons.

Each lesson also includes these special features:

Tips: These highlight shortcuts for performing common tasks or ways you can use your new FreeHand skills to solve common problems.

Power Tips: These highlight productivity shortcuts.

Notes: These provide background information about a feature or task.

Italic terms: Italics are used to indicate the exact text or file name you need to enter in a dialog box or panel as you work through the steps in a lesson.

Menu commands and keyboard shortcuts: Alternative methods for executing commands appear in special formats. Menu commands are shown like this: Menu › Command › Subcommand. Keyboard shortcuts are shown like this: Ctrl+Z (Windows) or Command+Z (Mac OS). The + between the names of the keys means that you should press both keys simultaneously. Both Windows and Macintosh commands are always included.

MACROMEDIA TRAINING FROM THE SOURCE

Each book in the Macromedia Training from the Source series includes a complete curriculum that has been reviewed by Macromedia's own product support teams. The lesson plans were developed by some of Macromedia's most successful trainers and refined through long experience to meet students' needs. We believe that Macromedia Training from the Source books offer the best possible training for Macromedia programs.

The instructions in this book are designed for those wanting to learn to use FreeHand MX.

The lessons assume the following:

- You are familiar with the basics of your operating system, including the use of the menu system and file management.
- FreeHand MX is installed, and your system meets the requirements needed to run it.

WHAT YOU WILL LEARN

By the end of this course, you will be able to:

- Use FreeHand to create colorful, vector-based graphics for print and the web
- Combine text and graphics to create multipage layouts
- Work with points and paths to create exciting illustrations
- Use layers to organize your drawings and create movies
- Use the Navigation panel to add links for HTML pages
- Use FreeHand with Macromedia Flash to create web animations
- Use the Connector tool to create a site map
- Globally change objects using symbols
- Use the Extrude tool to create 3D-like objects

SYSTEM REQUIREMENTS

Windows

- Macromedia FreeHand MX, Macromedia Flash MX, Macromedia Fireworks MX (In case you don't own copies of these applications, we've provided 30-day trial versions on the CD.)

- Intel Pentium II processor or equivalent, 300+ MHz

- Windows 98SE, Windows Me, Windows 2000, Windows NT version 4 (Service Pack 6), or Windows XP

- 96MB of available RAM (128MB recommended)

- 70MB available disk space

- CD-ROM drive

- Color monitor capable of 1024 x 768 pixel resolution and 16-bit display (thousands of colors, millions of colors recommended)

- Type Manager version 4 or later with Type 1 fonts, and a PostScript Level 2–compatible printer or later (recommended).

Macintosh

- Macromedia FreeHand MX, Macromedia Flash MX, Macromedia Fireworks MX (In case you don't own copies of these applications, we've provided 30-day trial versions on the CD.)

- Power Mac G3 or better

- Mac OS 9.1 or higher, or Mac OS X 10.1 or higher

- 96MB of RAM (128MB recommended)

- 70MB available disk space

- Color monitor capable of 1024 x 768 pixel resolution and 16-bit display (thousands of colors, millions of colors recommended)

- Adobe Type Manager version 4 or later with Type 1 fonts (Mac OS 9.x), a PostScript Level 2–compatible printer or later (recommended), and QuickTime 6 (Mac OS 9.x).

freehand basics

Macromedia FreeHand is a powerful application that you can use for your creative projects, whether they are for print or the web. Designed originally as a tool for creating line art for print, FreeHand has grown to be a tremendous tool for all your graphic projects and ideas. For example, you can use FreeHand to draw a logo for your company, create business cards and letterheads and other marketing materials, storyboard your web site, and even create Macromedia Flash presentations. Although Macromedia Flash is a powerful web animation tool, FreeHand has better drawing tools. The two applications work together, giving designers a commanding set of tools for creating everything necessary for print or motion graphics.

This lesson introduces you to the FreeHand MX interface and shows you how you can customize your workspace. You then use some of the basic drawing tools to create a logo for a fictitious company.

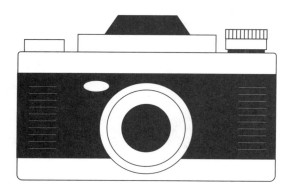

In this lesson, you will draw the camera using the basic drawing tools.

WHAT YOU WILL LEARN

In this lesson, you will:

- Learn about the FreeHand MX interface
- Customize your workspace
- Combine basic shapes to create a complex image
- Use the Knife tool to create two objects from one
- Group several objects into a single object

APPROXIMATE TIME

This lesson takes approximately 2 hours to complete.

LESSON FILES

Media Files:
None

Starting Files:
None

Completed Projects:
Lesson01\Completed\camera.fh11

LEARNING THE MX INTERFACE

When you first open Macromedia FreeHand MX, you see the MX workspace. If you are familiar with other Macromedia Studio MX products such as Macromedia Fireworks MX, Dreamweaver MX, or Macromedia Flash MX, you'll feel right at home using the FreeHand MX interface. If this is your first experience with an MX product, be sure to read the section "Floating and Docked Panel Groups" later in this lesson.

EXPLORING THE FREEHAND TOOLS PANEL

FreeHand has a variety of tools you can choose by clicking the tool on the **Tools panel** or by using the shortcut key shown in the following figure. If a tool has a small black triangle in the bottom right corner, it is part of a group of tools; hold down the mouse button on the tool to access the pop-up tool group.

For example, hold down the mouse button on the Rectangle tool to see the other tool (the Polygon tool) in this group. If the Tools panel is not open, choose Window > Tools. The shortcut key for the Rectangle tool is R; you can press this key to select that tool. When you roll over each tool on the Tools panel, tool tips display the tool name and the shortcut key.

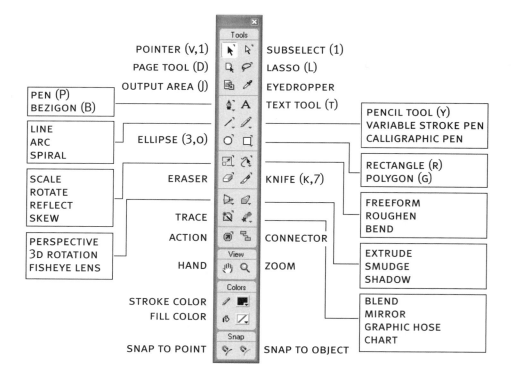

FREEHAND MX TOOLS PANEL

FLOATING AND DOCKED PANEL GROUPS

When you first launch FreeHand, you'll see some of the **panels** within their **panel groups docked** together in the docking area on the right side of the screen. You can move, separate, or customize these panel groups. The panels and panel groups can be opened, closed, docked, expanded, or collapsed. You determine the configuration based on your needs and monitor space. In Windows, the docked panels are part of the application window. In Mac OS, the docked panels **float** above the document window. The panels initially appear on the right side of the screen, but you can move them wherever you like.

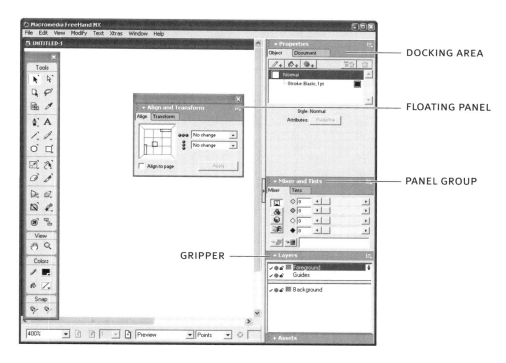

Not all of the panels are initially docked together. For example, choose Window > Align. A panel group named Align and Transform opens, floating on top of your workspace. This panel group consists of the Align and Transform panels. Click a panel tab to select a panel.

If you want to dock the Align and Transform panel group in the docking area, move the pointer over the left side of the panel, over the dotted area, called the **gripper**. The pointer changes to a four-pointed arrow in Windows and to a hand in Mac OS. When you see this pointer, drag the panel to the panel group. When you release the mouse button, the panel group is docked with the other panel group. To remove a panel or panel group from the docked group, move the pointer over the gripper until the pointer changes as before; then drag the panel or panel group from the docked area.

9

In Windows, you can collapse the docking area on the right to create a larger working area for your drawing. Click the expander arrow to collapse the docking area; click the arrow again to expand the docking area.

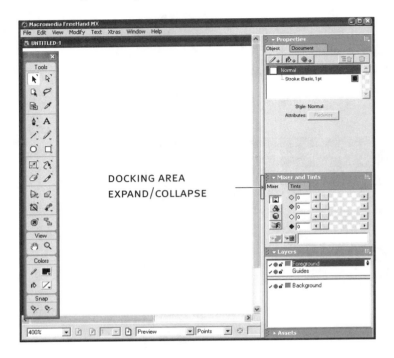

CREATING A NEW DOCUMENT

You will now see how to create a new document. Before you start, copy the Lessons folder from the CD provided with this book to your hard drive if you haven't done so already. Create a new folder within the Lessons folder and name it *Projects*. You will save all of the work you create within that folder. When you launch FreeHand, you will see the application window and menus, toolbars, and several panels.

1) Choose File > New to create a new, empty document.

A document window appears with a new page. Pages you create in FreeHand float on the **pasteboard**, an area 222 by 222 inches. You can place as many pages in your document as can fit within the pasteboard area. You can also use the pasteboard to temporarily store elements you are working with in your document. Just drag the elements outside the page boundaries to move them to the pasteboard until you need them again. Keep in mind that elements on the pasteboard will not print and won't be included when you export your pages.

After you finalize your drawing, you'll want to delete those objects still on the pasteboard. If you leave them on the pasteboard, they just increase the file size of your document.

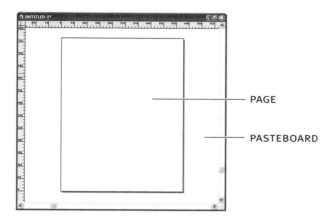

TIP   *If you don't see the entire page, choose View > Fit to Page.*

2) Choose File > Save As and save your file in the Projects folder and name it *camera.fh11*.

In Windows, the .fh11 extension is added automatically to the file name. In Mac OS, the extension is not added to the file name. Although it is not needed for Macintosh computers, it is always a good idea to add the correct extension for your files, especially if you share files with Windows users.

TIP   *When naming your files, think ahead to where you might be using them. For example, if you are creating a logo or graphic that will be used on a web page, don't use spaces in the file name. Instead of naming your file camera logo.fh11, name it camera_logo.fh11, adding an underscore in place of the space. In addition, use lowercase letters for the file name.*

ADDING RULER GUIDES TO THE PAGE

The page **rulers** are handy measuring tools that appear at the top and left of the document window. The page rulers do not appear by default, but they are easy to turn on and off as you need them. In fact, they are so helpful that you may want to change your default settings to include them each time you create a new document. You'll see how to do that in Lesson 2. For now, you'll simply turn on the rulers and drag some **guides** onto the page.

1) Choose View > Page Rulers > Show.

The rulers are added to the document window. A check mark appears next to the Show command to indicate that the rulers are on. When you want to hide the rulers, choose the command again.

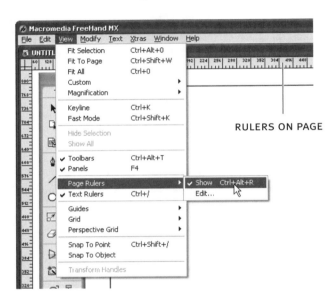

RULERS ON PAGE

The rulers use the current document measuring units. You can change the units to picas, inches, decimal inches, millimeters, kyus, centimeters, or pixels.

NOTE *A kyu (pronounced "Q") is a metric unit of distance used in typography, especially in Japanese text. It was originally written as Q and is equal to exactly 0.25 millimeter, or about 0.71 of a point.*

2) Click the Units pop-up menu and pick Points from the list.

The Units pop-up menu is located on the Status toolbar in Windows and at the bottom of the document window in Mac OS. If you are working in Windows and don't see the Status toolbar, choose Window > Toolbars > Status. The unit of measure you choose affects the ruler guides and all other measurements except for text-related settings; for example, text size is always expressed in points.

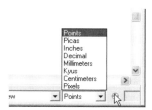

3) Position the pointer on the top ruler and drag down and onto the page.

As you drag, you'll see the blue horizontal line guide. When you have the guide where you want it to appear, release the mouse button. For this exercise, position the guide in the middle of the page. If you need to move the guide, position the pointer directly on the line and then drag the guide. The pointer changes to a cursor with a small arrow at the bottom right when it is on the guide.

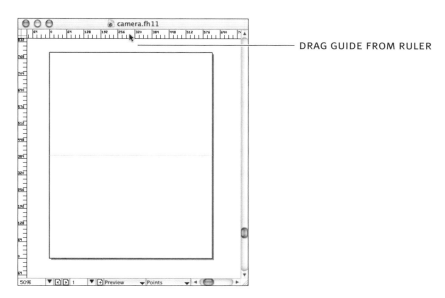

DRAG GUIDE FROM RULER

NOTE *Make sure the pointer is within the area of the page when you release the mouse button. Guides don't appear if the pointer is on the pasteboard when you release the mouse button.*

4) Position the pointer on the left ruler and drag right and onto the page.

Drag the vertical guide to the middle of the page.

Guides are nonprinting aids to help you place objects on the page. When you no longer need them, you can simply drag them off the page. If you want to leave the guides but not see them, choose View > Guides > Show to toggle them off and on.

NOTE *If you want to move a guide, drag the guide with the Pointer tool. When the pointer is on a guide, a down- or left-pointing arrow is added to the cursor. If you want to remove a guide, just drag it off the page.*

 POINTER OVER VERTICAL GUIDE

DRAWING THE CAMERA

The best way to learn the tools in FreeHand is to use them to draw something. In this exercise, you will create a simple drawing of a camera that will be used in the logo for a fictitious company, called Action Photos. You will use the basic drawing tools—the Ellipse, Line, and Rectangle tools—to draw the camera. You'll see that by combining simple shapes, you can draw complex objects, even if you think you can't draw a straight line!

The camera you will draw is composed of several elements that need to be centered on each other. FreeHand provides alignment tools that you can use to align objects to each other, but in this exercise you will use the intersection of the guides on the page to center the objects as you draw them.

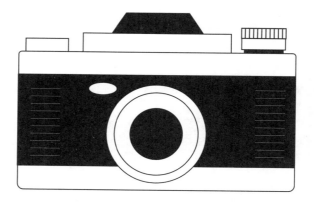

USING THE RECTANGLE TOOL

The Rectangle tool is one of the basic drawing tools. With it, you can draw rectangles (of course), squares, and rounded-corner rectangles and squares. You'll use this tool to draw most of the camera.

1) Select the Rectangle tool from the Tools panel.

If you don't see the Tools panel, choose Window > Tools.

The cursor changes to a plus.

RECTANGLE TOOL

2) Choose Window > Toolbars > Info.

The **Info toolbar** displays information about objects as you draw them. In Windows, some of the same information appears on the **Status toolbar**, so you may not need to open the Info toolbar.

TIP *The Info toolbar floats on top of the document window and can be moved to any location you wish. If you prefer to leave it open but out of the way, you can dock it below the menu bar. Drag the toolbar to the top of your screen. It will dock itself as it touches the menu bar. You can then move it left or right depending on the size of your monitor. To release it from the menu bar, drag it down. Other toolbars dock in this fashion as well. If you have a large monitor, you can dock those toolbars you use frequently to make them easier to access.*

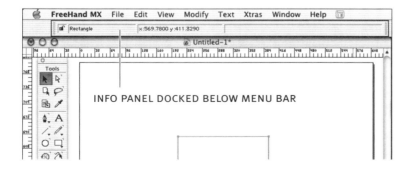

INFO PANEL DOCKED BELOW MENU BAR

3) Drag on the page to draw a rectangle approximately 370 points wide and 240 points high.

You'll see a blue outline of the rectangle as you drag. Release the mouse button when the shape is the size you want. This rectangle will form the body of the camera.

In Windows, look at the Status toolbar as you draw to see the width and height of the rectangle. In Mac OS, look at the Info toolbar to see the dimensions.

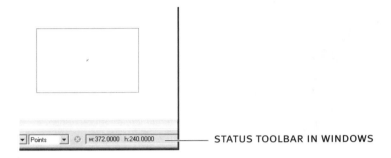

STATUS TOOLBAR IN WINDOWS

TIP *To draw a square, hold down Shift as you drag with the Rectangle tool.*

You want to center all of the components of the camera on each other, and you will do this by centering everything on the ruler guides. You will start by centering your rectangle on the intersection of the guides.

4) Select the Pointer tool from the Tools panel and start dragging the rectangle toward the intersection of the guides.

As you drag, you'll see a small X in the center of the rectangle, indicating the rectangle's center point. Make sure you drag the outline of the rectangle, not from the middle of the rectangle.

TIP *If an object has a fill color, you move it by dragging in the middle of the object. If an object has only a stroke, you move it by dragging the outline of the object.*

NOTE *The Pointer tool is the tool to use for selecting, moving, or editing objects on the page. It is easy to forget to switch to the Pointer tool before moving an object. If you do forget, you may inadvertently draw another rectangle.*

5) Drag the rectangle until the X is over the intersection of the guides; then release the mouse button.

If you don't see the small X in the center of the rectangle, you paused before you moved the mouse. Tap Alt (Windows) or Option (Mac OS) as you drag to view the small X.

If you hold down the mouse button briefly before you start to drag an object, you will see a preview of the entire object as you move it. For example, if you have an object with a fill and a drop shadow, you will see those properties as you move the object. This type of dragging is referred to as a preview drag. For complex objects, dragging may be a little slower if you use preview dragging. If you move an object quickly, as soon as you click the object, you see only the outline of the object as you drag. Tapping Alt or Option as you drag switches the drag type to Keyline or Preview.

This method of centering an object over a guide works well enough, but there is an even easier way. In the next step, you'll use that method. In FreeHand, there are usually two or more ways to accomplish a task. As you work through the lessons in this book, you will learn alternative methods. Experiment with the different methods to find the one that works best for you.

6) Select the Rectangle tool from the Tools panel. Move the pointer to the intersection of the guides. Hold down Alt (Windows) or Option (Mac OS) and drag to draw a second rectangle.

When you hold down Alt or Option, the pointer adds a circle to the cross cursor to indicate that you are drawing from the center outward from where you started dragging. Continue to drag until the sides of the rectangle match those of the first rectangle you drew. Make the vertical sides of this second rectangle shorter than those of the first one.

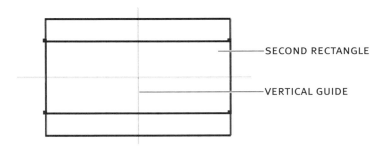

SECOND RECTANGLE

VERTICAL GUIDE

NOTE *If you are having trouble matching the sides of this new rectangle to the first one, you may not have correctly centered the first rectangle when you moved it. Select the first rectangle with the Pointer tool, delete it, and then draw it again, using the center-out method described in step 6.*

USING THE OBJECT PANEL

The **Object panel** contains information about the selected object. Since different types of objects have different properties, the panel changes based on the selected object. For example, when a rectangle is selected, the Object panel reports the X,Y location of the bottom left point of the rectangle plus the rectangle's width and height. Entering new values changes the shape and position of the rectangle. You can also use the Object panel to add or change the stroke, fill, or effect of an object.

1) Use the Pointer tool to select the larger rectangle on the page.

From now on, when this book instructs you to select an object, you are to switch to the Pointer tool and click the object. If you should use a different method, you will be instructed specifically to do so.

2) Look on the Object panel for information about the rectangle.

The Object panel is grouped by default with the Document panel in the Properties panel group. If you don't see the panel, choose Window > Object.

RECTANGLE INFORMATION —

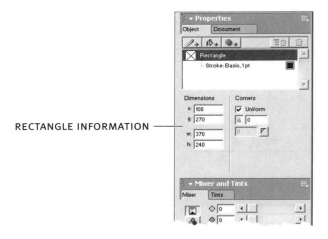

Note the width of your rectangle and its X value. The X (horizontal position) value is measured from the left of the page, and the Y (vertical position) value is measured from the bottom of the page.

3) Select the smaller rectangle and check its values in the Object panel.

You want the width and X value of both rectangles to be the same. If they are not, select the smaller rectangle and change its width in the Object panel to match that of the larger rectangle; then change the X value if needed. After you enter the new value in the Object panel, press Enter (Windows) or Return (Mac OS) to set the value.

TIP *You can copy the Width value of one rectangle and paste it in the Width text box for the other rectangle instead of trying to remember the value.*

Once the rectangles are positioned and sized correctly, you will use the Object panel to add a fill to one of the rectangles.

4) Select the smaller, inner rectangle. Click the Add Fill icon on the Object panel.

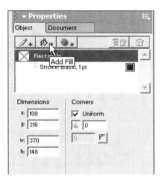

A basic black fill is added to the rectangle. Look in the top portion of the panel, and you'll see that the fill property was added after the stroke. Each time you add a new fill, stroke, or effect, that item is added to the list. The order in which a property appears in the list can affect the look of the object on the page. In this case, the order of the stroke and fill isn't significant.

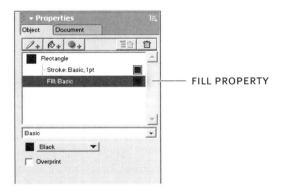

FILL PROPERTY

NOTE *The pointer changes when it is over a property on the Object panel. For example, in Windows the pointer changes to a hand, and in Mac OS X the pointer changes to a thick cross. You can then change the order of an object in the list by dragging the item up or down.*

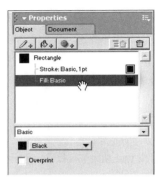

5) Select the Stroke property on the Object panel.

The area below the list items displays the properties for the selected object. For the stroke, you can change the color, size, and other parameters.

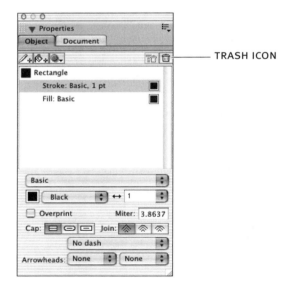

TRASH ICON

6) With the stroke item still selected, click the Trash icon on the Object panel to delete the stroke.

Once you have filled the rectangle with black, the stroke is no longer needed.

SNAPPING TO OBJECTS

In the next exercise, you will draw the other parts of the camera: the knobs and center section. They are simply more rectangles of varying sizes that are placed along the top edge of the camera body. To make the task of placing them easier, you will use the Snap to Object feature. When Snap to Object is turned on, objects snap to other objects as you move them near each other. Think of a magnet as it moves close to a metal object. The magnet and the object snap together when they come within a certain distance of each other. That distance is determined by the strength of the magnet. In FreeHand, the distance is determined by the snap distance set in your preferences.

There are instances in which you will find the snapping feature annoying, perhaps even a hindrance. For example, if you are trying to move an object close to, but not touching, another object, it may snap to that other object as you move it. As long as you recognize that snapping is on, you can simply turn it off before you get frustrated. In the task here, however, the snapping feature is helpful.

1) Choose View > Snap to Object if snapping is not already enabled.

A check mark next to the command indicates that it is enabled.

You can also click the Snap to Object button on the Tools panel to enable (or disable) snapping.

SNAP TO OBJECT

2) Use the Rectangle tool to draw the knobs and center section on the top of the camera.

You can draw the center section using the Alt-drag or Option-drag method you learned earlier and then move the rectangle down to place it exactly on top of the camera. To resize a rectangle, use the Pointer tool to drag one of the **selection handles**.

NOTE *Rectangles, elllipses, and polygons are drawn as grouped objects and are referred to as basic shapes. Because they are grouped, you can drag the selection handles to change the size of the rectangle or ellipse. If you ungroup the object and then select it, the selection handles are converted to points. Dragging a point changes the shape of the object. You will learn about points and paths in Lesson 3.*

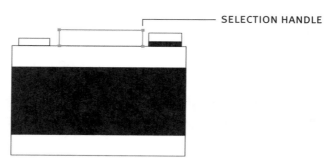

SELECTION HANDLE

◎ POWER TIP *As you draw your rectangles, you may not position them correctly. Instead of drawing them and then moving them later, you can reposition them as you draw, Just hold down the spacebar as you draw. A cross cursor appears, indicating that you can move the object. Continue to hold down the mouse button when you release the spacebar and then continue to draw the rectangle. In Windows only, you can press the right mouse button instead of pressing the spacebar.*

As you drag your rectangles toward the top of the camera body, they should snap to that object.

NOTE *When Snap to Object is on, a small circle appears at the lower right of the cursor when you are within snapping range of another object.*

If you don't think that the snapping distance is great enough, you can change the distance in your preferences.

3) Choose Edit > Preferences (Windows and Mac OS 9) or FreeHand MX > Preferences (Mac OS X); then select the General tab (Windows) or the General category (Mac OS).

Adjust the snap distance in the dialog box. This setting is in pixels. The smaller the number, the closer the object needs to be before snapping takes effect.

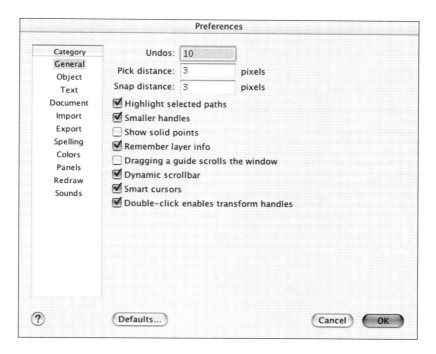

⊚ POWER TIP *Hold down Ctrl (Windows) or Command (Mac OS) as you drag an object to temporarily override snapping.*

4) Click OK to close the Preferences dialog box. Choose File > Save.

It is a good idea to save your work often. Keep the file open; you'll be adding more to the camera drawing.

CHANGING THE VIEW MAGNIFICATION

As you work with drawings, you will often find it helpful to zoom in or out of the page either to isolate an object or to see the entire image. For example, you might want to zoom in to make sure that the rectangles you added to the top of the camera coincide with the top of the camera body. There are several ways to accomplish this, using either menu commands or keyboard shortcuts.

1) Click the Magnification pop-up menu and select a larger number from the pop-up menu.

The Magnification pop-up menu is located on the Status toolbar in Windows and at the bottom of the document window in Mac OS. The page view changes to the magnification selected.

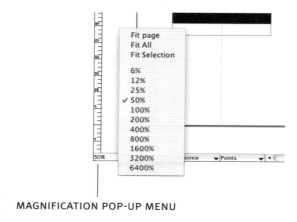

MAGNIFICATION POP-UP MENU

You can also use the View menu to change the magnification. Notice that the View menu has fewer options than the Magnification pop-up menu.

POWER TIP *You can also type any magnification value (from 6 to 256,000 percent) in the magnification text box. Press Enter (Windows) or Return (Mac OS) to set the magnification value for the page.*

2) Select the Zoom tool on the Tools panel and then click in the middle of the camera.

The cursor changes to a magnifying glass with a plus sign in the middle. The page magnification is centered on the point you clicked on the page. If you want to see a specific area, then click that area of the page. As you continue to click with the Zoom tool, the page magnification jumps to the next level. When you reach the greatest magnification level, the plus sign is removed from the pointer, indicating that you can't zoom in any closer. With a maximum zoom value of 256,000 percent, you shouldn't see that empty pointer often.

ZOOM IN AND ZOOM OUT POINTERS

○ POWER TIP   *If you drag around an area with the Zoom tool, FreeHand displays a dotted-line marquee. When you release the mouse button, the page is zoomed in on just that area. This procedure is sometimes more efficient than clicking several times with the Zoom tool.*

3) Hold down Alt (Windows) or Option (Mac OS) to change the Zoom In tool to the Zoom Out tool. Click the page to decrease the magnification level.

The tool switches to a magnifying glass with a minus sign in the middle.

TIP   *FreeHand also provides keyboard shortcuts for zooming in and out of a page. You can use these shortcuts no matter what tool is currently selected. In Windows, press Ctrl+spacebar for the Zoom In tool and Ctrl+Alt+spacebar for the Zoom Out tool. In Mac OS, press Command+spacebar for the Zoom In tool and Command+Option+spacebar for the Zoom Out tool.*

○ POWER TIP   *Double-click the Zoom tool to return the view magnification to 100 percent.*

USING THE LINE TOOL

The top right knob on the finished camera contains vertical lines to simulate the textured pattern on the knob. To draw this pattern, you will use the Line tool. You could draw each line individually, but then you would have the problem of spacing the lines equally. Instead, you will draw one line, make a duplicate of that line, and then use blending to draw the other lines in the pattern automatically.

1) Select the Line tool from the Tools panel.

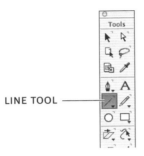

LINE TOOL

You will draw a vertical line within the rectangle for the knob. To make that task easier, you might want to zoom in on the knob.

2) Hold down Shift and drag down to draw a vertical line within the knob rectangle close to the left edge of the rectangle.

Holding Shift as you draw with the Line tool constrains the line to a vertical line. If the line is not positioned properly or is too long or short, use the Pointer tool to drag either the top or bottom point to make the line fit within the rectangle. If you need to move the line closer or farther away from the left edge of the rectangle, use the Pointer tool to move the line left or right.

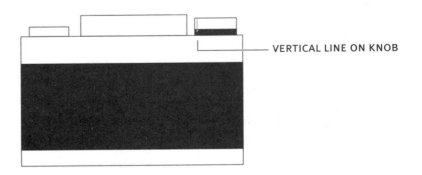

VERTICAL LINE ON KNOB

DUPLICATING AN OBJECT

FreeHand provides several ways to duplicate an object. For instance, you can use the familiar copy and paste method, the Clone command, or the Duplicate command. Here, instead of using any of these methods, you will use what is referred to as a duplicate drag.

1) Using the Pointer tool, select the vertical line.

The line changes to blue, indicating that it is selected.

2) Hold down Alt (Windows) or Option (Mac OS) as you drag the line to the right. Add the Shift key to keep the line from moving up or down as you drag.

The pointer displays a plus sign when you drag, indicating that you are making a copy. Position the new line approximately the same distance from the right edge of the rectangle as the first line is from the left edge.

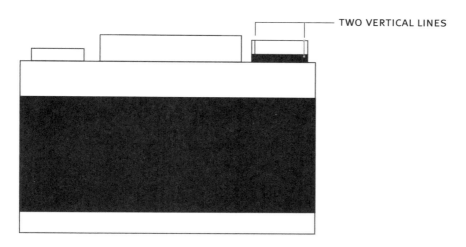

TWO VERTICAL LINES

NOTE *Make sure that you first press the mouse button on the line and begin to drag. Then, hold down the Alt or Option key. FreeHand confirms you are making a copy by adding a plus sign to the pointer. If you press the modifier key first, you will access the Subselect tool and will modify the line instead of duplicating it. The Subselect tool is covered in a later lesson.*

POWER TIP *For Windows only, right-mouse click and drag an object. When you release the mouse button, a menu appears where you can choose to move or make a copy of the object.*

3) Select the Blend tool from the Tools panel.

The Blend tool lets you create and modify blends from one object to another by dragging. You can specify a point on each object to control the way the blend is drawn. Here, you use the Blend tool to quickly draw lines equally spaced between the original two lines.

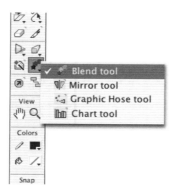

4) Using the Blend tool, drag from the top point of the first line to the top point of the second line.

As you drag, the Blend tool adds an anchor to the top of the first line; you then drag out a line (like a rubber band) from that point to the other point. When you release the mouse button, 25 lines (the default number) are created between the original two lines.

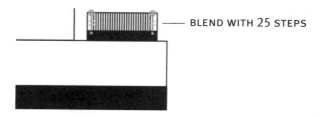

BLEND WITH 25 STEPS

TIP *Before you release the mouse button, you see a preview of the blend.*

5) On the Object panel, change the number of steps to *8*; then press Enter (Windows) or Return (Mac OS).

The number of lines in the blend change. Experiment with the number of steps in your blend to even out the vertical lines on your knob.

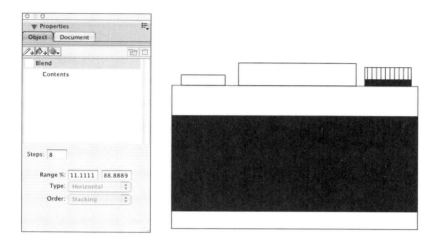

USING THE POLYGON TOOL

The Polygon tool can be used to draw equilateral polygons such as triangles and hexagons. (Polygons are closed geometric objects that have three or more sides. If all the sides are equal in length, the polygon is equilateral.) You can also use the Polygon tool to draw stars with three or more points. To draw the top section of the camera, you'll draw a six-sided polygon and place half of it behind the camera body. The Polygon tool is grouped with the Rectangle tool.

1) Hold down on the Rectangle tool. From the tool pop-up menu, choose the Polygon tool.

2) Double-click the Polygon tool on the Tools panel to open the Polygon Tool dialog box.

This dialog box is where you select either a star or a polygon and set the number of sides for the object.

3) Select Polygon for the shape type and then type *6* for the number of sides. Click OK.

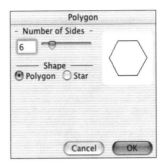

4) Hold down Shift as you drag with the Polygon tool to constrain the rotation of the polygon. Rotate as you drag to change the position of the polygon. You want two of the sides to be horizontal.

The Shift key constrains the rotation to 15-degree increments. Don't worry about the size of the polygon; you'll resize the shape in the next step.

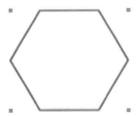

5) Switch to the Pointer tool and drag one of the corner handles of the polygon to stretch the shape horizontally.

You may want to move the polygon over the camera so you can size it based on your camera. Move it down so that only a small portion of the polygon is above the center rectangle.

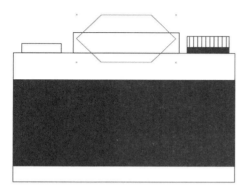

Since you want only the top portion of the polygon showing, you need to either cut off the bottom part or hide it. In the next section, you will learn how to slice the object with the Knife tool.

USING THE KNIFE TOOL

A **path** is a continuous line consisting of two or more **points**. For example, the line you drew with the Line tool is a path with two points: one at each end. A path can be either open or closed. The line you drew is an **open path**; an object where the first and last points are the same point is a **closed path**.

> **NOTE** *Points and paths are important concepts to grasp when using FreeHand. You will learn more about them in later lessons. In this section, you get just a brief introduction to them. Stick around. It gets better!*

As indicated by its name, the Knife tool is used for cutting paths. You can make a freehand cut or a straight cut. For the polygon, you want just the top part of the object, so you will use the Knife tool to cut away the bottom. You may want to move the polygon away from the camera body before you use the Knife tool so you don't accidentally cut it as well.

> **NOTE** *The Knife tool only cuts paths. When you use the Knife tool on an ellipse, rectangle, or polygon, FreeHand first converts those basic drawing objects to paths, then performs the cut.*

1) Double-click the Knife tool so you can set the options for the tool.

In the Knife Tool dialog box, you can select either a freehand or a straight cut, set the width of the knife, specify whether to close cut paths, and set the knife to make a cut that closely follows the motion of your hand as you use the tool.

2) For Tool Operation, select Straight, set the width to zero, and select Close Cut Paths. Click OK.

When you use the Knife tool on closed paths such as the polygon, you create two objects. By selecting the Close Cut Paths option, you create two closed paths when you slice through the polygon. Since you are making a straight cut, it doesn't matter whether the option to make a tight fit is selected. If you were making a freeform cut with the Knife tool, you would select that option to make sure that the cut followed the path of your hand movements with the mouse.

◎ POWER TIP *If Tool Operation is set to Freehand, you can still get a straight cut by holding down Alt+Shift (Windows) or Option+Shift (Mac OS) as you drag with the tool. For this step, you need to open the dialog box anyway so you can select Close Cut Paths.*

3) Hold down Shift as you drag left to right across the top of the polygon.

Start outside the polygon on the left and drag beyond the right side of the polygon. Even though you selected a straight cut, you still need to hold down Shift to make sure the cut is horizontal across both sides.

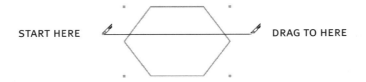

START HERE   DRAG TO HERE

NOTE *The Knife tool works only on selected objects. If you deselected the polygon, select it and then use the Knife tool.*

When you complete the cut, both the top and bottom sections of the polygon become outlined in blue, indicating that they both are selected. Since you want only the top section, you can delete the bottom section, but you will need to deselect the top section before you press the Delete key.

4) Switch to the Pointer tool and then press Tab.

All selected objects are deselected. Pressing Tab is a quick way to deselect everything. This approach is especially helpful when you are zoomed in on an area and don't realize that something else is selected that is outside your viewing area.

NOTE *The Tab key doesn't work for deselecting items if you are working within a text block entering text.*

5) Select the bottom portion of the polygon and then press Delete. Then move the remaining shape to the top section of the camera.

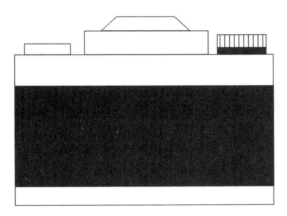

MOVING THE GUIDES

Your next task is to draw the circles for the camera lens. Look at the guides on the page. Remember that you placed them on the page to help you position objects as you draw them. By using Alt-drag or Option-drag to draw from the center, you centered the rectangles on the guides. The lens for the camera consists of three circles. Using that same technique, you can draw the three circles so they are aligned to each other as well.

The problem is that the interior rectangle is filled with black, making the intersection of the guides hard to see. By default, the guides are placed underneath the objects on the page. Normally, that is where you want them since they are less distracting that way. However, there are times when you will want to bring them to the front to make them easier to see.

You can control some aspects of the guides from the View menu. For example, you can show or hide them, or you can lock them so they can't be moved. If you want to move them in front of the objects on the page, you can use the Layers panel. You will learn more about the Layers panel in Lesson 4. For now, you will just use it to move the guides.

1) If you don't see the Layers panel in the docking area, choose Window > Layers.
If the Layers panel is in the docking area but not opened, click the triangle to open it. Guides are listed in the top section of the panel, below the Foreground layer. The Foreground layer contains all of the objects on the page.

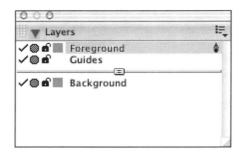

2) On the Layers panel, drag the Guides layer above the Foreground layer.
When you release the mouse button, the guides will appear on top of your camera.

3) Click the lock icon on the Guides layer.
Locking the layer prevents you from moving the guides as you perform the next steps.

LOCK ICON ON GUIDES LAYER ——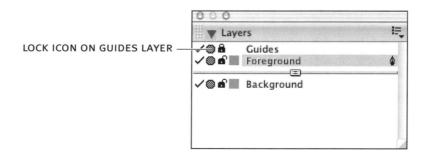

4) Select the Ellipse tool from the Tools panel. Position the pointer at the intersection of the guides. Hold down Alt+Shift (Windows) or Option+Shift (Mac OS) and drag to draw the largest circle for the lens.

Adding the Shift key constrains the ellipse to a circle; adding Alt or Option draws the circle from the center of the guides.

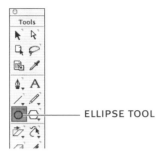

ELLIPSE TOOL

5) Click Add Fill on the Objects panel; then select White from the color pop-up menu on the panel.

6) Draw two more circles using that same method, making each circle smaller than the previous one. Add a black fill to the innermost circle.

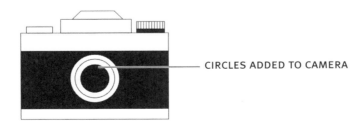

CIRCLES ADDED TO CAMERA

8) Save your file.

CREATING ROUNDED CORNERS

You've completed the basic camera; now you can make some changes to make it look even better. For example, the corners of the camera body are squared; you can round them to make the camera look more realistic.

1) Select the camera body rectangle.

Make sure that you select the larger rectangle, not the rectangle filled with black.

2) Choose Window > Object if the Object panel is not already open.

The Object panel shows the dimensions of the selected rectangle and a setting for the corners of the rectangle.

NOTE *Once a rectangle is created, you use the Object panel to change the corners. You can also change the corner setting for the Rectangle tool before you draw your objects. Double-click the Rectangle tool to open the Rectangle Tool settings and enter the corner radius you want. This setting remains in effect until you change it again.*

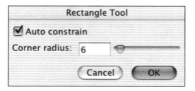

3) Deselect the Uniform option for Corners. Type *4* for the top values and *8* for the bottom values.

You can specify a corner radius for each corner of a rectangle. If you wanted all corners the same, you would leave Uniform selected.

> **NOTE** *The Object panel also has a setting for making the curve of the corner convex (the default) or concave. Click the concave button to toggle this option on or off.*

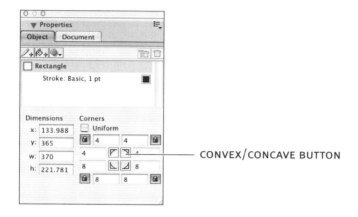

CONVEX/CONCAVE BUTTON

> **NOTE** *Polygons have corner radius controls similar to the controls for rectangles. You would apply the corner settings to the polygon before you cut the polygon with the Knife tool.*

4) Save your file.

ON YOUR OWN

Add black fill to the top part of the camera and to the bottom part of the knob on the right. Add some white horizontal lines on the black area of the camera to provide texture, and add a white oval to represent the view finder. In the next lesson, you will add some text so you can use the camera as a logo and then use it to create marketing materials.

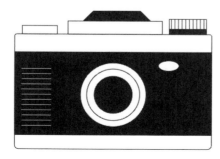

37

GROUPING ITEMS

As you create your drawings in FreeHand, you'll begin to notice that even simple drawings are composed of many elements. The camera you created in this lesson uses only lines, circles, and rectangles, but it consists of more than 10 objects. If you want to move the camera on the page or to resize it, you must first select all of its elements. With this example, that might not be too difficult, but as your drawings become more complex, keeping portions of your drawing grouped together as one object will make managing your documents easier.

To make sure that objects stay together when you move or resize them, you can group them. Once grouped, they behave as one object instead of many. You will use your camera drawing in several places. Grouping all of its elements will make it easier to copy the camera as one element for use in other documents.

1) Choose Edit > Select > All to select all of the objects on the page.

You can also use the selection rectangle to select all of the objects. Using the Pointer tool, place the cursor somewhere well outside the area of the camera, such as in the upper left corner of the screen, and drag across the camera to the opposite corner. You'll see a marquee (the selection rectangle) appear as you drag. All elements within that marquee are selected.

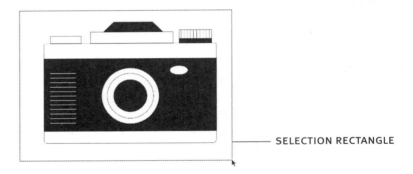

— SELECTION RECTANGLE

TIP *The Object panel reports the number of objects selected.*

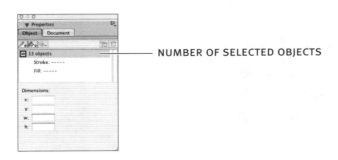

— NUMBER OF SELECTED OBJECTS

2) Choose Modify > Group.

All objects are grouped into one object. Now when you select the camera, you'll see four blue handles around the group. If you need to ungroup the objects, choose Modify > Ungroup.

You can also create **nested** groups. For example, the knob you created consists of three rectangles. You could select those three rectangles and group them together. Then you could select the remaining parts of the camera and group the knob group with the camera. The knob group would then be a nested group within the camera group.

⊚ **POWER TIP** *If you need to make a change to one of the objects in a group, hold down Alt (Windows) or Option (Mac OS) and click the object. This action does not ungroup the object, but allows you to modify an object within the group. This process is faster than ungrouping and then selecting the object.*

3) Save your file.

WHAT YOU HAVE LEARNED

In this lesson, you have:

- Explored the FreeHand MX interface (pages 8–10)
- Created a new document and saved it (pages 10–11)
- Added rulers and guides to the page (pages 12–14)
- Used the Rectangle tool (pages 15–17)
- Examined and used the Object panel (pages 18–20)
- Used Snap to Object to help position objects (pages 21–23)
- Changed the view magnification using the pop-up menu and the Zoom tool (pages 24–25)
- Used the Line tool (page 26)
- Duplicated an object and then used the Blend tool to create equally spaced objects (pages 27–28)
- Used the Polygon, Ellipse, and Knife tools (pages 29–37)
- Grouped items to make your objects easier to manage (pages 38–39)

adding pages and text

One unique aspect of FreeHand is that it lets you create multiple distinct pages in a single document. Of course, there is nothing unique about multiple pages in a document, but with FreeHand, each page can be a different size. This feature gives you tremendous flexibility in your projects. For example, you can create a corporate identity package, creating the logo on one page, business cards on another page, and letterheads and envelopes on other pages. Each page will be the size needed, and all of the design pages will be saved in one file. Instead of sending several files to the printer, you need to send just the one file.

You can create all of your marketing materials using FreeHand. You will use the text editing tools to format the text on each of the pages.

In this lesson, you will add some text to the camera you created in Lesson 1 to create a company logo. Then you will set up a document with multiple pages and combine the logo with some text to create a postcard, business card, and envelope.

WHAT YOU WILL LEARN

In this lesson, you will:

- Create a default document template
- Add new pages and change the page size
- Import graphics for your document
- Use the Text tool to enter and format text
- Apply kerning and range kerning to text
- Add special characters to your document
- Shift text off the baseline

APPROXIMATE TIME

This lesson takes approximately 2 hours to complete.

LESSON FILES

Media Files:
None

Starting Files:
Lesson02\Start\camera.fh11

Completed Projects:
Lesson02\Completed\corp_identity.fh11

CREATING A DEFAULT DOCUMENT TEMPLATE

In Lesson 1, you saw how helpful guides are for placing objects on the page. To use the guides, the page rulers must be visible. Although the rulers are easy to show and hide, you might want to customize FreeHand so that they appear each time you create a new page.

When you create a new page, FreeHand uses the **default document template** and opens it as an untitled document. If you find yourself changing the same settings or adding the same colors for every document, all you need to do is change the default template, and those changes will be made automatically for each new document.

1) Choose File > New to create a new document and then choose View > Page Rulers > Show.

If you want to change any other settings, make those changes as well. For example, if you like the Snap to Object feature, make sure that option is on.

2) Click the Units pop-up menu and pick Points from the list if it is not already selected.

Values you are instructed to use later in this lesson assume that you are using Points as your measurement system. If you use another system, you will need to adjust some of the values.

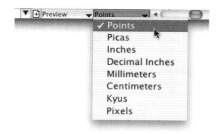

3) Choose File > Save As. In the Save Document dialog box, type *MyDefaults* as the file name and then choose FreeHand Template from the Save as Type (Windows) or Format (Mac OS) pop-up menu.

Templates are stored in the Macromedia > FreeHand > 11 > English > Settings folder within your user-specific Application Data (Windows) or Application Support (Mac OS) folder. Navigate to this location on your hard drive. Since this file will serve as your default FreeHand document, you want to save this file in a permanent location.

NOTE *The extension for a FreeHand template is .ft11.*

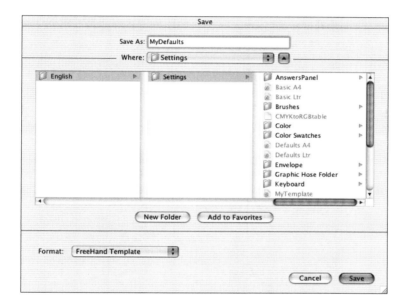

4) Click Save.

Your default template is saved.

5) Choose Edit > Preferences (Windows and Mac OS 9) or FreeHand MX > Preferences (Mac OS X) and click the Document tab (Windows) or Document category (Mac OS).

In the Document section of the Preferences dialog box, you can change the document view and window placement to control the way documents appear when they are opened.

6) From the New Document Template pop-up menu, choose MyDefaults. Click OK to close the Preferences dialog box.

Your new default document appears in the New Document template pop-up menu because you saved your document in the Settings folder. If you save your template in another location, you then need to click the ellipsis button next to the New Document Template pop-up menu and locate your template. The next time you create a new document, the page rulers (and any other settings you specified) will be turned on.

The template you just created will be used as the FreeHand default page, but you can create templates for any projects where you find yourself repeatedly using the same settings. For example, if you are creating documents for a client where you are always copying the corporate logo, create a template that contains that logo. Then you'll have it ready to go on the page. Instead of creating a new page, you can open the template. It will open as an untitled document with your settings and graphics.

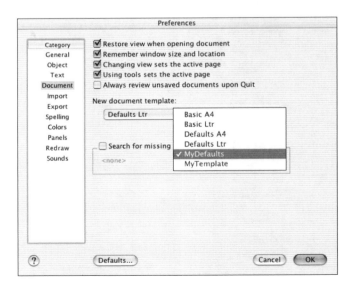

CHANGING THE PAGE SIZE

The camera you created earlier will be used as part of the logo for the Action Photos company. Instead of changing the camera file, you will import the graphic into another document and add some text. Then, in that file, you will add other pages of different sizes to create a business card, envelope, and letterhead.

1) Choose File > New to create a new document.

If you already have an untitled document open from the previous task, you can use that instead. The document contains one page with the default page size.

2) Change the measurement units to inches using the Units pop-up menu on the Status toolbar (Windows) or at the bottom of the document window (Mac OS).

The rulers change to display inches.

> **NOTE** *We changed the measurement system here to make it easier to define new page sizes. If you prefer to define your page size using different units, choose those units instead. You'll then need to make the conversion from inches to your measurement unit in step 5.*

3) Choose Window > Document to display the Document panel.

The **Document panel** is normally grouped with the Object panel in the Properties panel group. You can also click the Document tab in that panel group to select the panel.

4) Choose Custom from the Page Size pop-up menu on the Document panel.

You can choose from several preset sizes in the list, or you can define your own size using Custom.

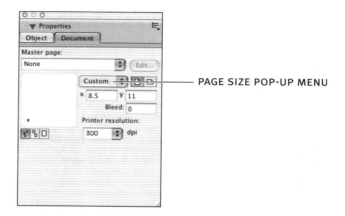 ———— PAGE SIZE POP-UP MENU

5) Select the value in the X text box and type _4_ as the width of the page. Press the Tab key to select the Y text box and type _6_ as the height of the page. Press Enter (Windows) or Return (Mac OS) to apply these changes to your page.

Your page changes to this new size.

6) On the Document panel, click the landscape page orientation button.

The page switches to 6 inches by 4 inches. You will use this page to create a postcard, and so it needs to be horizontal.

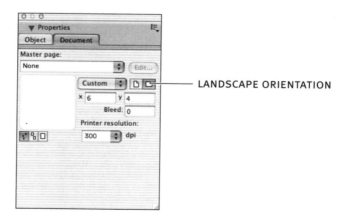 ———— LANDSCAPE ORIENTATION

7) Save your document as _corp_identity.fh11_ in the Projects folder.

ADDING CUSTOM PAGES

In this section, you will add more pages to your document, each page a different size. You will also move the pages around the pasteboard to make them easier to manage.

1) From the Document panel Options menu, choose Add Pages .

The Options menu is located at the top right of an open panel. It contains commands that are unique to each panel.

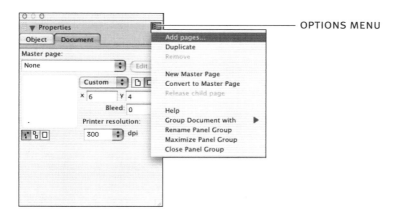

OPTIONS MENU

2) In the Add Pages dialog box, choose Custom for the page size, select landscape mode, and type *3.5* as the X value and *2* as the Y value. Click OK.

This new page you are adding will be for the business card. When you click OK, the new page is added to your document, to the right of the first page. You may not see it in the document area, depending on your view magnification. However, you should see a new page added in the page area of the Document panel.

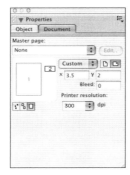

3) From the Magnification pop-up menu, choose Fit All.

You should now see both pages in the document window.

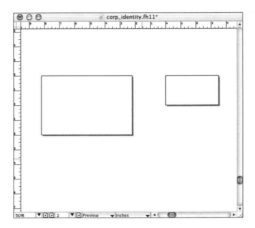

4) Select the Page tool from the Tools panel and click the second page.

PAGE TOOL

When you click to select a page, a blue outline with handles appears around the page.

The Page tool allows you to move, resize, or change the page orientation of a selected page. Move the pointer over one of the handles of the selected page. The cursor changes to either a straight double-arrow cursor or a curved double-arrow cursor. With the straight double-arrow cursor, you can drag to change the page size. With the curved double-arrow cursor, you can drag to change the page orientation. If you want to experiment with these options, look at the Document panel as you change the page. You'll see the new page size in the X and Y text boxes as you drag the handles. If you want specific page sizes, the easier approach is simply to enter the dimensions in the Document panel. If you want to make changes, just reenter the correct values to reset the page size.

5) Using the Page tool, drag in the center of the new page and move the page to the top right corner of the first page.

FreeHand won't let you place a page on top of another page. If you move the page so it overlaps another page, the selected page snaps back to its original location when you release the mouse button. If you get close to the other page, the two pages snap together.

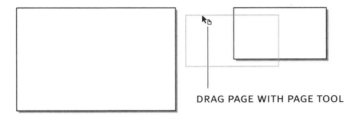

DRAG PAGE WITH PAGE TOOL

6) Position the Page tool over the second page. Hold down Alt (Windows) or Option (Mac OS) and drag down about 8 inches.

As you drag, you'll see a blue outline of the page. Holding the Alt or Option modifier key as you drag makes a copy of the page. Release the mouse button when the outline of this new page is below the first page.

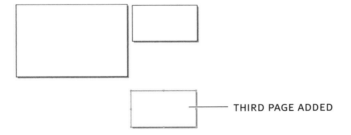

THIRD PAGE ADDED

NOTE *You can move pages around the pasteboard using the page icons in the Document panel, but the process is much easier with the Page tool. Below the page icons on the Document panel are three buttons that change the icon sizes.*

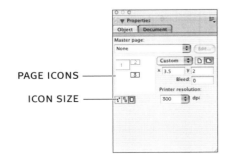

PAGE ICONS

ICON SIZE

7) Use the Page tool to select the third page. In the Document panel, change the X value to _9.5_ and the Y value to _4.125_. Press Enter (Windows) or Return (Mac OS) to apply the changes to the page.

This new page is the size of a #10 commercial envelope.

NOTE *If your third page is not placed below the first page, you may get an error message indicating that FreeHand can't change the page size because the page would overlap another page. Click OK to dismiss the dialog box, move your page with the Page tool, and then repeat step 7.*

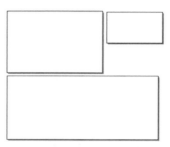

TIP *You can delete a page by selecting it with the Page tool and then pressing the Delete key.*

8) Select each page with the Page tool and note its page number in the Go to Page pop-up menu on the Status toolbar (Windows) or at the bottom of the document window (Mac OS).

The page number is determined by the placement of the page on the pasteboard, from left to right, not the order in which you created the page. You can use the Go to Page pop-up menu to move from page to page in your document.

POWER TIP *There are other shortcuts you can use with the Page tool. Hold down Alt (Windows) or Option (Mac OS) and double-click the page to open the Modify Page dialog box. Hold down Alt (Windows) or Option (Mac OS) and double-click the pasteboard to open the Add Page dialog box.*

IMPORTING GRAPHICS

Many times when you create your documents, you will want to use existing graphics or images. If you created a graphic in FreeHand, such as the camera you created in Lesson 1, you could just open the other document, select the camera, copy it, and then paste it in this document. But what if you don't have the application that created the other graphic? FreeHand imports several types of file formats, including: Macromedia Fireworks PNG, Adobe Photoshop PSD, Adobe Acrobat PDF, Adobe Illustrator EPS and AI files, GIF, JPEG, TIFF, and BMP. In the next task, you will import your camera and then add some text.

1) From the Go to Page pop-up menu, choose page 1.

The Go to Page pop-up menu displays the selected page, changing the view magnification to fit the page. The first page should be the postcard page.

2) Choose File > Import. Select your camera.fh11 file and then click Open. Click to place the imported camera on the postcard page.

You can use the camera.fh11 file in the Start folder of the Lesson02 folder if you can't find your camera file. The pointer changes to a corner cursor when you import files. Once the graphic is on the page, you can use the Pointer tool to move or resize it.

TIP *If you drag with the pointer instead of clicking, the imported graphic is sized to fit the area of the marquee you drag.*

3) Hold down Shift and drag one of the corner handles of the graphic to resize it.

The graphic is grouped. When you select it with the Pointer tool, you'll see four handles around the graphic. You want the camera to fill most of the area within the page, so resize it if necessary. Move the camera so there is some room at the top of the page for a headline.

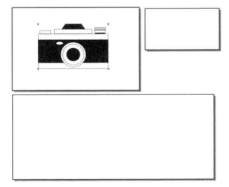

4) Save your file.

USING THE TEXT TOOL

FreeHand gives you almost all of the text-formatting tools you'll need to add and modify text on your pages. Although FreeHand is not designed for extensive page-layout duties, it can certainly serve your purposes for many of your designs. If you have a text-laden newsletter, stick to a page-layout program. If you have a product datasheet, you can create the graphics, import the text, and then format the text all in FreeHand.

NOTE *Check with your printer to make sure the company has FreeHand MX if you plan to send your files to be printed from FreeHand. If the printer doesn't have the current version but has an earlier one, you can export your file and save it as a FreeHand 8, 9, or 10 document.*

Before you can format text, you need to create the text. You can either type text directly in your FreeHand document or import it. In the next task, you will type some text using the Text tool. In a later lesson, you will import some text.

1) Select the Text tool from the Tools panel.

The pointer changes to the I-beam cursor, indicating that you are in text mode.

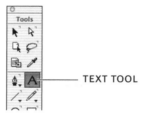 —— TEXT TOOL

2) Click at the top of the page.

When you click with the Text tool, you'll see the blinking cursor and the text ruler.

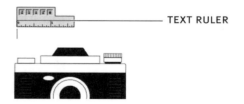 —— TEXT RULER

NOTE *If you don't like the text rulers, you can turn them off from the View menu. Choose View > Text Rulers to show or hide the text rulers.*

3) Type the following text: *We come to your event and capture the action.*

You should be able to type the text without its wrapping to the next line. Don't worry if the text does wrap; you'll fix that in a later step.

4) Click away from the text to exit text-editing mode; then click the text again.

Notice that you did not need to switch from the Text tool. FreeHand automatically switches to the Pointer tool when you move the pointer away from the text. Clicking the text now selects the text as an object—a text block.

We come to your event and capture the action

———— LINK BOX

The selected text block has handles on the corners and sides and a small box at the lower right corner—the **Link box**. If a small circle appears within the Link box, then the text box contains more text than what is displayed in the text block. You will need to delete some of the text, increase the size of the text block, or link the text to another text block.

TIP *The automatic switching to the Pointer tool is a preference that is set by default. If you want to remove that functionality, choose Edit > Preferences (Windows and Macintosh OS 9) or FreeHand MX > Preferences (Macintosh OS X), click the Text tab (Windows) or Text category (Mac OS), and deselect the option to switch the Text tool to the Pointer tool. If the option is deselected, then the Text tool remains the active tool until you change tools.*

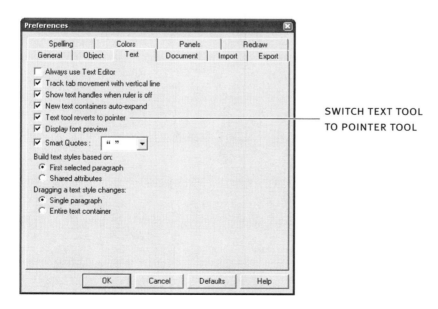

SWITCH TEXT TOOL
TO POINTER TOOL

5) Resize the text block by dragging the lower right handle (not the Link box) down and to the left.

Did the text block resize? If it springs back when you release the mouse button, look at the side handles on the text block. If the left and right side handles are hollow, then horizontal auto-expansion is on; if the bottom handle is hollow, then vertical auto-expansion is also on.

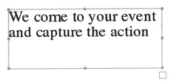

Auto-expanding text blocks expand either horizontally or vertically as you type within them. If auto-expansion is on, you can't drag the corner handles to change the width of the text block.

6) If the bottom and right side handles are hollow, double-click them to remove auto-expansion and then drag the lower right handle to the left to resize the text block.

The handle should be solid. If it is not, double-click it again. Resize the text block so that the text "We come to your event" is on the first line and the remaining text is on the second line. Don't worry if you have some empty space at the bottom of the text block. In the next step, you will delete the space.

We come to your event
and capture the action

The Object panel also displays auto-expansion buttons that you can use to turn the expansion option on and off. With the text block selected, select Text Block in the property list of the Object panel. Next to the width and height dimensions of the text blocks are the horizontal and vertical expansion buttons. Click each button to turn the option on or off.

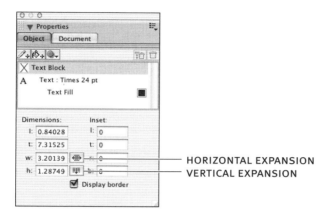

HORIZONTAL EXPANSION
VERTICAL EXPANSION

7) Double-click the Link box.

The text block resizes vertically to fit the text. The Link box is also used to link text blocks, which you will do later in this lesson.

FORMATTING TEXT

Once you have the text on the page, you can format it to your liking, changing the font, size, color, and paragraph formatting such as alignment and line spacing. You can use the Text menu, Text toolbar, or Object panel to apply your formatting. The advantage of the Object panel is that you can see all current settings in just a glance.

If you select the entire text block, you can apply formatting to all of the text within the text block. If you select specific text within the text block, you can apply formatting to just the selected text.

1) Use the Pointer tool to select the text block and then select the Text property on the Object panel.

Text formatting options appear on the Object panel. The left column contains five text attribute buttons: Character, Paragraph, Spacing, Columns, and Adjust Columns. When you click one of these buttons, the Object panel changes to display a different set of formatting controls.

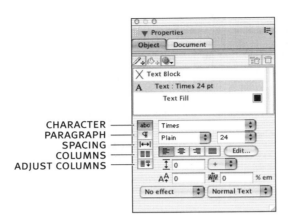

2) Click the Character attribute button (the abc button), choose a font from the Font pop-up menu, and choose a point size from the Size pop-up menu. Select Center alignment.

This text is a headline, so use a big, bold font such as Arial Black with a size of 24 points.

All of the text changes to that font and size. If the font you choose is larger than the original font size, your text may overflow the text block; in this case, a circle will appear in the Link box. Resize the text block to show all the text.

3) On the Object panel, type *4* in the Leading text box. Choose + from the Leading Method pop-up menu.

The spacing between the lines in the heading increases.

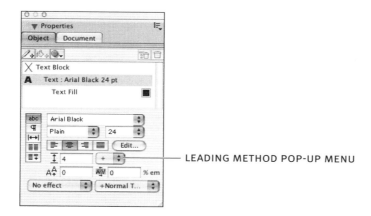

LEADING METHOD POP-UP MENU

Text characters sit on an imaginary line called the **baseline**. **Leading** (pronounced "ledding") is the distance between one text line to the next one. When you increase the leading amount, you are increasing the spacing between the lines.

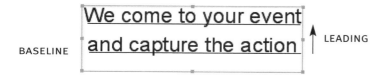

BASELINE

LEADING

FreeHand gives you three ways to set the leading: by adding extra leading, by setting the absolute leading amount, and by using a percentage. Next to the Leading text box is a pop-up menu that you can use to pick the method you want to use. Select the plus sign to add extra leading, select the equal sign to use a fixed value, or select Percentage to use that method.

The extra leading method adds the point size of the largest character in your text block to the number you enter in the Leading text box. The percentage method uses a leading value equal to a percentage of the largest character in the text block. If you choose either of these methods, the leading value changes if you change the point size of your text. If you choose the absolute leading amount, the leading remains at that value even if you increase or decrease the point size.

57

⊙ **POWER TIP** *You can also increase or decrease the leading amount by dragging the center handle on the bottom of the text block. This is a faster way to increase or decrease the leading amount when you are more concerned about the way the text looks on the page than using a specific amount.*

DRAG HANDLE TO CHANGE LEADING

4) Add the text *ACTION PHOTOS* to the page. Place that text on the top white part of the camera body. Change the font and size so the text fits within that area.

Make sure that you type the text in all uppercase letters.

You entered the company name in all uppercase letters. But what if your design changes? Or what if you just don't like the way the text looks? You could retype the text, but an easier method is to use the Convert Case command.

58

5) Choose Text > Convert Case > Title.

Your text is retyped using uppercase for only the first letter of each word. Convert Case can change the case of a text selection to uppercase or lowercase, small caps, title caps, or sentence caps.

When you change case, you may have some words, such as company names, that you don't want changed. You don't need to fix these manually. Instead, you can add these words to an exception list.

6) Choose Text > Convert Case > Settings. Select all of the options for the exceptions (Upper Case through Sentence Case) and then click Add. Type *USA* in the exception field that FreeHand adds to the list. Click OK.

The case of the word doesn't matter in the exception field; you could have also typed *usa*. Continue to click Add to add other words to the list, such as company names or abbreviations you typically use. The words you add to the exception list will be ignored when you use the Change Case command.

7) Use the Text tool to enter the following address and then move this text box to the lower left corner of the camera. Format the text to fit within this area.

555 Main Street
Adventure Town, USA

8) Add another text block for the phone number and type *1-800-555-1234*. Move this text block to the lower right corner of the camera.

9) Choose Window > Toolbars > Text. Change the font and size of the address and phone text blocks to your liking using the Text toolbar.

The Text toolbar is also convenient for changing the font, size, and leading. It doesn't contain all of the formatting controls of the Object panel, but it provides another quick way to format text.

TIP *If you have a large monitor, you can dock the Text toolbar below the top menu bar. Drag the toolbar to the top of your screen, and it will dock itself below the menu bar. If you have already docked the Info toolbar, the Text toolbar is docked below it.*

10) Save your file.

KERNING AND RANGE KERNING

When you use headings or large text in a logo, you may find that the space between each letter in the heading or logo is too large or too small. You can control that spacing using the kerning and range kerning controls. **Kerning** is the adjustment of the space between two characters; **range kerning** (sometimes called tracking) is the adjustment of two or more selected characters.

FreeHand kerns in percentages of an em. An em is a unit of measure used in typography that was originally equal to the width of the letter M. You can think of an em as being equal to the size of the type. For example, if you are using 24-point type, an em will be 24 points. In FreeHand, you can kern your type in increments as small as 0.01 percent of an em, either adding or subtracting that amount to the spacing.

Text Text THE SPACING BETWEEN THE T AND E
IS KERNED IN THE LEFT EXAMPLE

1) Using the Text tool, position the insertion point between the *A* and the *c* in the word *Action*.

When the insertion point is between two characters, you are adjusting the spacing between only those characters.

NOTE *Some fonts contain kerning values that FreeHand recognizes and displays in the kerning text box.*

2) Select the Text property in the Object panel and then click the Character options button. Type *–1* in the Kerning text box and then press Enter (Windows) or Return (Mac OS) to apply the kerning.

When you enter a negative number, the letters move closer together. A positive number increases the spacing.

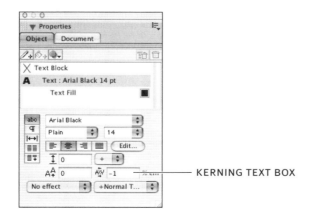

KERNING TEXT BOX

3) Select the text block with the Pointer tool and then repeat step 2.

When you select the text block or select multiple characters, you are performing range kerning. In this instance, all of the letters are tightened by –1 percent of an em. The spacing between the *A* and the *c* still retains the kerning you applied in step 1, with the range kerning amount added to the kerning amount between the two letters.

Action Photos —— NONKERNED TEXT
Action Photos —— KERNED TEXT

You can also use keyboard shortcuts for kerning:

Amount	Windows	Macintosh
0.1 em closer	Ctrl+Alt+Shift+Left Arrow	Command+Option+Shift+Left Arrow
0.01 em closer	Ctrl+Alt+Left Arrow	Command+Option+Left Arrow
0.1 em farther apart	Ctrl+Alt+Shift+Right Arrow	Command+Option+Shift+Right Arrow
0.01 em farther apart	Ctrl+Alt+Right Arrow	Command+Option+Right Arrow

ADDING A REGISTER MARK

There are several characters that don't appear on your keyboard; you have to use a combination of keystrokes to enter the character. For example, the registered mark (®) doesn't appear on the keyboard. How do you type it on the page? If you are familiar with word processing or page layout programs, you may have come across this question before.

In Windows, you can use Character Map (Start > Programs > Accessories > System Tools > Character Map) to find the character you need, copy it, and then paste it in your document. In Mac OS, you can choose Keycaps from the Apple menu (OS 9) or the Character palette (OS X).

NOTE *In Macintosh OS X, open System Preferences and choose International. Click the Input Menu tab and then choose Character Palette. The Input menu is added to the menu bar, allowing you to access the Character palette from any application.*

In the next task, you will enter the registered mark after the company name and then resize it and move it up off the baseline.

1) Position the insertion point after the last character in the company name. Use the character utility for your platform to insert the registered mark.

In Mac OS, you can press Option+R to enter the registered mark.

⊚ **POWER TIP** *In Windows, when you select a character in the Character Map, the keystroke is displayed at the bottom right of the dialog box. For example, the registered mark keystroke is Alt+0174. To enter this, you hold down the Alt key and then type the numbers on the numeric keypad. When you release the Alt key, the character is inserted in your text block. You must use the numbers on the numeric keypad, and you must type all four numbers, including the zero.*

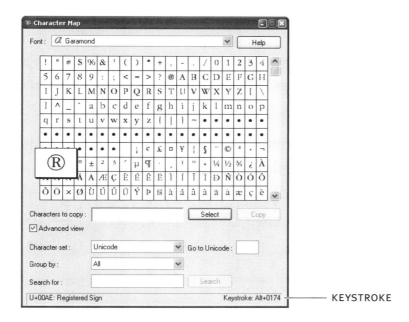

KEYSTROKE

2) Select the registered mark and make the point size smaller.

The registered mark should be readable but should not detract from the company name.

Action Photos®

USING BASELINE SHIFT

If you need to adjust the baseline of a character so it is different from the baseline of other text in the text block, you can use the baseline shift controls. You can move the character baseline either above or below the baseline of the other characters. For example, if you want the expression H_2O on your page, you can use baseline shift to move the 2 down. In this exercise, you want to move the registered mark above the baseline.

1) Change the measurement units to points.

When shifting text off the baseline, as you will do in the next step, it is easier to use points instead of another measurement system since text size is expressed in points.

2) Select the registered mark with the Text tool. Select the Text property on the Object panel and then click the Character button. Type 4 in the Baseline Shift text box and then press Enter (Windows) or Return (Mac OS) to apply the setting to the text.

A positive number moves the character up; a negative number moves the character down. You may need to adjust the number to match your text.

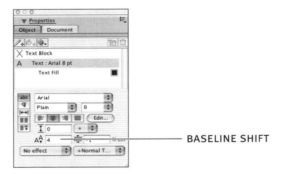 — BASELINE SHIFT

⊙ POWER TIP *You can also use keyboard shortcuts to adjust the baseline. Press Ctrl+Alt+Up Arrow (Windows) or Option+Up Arrow (Mac OS) to move the baseline up one point, or press Ctrl+Alt+Down Arrow (Windows) or Option+Down Arrow (Mac OS) to move the baseline down one point.*

3) Position the insertion point before the registered mark and kern the spacing tighter between the last letter and the registered mark.

Try using the keyboard shortcuts to kern between the letters.

4) Save your file.

ON YOUR OWN

Make a copy of the camera logo from the postcard page and paste it on the business card and envelope pages. You'll need to make the logo smaller to fit those pages. Remember: since the camera object is grouped, you can resize it by holding down the Shift key as you drag a corner handle. Add your name and address, plus the phone number. Format the text to your liking.

WHAT YOU HAVE LEARNED

In this lesson, you have:

- Created a default document template using your FreeHand preferences (pages 42–44)

- Added new pages, changed the page size, and rearranged the pages of your document (pages 45–50)

- Imported graphics for your document (page 51)

- Used the Text tool to enter text and formatted the text (pages 52–60)

- Applied kerning and range kerning to text to improve its appearance (pages 61–62)

- Added a special character to your document (page 62)

- Used baseline shift to move text off the baseline (page 64)

colors, gradients, and styles

We live in a full-color world. Color adds interest to artwork, whether printed or displayed on a web page. Color provides visual clues about objects around us: when we see a red sign, we know to stop; when we see a green light, we know to go. The color you add to the object you draw in this lesson may be enough to suggest a brand name, even though you don't add the company name to the product.

We see color when a light source reflects on an object. Our eyes receive the reflected light and transmit a message to our brain, causing us to see a particular color. How you reproduce the color on your computer depends on the way you want to use the drawing. Are you creating an image to be used on the web? Or do you want to include the image in a page-layout program or print directly from FreeHand? If you want to print, do you want to print on a color printer or to send your project to a commercial printer? Your answers to these questions determine how you create colors in FreeHand. Once you create colors for a particular output device, however, you can easily convert the colors for other uses.

To create the film canister for this lesson, you will split an ellipse and then use a portion of the ellipse for one side of the canister. You then will make a copy of that shape and flip it for the other side. You will add colors and a gradient fill to create the illusion of a 3D object.

In this lesson, you will mix a color, save the color, and apply it to an object. Before you do that though, you need to draw the object you want colored. First, you will create a film canister to be used in an advertisement and on a web page. You will draw half of the canister and then use tools to make a copy and reflect the copy for the other half. Once the film canister is almost complete, you will add some color and a gradient fill to make the cylindrical canister look more realistic. In the next lesson, you will draw a strip of film and use the 3D Rotation tool to make the film appear as if it is jutting out from the canister. In another lesson, you will animate the film moving out from the canister.

WHAT YOU WILL LEARN

In this lesson, you will:

- Learn about splitting and joining paths

- Learn to reflect, scale, and rotate objects

- Use the Mirror tool

- Use the transformation handles to scale an object

- Use the Color Mixer and Tints panels to create colors

- Add colors to the Swatches panel

- Create gradients and add them to objects

- Save graphic properties on the Styles panel

- Use the Subselect tool

- Use the Arc tool

APPROXIMATE TIME

This lesson takes approximately 3 hours to complete.

LESSON FILES

Media Files:
None

Starting Files:
None

Completed Projects:
Lesson03\Completed\film_canister.fh11

USING SPLIT AND JOIN

In Lesson 1, you were introduced to the concepts of points and paths. When you used the Knife tool to cut the polygon, you split the closed path of the polygon, creating two open paths. If a point already exists on a path, you can use the Split command to create new paths. Of course, you could also use the Knife tool to cut the path, but you may have difficulty cutting exactly on the point. Using the Split command makes the cut more quickly and more precisely.

An object must be a closed path if you want to add a fill color. Once you split an object, you may then want to move the points to change the shape. Then you can use the Join command to combine two open paths or to add a line connecting two selected points.

1) Create a new document and save it as *film_canister.fh11* in your Projects folder. Turn on the page rulers if they are not visible. Drag horizontal and vertical guides to the middle of the page.

The film canister consists of an ellipse at the top for the end cap, a colored right side, and a black left side. Since the left and right sides are identical, you will draw one side, make a copy of it, and then reflect the copy for the other side. The guides will help you create one side and the reflected copy.

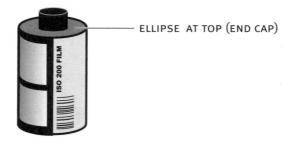

ELLIPSE AT TOP (END CAP)

2) Select the Ellipse tool and draw a horizontal ellipse from the center of the intersection of the guides. Make the ellipse approximately 100 x 30 pixels.

In Lesson 1, you learned to hold down Alt (Windows) or Option (Mac OS) to draw from the center of a rectangle or ellipse. You will use the ellipse you just created to draw the base of the canister and then make a copy of the ellipse to draw the end cap of the canister.

To achieve the perspective of a three-dimensional object, do not make the ellipse too tall vertically. Move the mouse up or down to change the height. If you do not like the drawn figure, delete it and draw it again. You can also resize it with the Pointer tool by dragging one of the handles; however, if you do this, you may move the center away from the intersection of the guides.

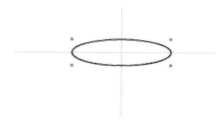

3) Choose Edit > Copy and then choose Edit > Paste. Move the copy to the pasteboard.

You've moved your drawing to the pasteboard for safekeeping. You will use this copy of the ellipse as the end cap in later steps.

4) Select the original ellipse and then choose Modify > Ungroup.

The basic shapes you draw with the Ellipse and Rectangle tools are grouped as one object by default. Since they are grouped, you see the four corner handles of the bounding box of the selected object instead of individual points. When you ungroup the object, you see the points on the object that control its shape. You want to split the ellipse at those four points, breaking the ellipse into four separate pieces.

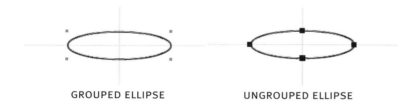

GROUPED ELLIPSE   UNGROUPED ELLIPSE

5) Using the Pointer tool, drag around the entire ellipse with the selection rectangle.

All points on the ellipse should now be selected. Selected points have hollow squares instead of solid squares. You should also see handles jutting out from the selected points. You'll learn more about these handles in a later lesson.

NOTE *When you drag the Pointer tool on the page, you see a dashed rectangle. All objects within that rectangle, called the selection rectangle, are selected when you release the mouse button. In later lessons, you will use the selection rectangle to select multiple items on the page.*

6) Choose Modify > Split.

The ellipse is split into four objects. You want to use the lower left arc to draw the left half of the canister base. Look at the Object panel. It should show that you have four objects selected.

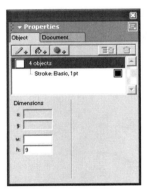

7) Press Tab to deselect the four sections of the ellipse. Using the Pointer tool, select and then delete the top two sections and the lower right section, leaving only the lower left arc.

Another method is to hold down Shift and click the lower left arc with the Pointer tool. This deselects only the lower left arc. You can then delete the three remaining selected arcs. The Shift key works as a toggle, adding to or subtracting from the selection.

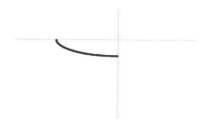

8) Hold down Alt (Windows) or Option (Mac OS) and drag down to create a copy of the arc. Add Shift as you drag to prevent the copy from moving left or right.

The copy of the arc is the bottom section of the left side of the canister. The film canister is tall and skinny. Drag the copy down approximately three times the width of the arc. To complete the left side of the canister, you just need to connect the two arcs with two vertical lines. The quickest way to do this is to join the two arcs, which you will do in the next step.

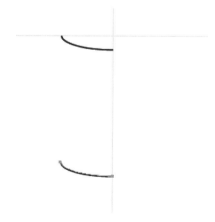

71

9) Hold down Shift and select the top arc with the Pointer tool; then choose Modify > Join.

A vertical line is drawn, connecting the two arcs on one side.

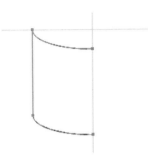

NOTE *The Join command does not always work as expected. If you do not get a connecting line as shown, draw a vertical line with the Line tool between the arcs and then use the Join command to connect the line to the two arcs.*

10) Click Closed in the Object panel.

FreeHand draws a line connecting the other two points in the arcs, creating a closed path.

 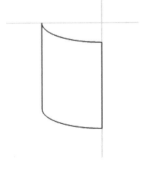

REFLECTING OBJECTS

Reflecting flips a selected object or objects about a specific axis. Often you will want mirror images of the objects you draw. For example, the shape you just created is the left side of the canister. The other side is the same shape flipped to the right. FreeHand provides several ways to reflect objects: using the Reflect tool, the Reflect panel, and the Mirror tool. The Reflect panel and the Reflect tool accomplish the same tasks. Depending on your preferences, you may find one easier to use than the other. For example, with the Reflect tool, you see the results on the screen as you use the tool. With the Reflect panel, you enter the axis angle you want to use for the reflection.

You will now make a copy of the shape you just created and then use the Reflect tool to flip it about the vertical axis. Later in this lesson, you will use the Reflect panel and the Mirror tool.

1) Select the shape and then choose Edit > Clone.

Cloning an object makes an exact copy and places it directly on top of the original. The clone is currently selected.

2) Hold down the mouse on the Scale tool and choose the Reflect tool from the tool group.

Three other tools are grouped with the Scale tool: the Rotate tool, the Reflect tool, and the Skew tool. Selecting any of these tools changes the cursor to a star.

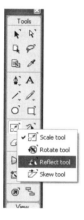

The **Scale tool** allows you to scale a selected object by dragging. If you hold down Shift as you drag, the object is scaled proportionally. You will scale one of your objects later in this lesson.

The **Rotate tool** allows you to rotate a selected object by dragging. You will rotate an object later in this lesson.

The **Skew tool** allows you to skew (or distort) a selected object by dragging.

73

3) Move the pointer over the right side of the object. Hold down Shift and drag down.

The clone of the shape flips about the vertical axis. Holding down Shift as you drag constrains the reflected angle to 90-degrees. Release the mouse button when you see the mirror image of the shape.

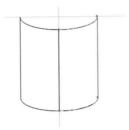

N O T E *If you are confused about the concept of dragging down to flip an object about the vertical axis, you may find this explanation helpful. Look at the palm of your hand, with your fingers pointing toward the ceiling. Flip your hand, leaving your little finger in the same space. You've reflected your hand about the vertical axis. The dragging down (or up) motion tells FreeHand to use the vertical axis. If you drag to the left or right, you flip the object about the horizontal axis.*

4) Choose Edit > Special > Paste in Front.

The copy of the original ellipse is pasted at the top of the body of the canister.

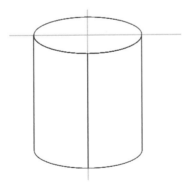

N O T E *If you cleared your clipboard by closing the application or making a copy of an object other than the ellipse, you will need to make a copy of the ellipse that you placed on the pasteboard earlier.*

5) Save your file.

ON YOUR OWN

On the top of the film canister is a spindle for winding the film. To create this part, you repeat the steps you used to draw the left side of the canister. The exception is that when you split the ellipse, this time you split it only on the left and right sides. To do that, select the left point after you ungroup the ellipse and then hold down Shift and select the right point. Move the spindle to the middle of the top ellipse of the canister.

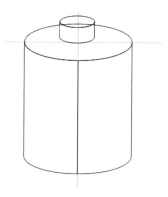

SCALING OBJECTS

You can use several methods to change the size of objects. You can use the Scale tool or the Scale panel, or you can drag a selection handle of a basic shape or use the transform handles on the object. If you want to scale an object by an exact percentage, use the Scale panel. If you want to scale the object visually, you can use any of the other methods.

In the next steps, you will make a copy of the left side of the canister and use the transformation handles to make it smaller. Then you will make a copy of this smaller object. Later in this lesson, you will apply a gradient fill to add some dimension to the film canister.

1) Using the Pointer tool, select the left side of the canister with the Pointer tool and then choose Edit > Clone.

The clone of the object is selected.

2) Double-click the outline of the cloned object.

The object displays transformation handles.

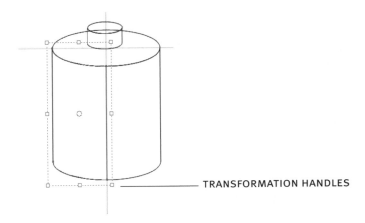

TRANSFORMATION HANDLES

3) Position the pointer over one of the corner handles and drag toward the middle of the object. Press Tab to release the transformation handles.

As you drag, the object gets smaller. You want the object less than half the height and about 70 percent of the width of the original object. If you drag a corner handle, you change both the width and the height. If you need to change just the height or the width, drag one of the side handles. To scale the width and height proportionally, hold down Shift as you drag a corner handle.

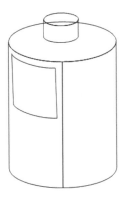

NOTE *If you want to change the shape of the curve of the interior object, use the Pointer tool to select a point and then use the arrow keys to nudge the point upwards or downwards.*

4) Position the new object toward the top of the left side of the canister. Hold down Alt (Windows) or Option (Mac OS) and drag to make a copy of the new shape. Add Shift as you drag to constrain the copy as you drag.

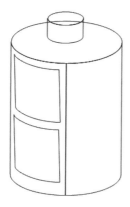

5) Save your file.

USING THE REFLECT PANEL AND THE MIRROR TOOL

If you know the exact angle that you want an object reflected, you can use the Reflect panel instead of the Reflect tool. Using the Reflect panel, you can reflect a single object, or you can make copies of the object as you reflect it. By default, the object is reflected around its center point, but you can change the reflection point if you prefer.

The Mirror tool lets you clone and reflect an object a specific number of times in one click. You could have used this tool to clone and reflect the canister body; it is also great for creating geometric patterns and designs.

You've already used the Reflect tool on your image, but you will now experiment with the Reflect panel and the Mirror tool to see how they work as well. In the next steps, you will type some text off to the side of your page and use the Reflect panel and then the Mirror tool to create and then reflect a copy.

1) Select the Text tool and type some text on the pasteboard; for example, type your name.

Remember that the pasteboard is anywhere outside the boundaries of the page. Since you are just experimenting with other reflection methods, the pasteboard is a convenient location to place your text.

2) Double-click the Reflect tool on the Tools panel to open the Reflect panel.

The Reflect panel is in the Align and Transform panel group along with the Scale, Rotate, and Skew panels. Here you can enter the reflection axis in degrees, specify the center point of the reflection, and select options to reflect the contents and fills of the object.

The X and Y values indicate the center point of the text block. If you reflect the text and make a copy, the copy is placed on top of the original, reflected on that center point. However, you want the copy reflected and placed to the right of the original text. In the next step, you'll change the center point of the reflection.

3) Hold down Alt (Windows) or Option (Mac OS) and click the right side of the text block.

The X and Y values for the center point change to the position where you clicked the text block.

NOTE *You must have the Reflect tool selected when you press the Alt or Option key to change the center point of the selected object. If you don't see the star cursor, the Reflect tool is not selected.*

4) Enter *90* as the reflection axis angle, enter *1* as the number of copies, and click Reflect.

A copy of the text is reflected to the right of the original text block, flipping over the new center point. When you enter 90 degrees as the reflection angle, you reflect the object across its vertical axis. If you'd entered 180 degrees as the reflection angle, the object would be reflected across its horizontal axis. Positive numbers reflect the object counterclockwise; negative numbers reflect the object clockwise.

5) Select the Polygon tool; then double-click the tool to open the Polygon Tool dialog box. Select Star as the shape, type *5* as the number of sides, and select Automatic as the Star Points option. Click OK. Drag to draw a star.

You will next use the Mirror tool to reflect the star multiple times.

6) Choose Window > Toolbars > Xtra Tools.

MIRROR TOOL

7) Double-click the Mirror tool to open the Mirror dialog box. Select Multiple from the pop-up menu, type *12* as the number of copies, choose Rotate, and click OK.

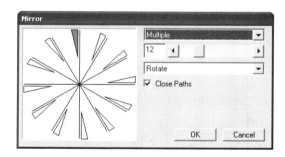

In the top pop-up menu, you can choose the reflection angle you want to use: Vertical, Horizontal, Horizontal and Vertical, or Multiple.

8) Drag the star. Release the mouse when you see a pattern of stars.

The Mirror tool reflects objects around a center point. As you drag, you see a preview of the objects you are reflecting. In this case, you are creating 12 stars.

You don't need the text or the star pattern you drew to experiment with these tools. You can delete them, or you can leave them if they are on the pasteboard.

USING THE COLOR MIXER

You can add colors to objects in a variety of ways, and you can easily add, edit, or change the colors you use in your drawings.

You have a choice of three **color models** for mixing colors: CMYK, RGB, and Spot. The color model you choose depends on how you plan to use your drawing. If you are planning to export your drawing and use it in a print publication that includes color photographs, for example, choose CMYK because you will need to use at least the four process inks (cyan, magenta, yellow, and black) to print the photographs. If you are printing your document with spot colors, choose either CMYK or RGB.

If your drawing is destined for online distribution (for use on a CD or the web), choose RGB or the System color model. If your drawing is headed for the web, you may also want to stick to web-safe colors.

The number of colors computer monitors display depends on the bit depth of the monitor. An 8-bit monitor displays 256 colors; a 24-bit monitor displays 16,777,216 colors (or millions of colors). In the early days of the Internet, color monitors displayed only 256 colors. To make web pages display colors correctly, you need to create your artwork using only 256 colors. In addition to the 256-color restriction, web browsers have a palette of only 216 colors common to both Windows-based and Macintosh computers. These colors are commonly called **web-safe colors**. Using a web-safe color ensures that your colors are displayed correctly on any computer.

If you don't use web-safe colors, then the colors in your graphics won't appear exactly as they were defined for users with only 8-bit color monitors. Colors other than web-safe colors **dither** on the screen. Dithering is a process of combining two colors to fake a color. For example, to achieve an orange color, the monitor might alternate red and yellow colors instead of displaying one solid color. The problem with dithering is that the resulting color looks grainy.

In the next steps, you will use the **Color Mixer** to mix a color and then save that color on the Swatches panel.

1) Choose Window > Color Mixer to open the Mixer panel.

The Color Mixer is in the Mixer and Tints panel group. You can also open that panel group to access the panel if it is within the panel docking area.

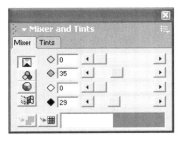

2) Select RGB as the color model; then type *252* in the R text box, *237* in the G text box, and *0* (zero) in the B text box.

As you enter the values, the color ramp displays the mixed color. You should see a yellow color on the ramp.

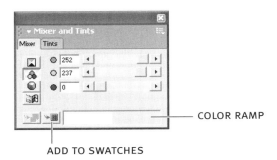

COLOR RAMP

ADD TO SWATCHES

3) Click Add to Swatches on the Color Mixer panel. In the Add to Swatches dialog box, choose Spot and then click Add.

After you mix a color, you can save it on the Swatches panel for coloring other objects in your drawing.

NOTE *Due to a bug in Freehand, the numbers you add to the Swatches panel are often off by one. This is the result of a numeric roundoff problem, but your values should match just fine.*

USING THE SWATCHES PANEL

You use the **Swatches panel** to store your mixed colors, name your colors, apply colors, duplicate colors, import colors from color libraries, and convert colors from spot to process, process to spot, and RGB to CMYK. The panel includes selectors for applying colors to the fill or the stroke, or to both the fill and the stroke, of an object.

1) Choose Window > Swatches to open the Swatches panel if it is not already open.

The Swatches panel is in the Assets panel group. You can also access the Swatches panel by opening this panel group if it is closed. The panel should display the yellow color you just created. The name of the color is the name of your color mix: 252r 237g 0b.

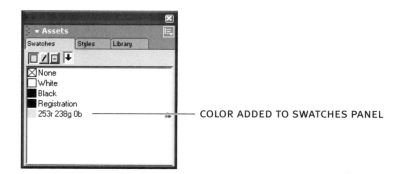

COLOR ADDED TO SWATCHES PANEL

NOTE *If the color is a process color, the name of the color appears in italics. The names of spot colors appear in plain text, as shown for your yellow color.*

2) Drag the yellow color chip from the Swatches panel and drop it on the right side of your film canister.

FreeHand provides several methods for applying colors to objects on a page. The film canister is a large target, so in this case you can use the drag-and-drop method. For smaller objects, you can first select the object and then drop the color chip on the fill selector on the Swatches panel. You can also add a fill from the Object panel and then change the color from the color pop-up menu on the panel.

DRAG COLOR CHIP...   ... TO HERE

USING THE TINTS PANEL

Tints are lighter versions of a color. Shades of gray, for example, are just percentages or tints of black. Once you create your color, you can use the Tints panel to create the tints. In this task you will create several tints of black and then use them to color portions of your film canister. Then you will use the tints as part of a gradient.

NOTE *Tints retain a relationship to their parent color. This means if you alter the parent color, the tint changes as well. If you make a tint from a spot color, the tint prints on the same plate as the parent color.*

1) Click the Tints tab in the Mixer and Tints panel group.

The Tints panel is initially grouped with the Color Mixer in the Mixer and Tints panel group.

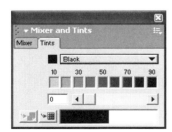

2) Choose Black from the color pop-up menu.

All of the colors that you have added to the Swatches panel, plus black and white, appear in the pop-up menu. After you pick the color, you'll see nine tints ranging from 10 percent to 90 percent. You'll also see a color slider and percentage text box where you can enter any number between 0 and 100.

3) Click the 50 percent color chip to select that tint.

You could also drag the slider to 50 or type *50* in the percentage text box.

When you select a tint, the color ramp is divided into two sections. The left side displays the original color; the right side displays the selected color.

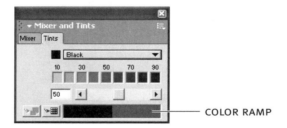

COLOR RAMP

4) Position the pointer on the gray color on the ramp and drag it to the Swatches panel.

As you drag, you see a gray color chip. After you release the mouse button, the color is added to the Swatches panel.

POWER TIP *Hold down Alt (Windows) or Option (Mac OS) and click a color on the Swatches panel to open the Tints panel with that color.*

5) Repeat steps 3 and 4 and add 80 percent and 30 percent black to the Swatches panel.

The colors you add to the Swatches panel are added at the bottom of the list. If you want to change the order in the list, drag the name of the color up or down in the list.

NOTE *You can also drag the tint color chip on the Tints panel to the Swatches panel.*

6) Drag the 50% black tint from the Swatches panel to the top ellipse of the film canister.

As long as the object is large enough for the color chip, you can drop a color on an object even though the object is not selected. If your object is too small, you may need to select it first or change the view magnification to make the object larger.

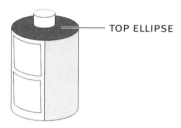

TOP ELLIPSE

7) Select the bottom part of the spindle on top of the film canister.

Since this part is small, you will use another method to change its fill color.

BOTTOM PART OF SPINDLE

8) Drag the 80% black color chip from the Swatches panel to the Fill selector at the top of the panel. Drag the black color chip to the Stroke selector.

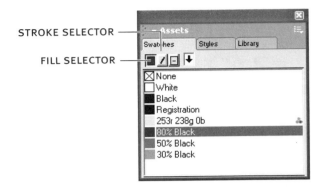

STROKE SELECTOR

FILL SELECTOR

9) Select the top ellipse of the spindle. Drag the black color chip to the Fill selector and the 30% black color chip to the Stroke selector.

Adding a lighter color to the stroke should make the top part of the spindle more prominent.

10) Change the fill color of the two shapes on the left side of the canister to 30% black and then change the left side of the canister to black.

If you'd first changed the fill of the left side of the canister, you wouldn't see the outlines of the two shapes on top since their strokes are black. However, you could still drop the gray color on them even without being able to see them.

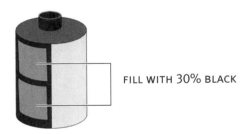

FILL WITH 30% BLACK

11) Save your file.

ADDING GRADIENTS

Adding colors to your film canister makes it look better, but the colors are flat and don't show the viewer the three-dimensional quality of the item. To aid in that illusion, you will add a **gradient** fill, which provides a smooth transition from one color to another. Look at any shiny, round object and you'll see a variation in color where light hits the surface.

To add some dimension to your film canister, you will add a gradient to the two shapes on the left side of the canister.

1) Select the top left shape on the canister. Select the Fill property on the Object panel. Choose Gradient from the Fill Type pop-up menu.

When you change the fill type, the Object panel changes to display options for that fill type. The default gradient is Linear. Your selected shape should now contain a linear gradient, from 30% black to white. FreeHand uses the original fill color of the object as the first color and uses white as the second color. Those colors should appear on the gradient ramp on the Object panel.

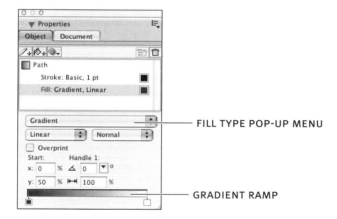

FILL TYPE POP-UP MENU

GRADIENT RAMP

TIP *You can click the color pop-up boxes on the gradient ramp to change the colors of the gradient.*

COLORS, GRADIENTS, AND STYLES

On the selected object, you will see a start point (a filled circle) and a **gradient handle** (a filled square) for the gradient. (Radial and Rectangle gradients display two gradient handles.) You can drag the start point and the handle to change the effect of the gradient within the object. Dragging the handle up or down changes the angle of the gradient.

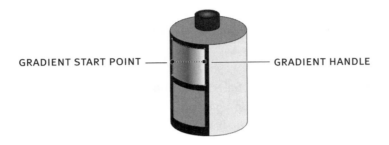

GRADIENT START POINT ——————— GRADIENT HANDLE

NOTE *The gradient handles of a selected object appear only when the Gradient fill property is selected on the Object panel.*

The Object panel displays the X and Y values for the start point, the angle of the handle, and the length of the handle as percentages of the width of the object. You might want to experiment by moving the handle and the start point to see the effects on the gradient in the object. To return the gradient start point to the edge of the object, drag the start point back, or type *0* in the X text box on the Object panel. To extend the handle to the other side of the object, type *100* as the length percentage.

⊙ POWER TIP *Double-click either the start or the end point of the gradient handle to quickly return the point to its original position.*

You can specify the type of gradient you want and the behavior of the gradient. FreeHand offers six types of gradient: Linear, Radial, Contour, Logarithmic, Rectangle, and Cone. You want the Linear gradient for this exercise, but you may want to experiment with the other types to see the different effects you can achieve. Use the pop-up menu on the Object panel to change the gradient type.

You can also change the gradient behavior by selecting an option from the behavior type pop-up menu. Your choices here are Normal, Repeat, Reflect, and Auto Size. When you choose Normal, the position of the end points determines the length of the gradient. When you choose Repeat, the gradient repeats a specific number of times. When you choose Reflect, the colors in the gradient transition from one end of the color ramp and then back, repeating the number of times specified. When you choose Auto Size, the length of the gradient is set to the exact width and height of the object. The gradient handles do not appear when you choose Auto Size; if you want to adjust the gradient, use the attribute settings on the Object panel.

2) Drag the 50% black color chip from the Swatches panel to the middle of the gradient ramp on the Object panel.

You just added a new color to the gradient, and you should see the results in the object. You can move the color chip left or right to change the position of the color in the gradient. Try moving it closer to the left color chip to see if you get the effect of a cylinder.

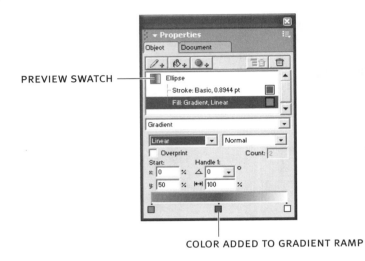

PREVIEW SWATCH

COLOR ADDED TO GRADIENT RAMP

NOTE *You can add up to 32 colors on a gradient ramp. To delete a color from the gradient ramp, just drag it away from the ramp.*

3) Select the top ellipse of the spindle on the top of the film canister. Select the Fill property on the Object panel and change the fill type to a Radial gradient. Drag the black color chip to the left chip in the gradient, and drag the 50% black color chip to the right chip in the gradient.

You should see a subtle change in the ellipse; it should look like a hollow cylinder. Experiment with other tints of black if you want to change the look even more.

POWER TIP *You can drag the preview swatch on the Object panel of a selected object and drop it on other objects. The attributes of the selected object are copied to the target object.*

USING THE STYLES PANEL

As you create the fills and effects for your objects, you may need to use the exact fill that was applied to other objects. For example, you just applied a gradient to one of the shapes you added to the film canister. That gradient needs to be applied to the other shape you added as well. You could just delete the second shape and then make a copy of the shape with the gradient. That method would work just fine; that is how you originally created the second shape. FreeHand provides another way as well: you can save the gradient fill in the **Styles panel** and apply it from there.

Styles are simply named collections of formatting attributes. If you are familiar with style sheets in word processing or page layout programs, you probably already have a good idea of how styles work. Not only can you save text styles for your work in FreeHand, but you can also save graphic styles. You'll work with text styles in Lesson 7, "Page Layout and Printing." For now, you will learn only about graphics styles.

Whenever you find yourself choosing the same formatting attributes for objects, you should consider saving those attributes as a style. Not only will this speed up your production time, but it will also ensure consistency throughout your document. In addition, if you change an attribute of a style, all objects using that style will be changed automatically when you redefine the style. For example, suppose your drawing uses a red color that matches the red of a company logo, and the company changes the logo color and you need to update your drawing. Instead of having to change the color of each individual object, you simply need to redefine the style with a different color, and your entire document will be updated instantly.

In FreeHand, the best way to create a style is by example. You've already created the gradient. In the next steps, you will save your gradient as a style and then apply it to the other shape.

1) Choose Window > Styles to open the Styles panel.

The Styles panel is grouped with the Swatches and Library panels in the Assets panel group. If the panel group is already open, you can also click the Styles tab to open the panel. The panel has three default styles: Normal for graphics, Normal for text, and Normal for connectors. (Connectors are covered in a later lesson.)

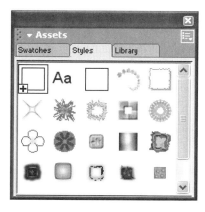

COLORS, GRADIENTS, AND STYLES

2) Choose Large List View from the Options menu on the Styles panel.

The Options menu is located at the top right on all panels. Click the icon (which looks like a series of three dots and lines) to access the menu.

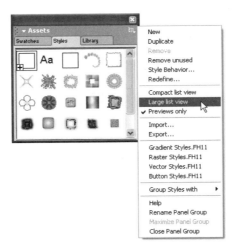

You can view styles in three ways on the panel: using Compact List View, Large List View, and Previews Only. Previews Only (the default) displays only a picture of the style and is not very informative. The two list views display a picture and the style name. If you have many styles defined, you may prefer the compact view so you can see more styles on the panel.

3) Select the shape that contains the gradient. Choose New from the Styles panel Options menu.

A new style with the attributes of the selected object is added to the end of the style list and named Style-1.

○ **POWER TIP** *You can also create the new style by dragging the object onto the Styles panel or dragging the preview swatch of the object onto the Styles panel.*

4) Double-click the default name of the new style, Style-1. Type *Gradient* as the style name and press Enter (Windows) or Return (Mac OS) to apply the name to the style.

The name of your style is not limited to a single word, as you've used here. If your document uses several gradient styles, name each one to describe its attributes.

STYLE SWATCH ——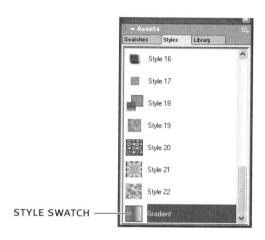

5) Select the second shape on the left side of the canister and select the new Gradient style from the Styles panel.

The style is applied to the shape. The two shapes are now identical.

⊙ POWER TIP *You could also drag the style swatch and drop it on the second shape to apply the style to the object.*

TIP *When you applied the style, all of the attributes (the stroke and fill, for example) were applied to the new object. You could change the style so that only the fill is applied to objects. Select the style name on the Styles panel and choose Style Behavior from the Style Options menu. Choose Fill Attributes from the Style Effects pop-up menu in the Edit Style dialog box.*

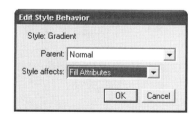

DRAWING THE BAR CODE

Your film canister is almost complete, but you still need to add some text and the bar code. In Lesson 1, you used the Blend tool to create a specific number of equally spaced lines. To create the bar code, you will use a similar method. First, you need to create one of the lines that will be used for the bar code. The line needs to mimic the curvature of the canister bottom. There are several methods for creating the arc. Here, instead of trying to draw the arc, you will make a copy of the right side of the canister, split the object, and then use the Knife tool to make the arc smaller. You've already learned all of the skills needed for this task, making this next exercise a good review. You may want to try drawing the bar code on your own. If so, just skip the following steps.

1) Make a copy of the right side (the yellow side) of the canister and move it off to the side.

Use any method you've learned to make the copy.

2) Drag the selection rectangle around the copy to select all of the points.

The four points of the object should be hollow, indicating that the points are selected.

3) Choose Modify > Split. Press Tab to deselect everything. Select and delete the top and side objects.

You need only the bottom portion of the split object.

4) Move the arc over the yellow part of the canister, toward the bottom.

This curved line is the bottom line of the bar code. It is longer than the canister and needs to be cut. In the next step, you will use the Knife tool to make the line smaller.

5) Select the Knife tool and drag it vertically through the selected curved line to make the cut. Press Tab to deselect everything and then select the line to the right of your cut. Delete this portion.

The resulting curved line should follow the curvature of the bottom of the canister. Now you just need to make some copies of the line and blend them to create the bar code.

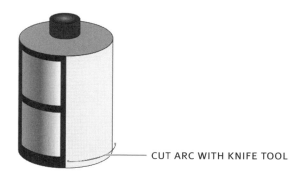

CUT ARC WITH KNIFE TOOL

◎ P O W E R   T I P *The Knife tool works only if the object is selected. If the object is not selected when you choose the Knife tool, you can press Ctrl (Windows) or Command (Mac OS) to change to the Pointer tool and then select the line. When you release the Ctrl or Command key, the cursor returns to the Knife tool. This shortcut for the temporary Pointer tool works with any of the other tools and is a real time saver.*

6) Use the Alt-drag or Option-drag method you've learned to make two copies of the new curved line. Hold down Shift as you drag to constrain the movement.

You don't want the two new lines equally spaced. Make the space between the first and second lines bigger than the space between the first line and the original line.

THREE ARCS

COLORS, GRADIENTS, AND STYLES

7) Hold down Shift and select the three lines. Choose Modify > Combine > Blend. On the Object panel, change the number of steps for the blend to *8*.

You can experiment with the number of steps to see what results you like the best.

8) Save your file.

USING THE SUBSELECT TOOL

You use the Subselect tool to select items in a group or, in this case, to select the lines that make up the bar code. If you select the bar code with the Pointer tool, you'll see that the lines are grouped. You could ungroup the objects, but then you'll need to select them all again to regroup them. By using the Subselect tool, you can select and change an element within a group. When you deselect the item, it remains grouped with the other items.

To make the bar code look more realistic, you will change the point size of each of the three lines of the blend.

1) Select the Subselect tool from the Tools panel.

The cursor changes to the hollow pointer of the Subselect tool.

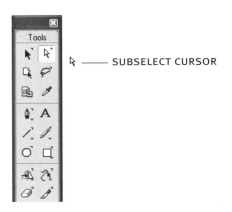

SUBSELECT CURSOR

2) Select the bottom line of the bar code. On the Objects panel, change the size of the stroke to *1.75* points. Select the middle line in the bar code and change its stroke to *1.5* points. Select the top line of the bar code and change its stroke to *0.5* points.

The widths of the lines in the blend now vary from 0.5 to 1.75 points.

⊙ **POWER TIP** *You can temporarily access the Subselect tool by holding down Alt (Windows) or Option (Mac OS) when you have the Pointer tool selected. If you have another tool selected, hold down Ctrl+Alt (Windows) or Command+Option (Mac OS) to access the Subselect tool. Using one of these methods is generally faster than choosing the tool from the Tools panel. When you release the modifier keys, you are returned to the originally selected tool.*

3) Save your file.

NOTE *When you use the Subselect tool or the Subselect shortcut on a blend, you can select only the original items used to create the blend; you can't select the items created by the blend. If you want to make a change to each individual item, you will have to ungroup the blend. Choose Modify > Ungroup twice to access the individual lines. Once you ungroup the blend, it is no longer a blend, which means that you can't change the number of steps.*

USING THE ARC TOOL

An alternative method for drawing the bar code is to use the Arc tool. The Arc tool draws a quarter of an ellipse. The advantage to drawing the arc as you did previously is that the curvature of the arc exactly matches the curvature of the canister. Using the Arc tool is faster but may not be as accurate.

1) Choose Window > Toolbars > Xtra Tools.

ARC TOOL

2) Double-click the Arc tool to access the Arc tool options. Select Create Open Arc and Create Flipped Arc. Leave the other option deselected. Click OK.

FreeHand gives you three options for creating an arc:

- **Create Open Arc** creates a single-line path between the end points of the arc. When this option is not selected, FreeHand joins the paths to create a pie shape.

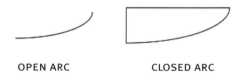

OPEN ARC   CLOSED ARC

- **Create Flipped Arc** flips the orientation of the arc.
- **Create Concave Arc** creates an arc with an outer corner.

CONCAVE ARC

98

3) Position the pointer just above the bottom of the film canister on the right side. Drag to draw the arc.

As you drag, you control the curvature of the arc. Drag up to make the curvature more pronounced. If you are not happy with the shape of the arc, you can delete the arc and try again. You can also use the Pointer tool to select one of the end points and then use the arrow keys to slowly adjust the arc.

4) Repeat from step 6 in the section "Drawing the Bar Code" to draw the remaining parts of the bar code.

If the arc is too long on one side, you can use the Knife tool to cut off that end. Make the cut before creating the additional copies.

ROTATING ITEMS

You are almost done; but don't take a break yet. The last task to complete the film canister is to add some text. You want the text to appear vertically on the canister. You can rotate items in several ways: you can use the Rotate tool, the Rotate panel, or the transformation handles.

1) Select the Text tool and type the following text: ISO 200 FILM. Format the text as Arial Black, 10 points.

Place the text to the side of the film canister for now. You will move it on top of the canister after you rotate it.

NOTE *The size of the text depends on the size of your canister. You can change the point size if you need to after you rotate the text.*

2) Choose Window › Toolbars › Info.

The Info toolbar displays the X,Y position of the pointer and the center point and angle of rotation as you rotate the text.

NOTE *In Windows, the information is also displayed in the Status toolbar.*

3) Select the Rotate tool on the Tools panel.

Remember that the Rotate tool is grouped with the Scale and Reflect tools. You get the same star cursor as with the Reflect and Scale tools.

4) Click within the text block and hold down the mouse button. Move the pointer away from the text block and drag up until you see "angle:90" displayed in the Info panel.

The place you clicked becomes the center of rotation. By moving the pointer away from the center point, you can more easily control the angle of rotation. The closer the pointer is to the center point, the faster the object rotates around the center point. If you add Shift as you rotate the object, the rotation is constrained to 45-degree angles.

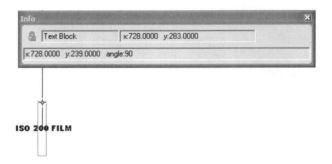

5) Use the Pointer tool to move the text block above the bar code.

After you place the text block, you may need to change the point size. You can still change the size even though the text block is rotated. Use the Object panel as you normally would to change the size.

6) Save your file.

Although the Rotate tool is easy to use, there are times when you may prefer to use the other methods of rotating objects. For example, if you know the angle you want to use, you can enter the angle on the Rotate panel instead of dragging the object around a center point. To access the panel, double-click the tool as you did to access the Reflect panel. Type the rotation angle and then click Rotate. Notice that you can choose to rotate only the object and not the contents and fills. (Deselect both

Contents and Fills on the panel to rotate only the outline of the object.) This option is available only when you use the Rotate panel.

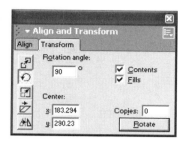

You can also double-click the object with the Pointer tool to display the transformation handles. Move the pointer to one of the corner handles until you see the curved double arrow. Hold down Shift as you drag around the object to constrain the rotation. Press Tab to release the transformation handles.

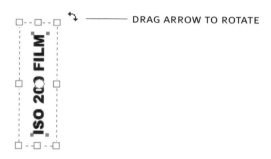

WHAT YOU HAVE LEARNED

In this lesson, you have:

- Split and joined paths (pages 68–72)
- Reflected and scaled objects (pages 72–77)
- Used the Reflect panel and the Mirror tool to flip objects about an axis (pages 77–80)
- Used the Color Mixer and Tints panel to create colors and added those colors to the Swatches panel (pages 80–86)
- Created gradients and added them to objects (pages 87–90)
- Used the Styles panel to save attributes of a graphic (pages 90–93)
- Used the Subselect tool to select items in a group (pages 96–97)
- Used the Arc tool to draw an arc (pages 98–99)
- Used the Rotate tool to rotate text (pages 99–101)

using layers

As you create drawings that are more complex, you will want to organize and control the elements on the page. You can do that with layers. **Layers** are transparent planes on which you place your objects. You can choose to show or hide a layer, which shows or hides all of the objects on that layer. You can move a layer up or down, changing the stacking order in which objects appear on a page.

Say, for example, that you are drawing a complex map of an area. The map contains streets and highways, rivers, railroads, and descriptive text. While you are concentrating on the streets, you don't want to be distracted by the rivers and the railroads. If you put all of the streets and highways, rivers, railroads, and text each on a separate layer, you can quickly hide and then show the layers as you work on a part of the map.

Using layers in your drawings makes managing multiple objects easier, as you will learn in this lesson.

In this lesson, you will add some layers to the document containing your film canister. Then you will draw a strip of film and change its perspective using the 3D Rotation tool.

WHAT YOU WILL LEARN

In this lesson, you will:

- Move objects above and below other objects
- Add layers and move objects to those layers
- Change the order of layers
- Hide, show, and lock layers
- Align and distribute objects
- Rotate an object in 3D space
- Change the color of a layer

APPROXIMATE TIME

This lesson takes approximately 2 hours to complete.

LESSON FILES

Media Files:

None

Starting Files:

Lesson04\Start\film_canister_start.fh11

Completed Projects:

Lesson04\Completed\film_canister.fh11

USING THE ARRANGE COMMANDS

You may have noticed that each object you've drawn on the page has been placed on top of the last object you drew. You haven't defined any layers, but you are stacking objects as you draw them. All of the objects you've drawn up to now have been placed on the default layer: the Foreground layer. If you have followed the step-by-step instructions, you've drawn the objects in the proper sequence, and you may not have noticed the stacking order of the objects.

To see how the stacking order affects the objects on your page, you will use the Arrange commands to move your objects in front of or behind other objects. The FreeHand commands to bring objects to the front and send objects to the back work like similar commands in other graphics programs. If you are familiar with these concepts, you can skip this section and jump to the section "Using the Layers Panel."

1) Open the film_canister.fh11 file if it is not already open. Select one of the two shapes (with the gradient) on the left side of the canister.

You can also use the film_canister_start.fh11 file in the Start folder within the Lesson04 folder if you no longer have your file.

SELECTED SHAPE

You are going to experiment with the Arrange commands.

2) Choose Modify > Arrange > Send to Back.

The shape moves behind the black object. It is hidden except for its blue outline, indicating that it is still selected. Leave it selected.

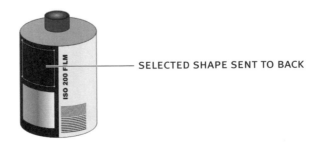

SELECTED SHAPE SENT TO BACK

3) Choose Modify › Arrange › Bring to Front.

The item returns to its original position, in front of the black object.

Although you didn't need to change the arrangement of this item, there will be times when you want to move objects in front of or behind other objects. Remember that objects with fills hide the objects behind them. In a later lesson, you will apply transparency to objects. When you apply transparency, the opacity level of the top object determines how much of the object below it you see. For now, though, just remember that filled objects are opaque.

> **NOTE** *If you deselected the object before bringing it back to the front, you'll discover that it is a bit difficult to select it again. An easier approach in this case is to select the black portion of the film canister and send it to the back. The smaller piece is then on top again.*

The Arrange commands not only allow you to move objects to the very front or to the very back, but also forward or backward in the stack one object at a time. The left side of the film canister is only two objects deep, so choosing Send Backward would be the same as choosing Send to Back. If you'd like to experiment with the other commands, draw a filled rectangle on top of the left side of the film canister and place it so a portion of it is off the canister so you can see it move forward and backward.

USING THE LAYERS PANEL

The Arrange commands you experimented with in the previous section control only items on a single layer. Using the **Layers panel**, you can add separate layers for your objects and change the order of each layer. Note the distinction between the stacking order within a layer and the layer order: if an object is on the top layer and you send it to the back, it will be the bottom object on that layer, but it will still be above any object on a layer below it.

FreeHand has three default layers: Foreground, Guides, and Background. You can add multiple foreground and background layers. The Foreground layer is the default layer for objects on the page. The Guides layer holds all of the guides you use for aligning elements in your document. One use of a background layer is to place objects that you want to trace. For example, you might have a logo or a piece of artwork that you've scanned and want to use as a guide for your drawing. Objects on a background layer are screened to 50 percent of their original color, making them easier for you to trace. In Lesson 5, "Using Points and Paths," you will place some artwork on the Background layer to use as a guide for drawing.

The Layers panel is divided into two sections: the top section contains foreground layers; the bottom section is for background layers. Any layer (except the Guides layer) above the separator line on the Layers panel is a printing layer. Any layer below the separator line is a nonprinting background layer.

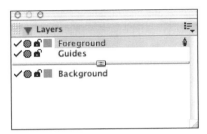

In the next section, you will add layers to your document and move objects onto the layers.

1) Open your film_canister.fh11 file if it is not already open.

You can also use the film_canister_start.fh11 file in the Start folder within the Lesson04 folder if you no longer have your file.

2) Select the text block on the film canister.

Look at the Layers panel. The Foreground layer is highlighted, indicating that the selected object is on that layer.

3) Choose New from the Layers panel Options menu.

A new layer, named Layer-1, is added at the top level on the Layers panel.

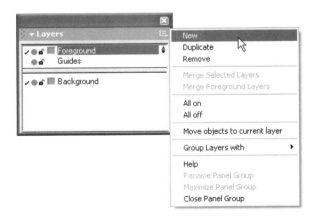

4) Select Layer-1 on the Layers panel.

The selected text block moves to the layer.

NOTE *This is the default behavior, but you can change this in your preferences. If this step doesn't work as described, check the Panel section of the Preferences dialog box and verify that the option to click the layer name to move selected objects is selected.*

5) Double-click the Layer-1 name to select it and then type *text*. Press Enter (Windows) or Return (Macintosh) to rename the layer. Press Tab to deselect the text block.

It is very easy to move an object to a layer. You select the object or objects and then select the name of the layer on the Layers panel. It is also just as easy to inadvertently move objects to the wrong layers. Just remember that anything that is selected when you select a layer is moved to that layer. When you are changing a layer name or moving a layer, be sure to press Tab to deselect all objects on the page before making the change to the layer.

NOTE *If you find yourself continually moving objects to the wrong layer, deselect the option in the Panel section of the Preferences dialog box and deselect the option to click the layer name to move selected objects.*

If you are drawing a new object and want it placed on a layer, deselect everything, select the layer, and then create the object. It will be placed on the selected layer. If you later decide to move the object to another layer, select the object and then select the new layer while the object is still selected.

NOTE *The Layers panel displays a small pen icon to the right of the text layer you just created. That icon indicates the active layer. New objects you create are always placed on the active layer. The blue bar across the layer name doesn't represent the active layer unless you see the pen icon as well. Select the yellow object on the page. The Layers panel highlights (with the blue bar) the layer name, but the pen icon remains on the text layer. If you draw a new object on the page, it will be placed on the text layer.*

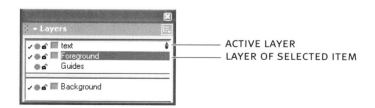

ACTIVE LAYER
LAYER OF SELECTED ITEM

6) Create a new layer, name it *bar code*, and move the bar code object to that layer.

You now have three foreground layers in addition to the Guides layer.

7) Click the lock icon to the left of the bar code layer name.

When a layer is locked, you can't select any objects on that layer. You also can't move an object to that layer. When working on complex drawings, it is very handy to lock a layer you are not currently modifying or using. That way, you can't inadvertently delete or move the contents of the layer. However, you can still change the stacking position of a layer when it is locked.

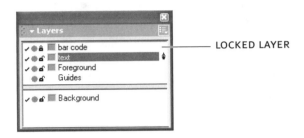

LOCKED LAYER

⊙ POWER TIP *To quickly lock or unlock all layers, hold down Ctrl (Windows) or Option (Macintosh) and click the lock icon to the left of any layer name.*

8) Click the check mark to the left of the bar code layer name to hide the layer; then click the same area again to display the layer.

When the check mark is gone, the text block, and any other objects on that layer, is hidden. The text is not deleted; it is just hidden from view. Click the same area again to redisplay the check mark and show the layer.

HIDDEN LAYER

Showing and hiding layers is another way to make complex drawings easier to work on. Think again of the map example. You have streets and street names. Perhaps you are trying to modify the curve of a street, but the street name is in the way, and you keep selecting the street name instead of the street. If you've placed all of the text on a separate layer, you can hide the text layer and just concentrate on the streets.

◎ POWER TIP *To quickly hide or show all layers, hold down Ctrl (Windows) or Option (Macintosh) and click the check mark (or check mark area) to the left of any layer name.*

◎ POWER TIP *To select all objects on a layer, hold down Alt (Windows) or Option (Mac OS) and click the layer on the Layers panel.*

9) Save your file.

ALIGNING OBJECTS

In the next steps, you will draw a strip of film to add to the page. You've already learned the skills to complete this exercise, so this will just be more practice for you. The strip of film consists of several large rectangles representing the frames of the film plus two rows of small rectangles with rounded corners down the sides of the strip representing the sprocket holes. You will create a new layer to make it easier to manage the strip of film.

1) Create a new layer and name it *film*. Drag it below the Foreground layer.
You want the illusion of the film canister sitting on the strip of film, so this layer needs to be below all of the other layers. As long as this layer is selected, all items you create are placed on that layer.

2) Draw a tall, skinny rectangle. Make the rectangle approximately the same width as your film canister and twice as long. Fill the rectangle with black.
You may want to move the rectangle off to the side of the film canister to make it easier to manage. This rectangle will form the filmstrip.

109

3) Draw a smaller rectangle within the filmstrip for one of the frames of the film. Fill this rectangle with 30% black.

The frame needs to be centered on the filmstrip and placed toward the top of the filmstrip. In the next step, you will align the frame to the filmstrip. You want some room on either side of the frame to draw the sprockets, so don't draw the frame too wide.

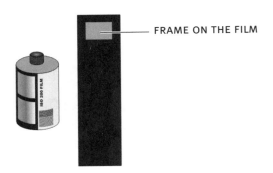

FRAME ON THE FILM

4) Select both rectangles. Choose Modify > Align > Center Vertical.

The small gray frame is centered within the filmstrip.

5) Draw a small rectangle for the sprocket. Fill the shape with white and add a 1-point curve to the corners. Move the rectangle to the top left of the filmstrip.

Remember that to add a corner radius, you use the Object panel. Select the Rectangle item in the panel list and then type *1* in the Corner text box.

SPROCKET ON THE FILM

6) Make a copy of the rectangle using the Alt-drag or Option-drag method, holding down Shift as you drag to keep the copy aligned with the original. Move the copy just below the first rectangle. Choose Edit > Duplicate to make another copy. Repeat the Duplicate command until the rectangles fill the left side of the filmstrip.

The number of rectangles depends on the size of your elements. Don't worry how many you have. You are more interested in achieving the look of sprocket holes on a filmstrip. When you've finished making the duplicates, you may notice that they are not evenly spaced within the filmstrip. They are equidistant from one another, but they may not be spaced equally on the top and bottom of the filmstrip.

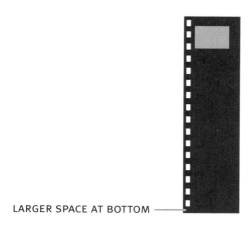

LARGER SPACE AT BOTTOM

Later you will use the Align panel to distribute the items so they are spaced evenly. Before you can do that, though, you need to position the top and bottom sprockets on the filmstrip.

7) Use the arrow key to move the last sprocket down until the distance between the bottom of the sprocket and the bottom of the filmstrip is the same as the distance between the top of the first sprocket and the top of the filmstrip.

MOVE SPROCKET DOWN

8) Select all of the sprocket rectangles.

There are many ways to select just those items. You can use any method you've learned. One way is to use the selection rectangle and drag around all of the items. This selects all of the sprockets, the filmstrip, and the gray frame. Then hold down Shift and click the frame and the filmstrip to deselect them, leaving just the sprockets selected.

9) Choose Window > Align.

The Align panel aligns selected objects on their edges or their centers or spaces them equally. You could have used the Align panel instead of the Modify menu to align the frame in step 4.

The Align panel has two pop-up menus with horizontal and vertical options and a preview pane with three rectangles illustrating your align selection.

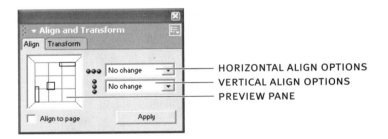

HORIZONTAL ALIGN OPTIONS
VERTICAL ALIGN OPTIONS
PREVIEW PANE

10) Choose Distribute Centers from the Horizontal pop-up menu. Click Apply (Windows) or Align (Mac OS).

Your rectangles are equally spaced within the filmstrip.

N O T E *When you choose a distribute option from the pop-up menu, another rectangle is added to the preview pane.*

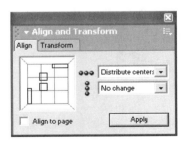

112

11)   While all of the sprockets are still selected, use the Alt-drag or Option-drag method again to make a copy of them for the right side of the filmstrip. Use that method again to add frames to the filmstrip.

If your frames aren't spaced the way you want them, you can use the Align panel to distribute them.

12)   Save your file.

TIP   *You can also use the preview pane on the Align panel to quickly align selected objects. For example, if you want objects aligned to their left edges, you can click anywhere within the far left polygon in the Align panel. You'll see the preview rectangles in the pane move to the left edge. You can click any of the bounding polygons or any of the interior rectangles to change the alignment method.*

CLICK TO ALIGN LEFT ——

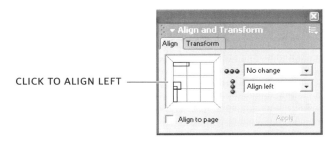

USING THE 3D ROTATION TOOL

The 3D Rotation tool applies simple 3D rotation to your 2D objects. You have just completed your filmstrip. To add perspective to your drawing, you will use the 3D Rotation tool to rotate the filmstrip back away from you in 3D space. The resulting image will be larger at the bottom and smaller at the top.

The 3D Rotation tool is fun to play with and can create some cool effects. But it does have a drawback in that you can distort your image more than the desired amount. Even the multiple number of undo's that FreeHand has may not be enough to return your image to its original state. When working with this tool, it is a good idea to make a copy of the image and move it to the pasteboard. That way, you can always return to the copy if needed.

1) Select all of the elements in your filmstrip and group them. Make a copy of the filmstrip and move it to the pasteboard.

Remember that to group objects, you choose Modify > Group. Grouping the filmstrip makes it easier to manage. In the next step, you are going to apply the 3D Rotation tool to all of the objects in the group. The copy of the filmstrip is used only if you need to return to the original image.

2) Choose Window > Toolbars > Xtra Tools. Double-click the 3D Rotation tool and then select Expert.

The 3D Rotation dialog box allows you to choose either the Easy or Expert mode. The Expert mode gives you a few more options for controlling the rotation.

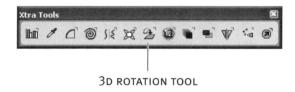

3D ROTATION TOOL

114

3) From the Rotate From pop-up menu, choose Center of Selection, drag the Distance slider to about 374, and from the Project From pop-up menu, choose Mouse Click.

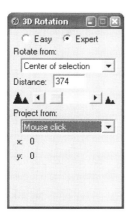

The Rotate From pop-up menu has four options:

- **Mouse Click** rotates from the point you click with the mouse pointer.
- **Center of Selection** rotates from the center of the selected object.
- **Center of Gravity** rotates from the visual center of the object.
- **Origin** rotates from the lower left corner of the object.

The Distance value you enter determines the amount of distortion of the rotation; smaller values result in more distortion.

In Expert mode, you also can select a point of projection from the Project From pop-up menu:

- **Mouse Click** makes the projection extend to the point you click with the mouse pointer.
- **Center of Selection** makes the projection point behind the selected object.
- **Center of Gravity** makes the projection point behind the visual center of the object.
- **Origin** makes the projection begin at the lower left corner of the object.
- **X/Y Coordinates** lets you enter X and Y values for the projection. The values default to the last coordinates of your pointer.

4) Position the pointer toward the top of your filmstrip. Hold down Shift and slowly drag up.

As you drag, you'll see a preview of the rotation of the filmstrip. Holding Shift as you drag constrains the 3D rotation. Before releasing the mouse button, you can experiment with releasing Shift and moving the mouse left and right. You want the appearance of perspective.

> **NOTE** *Dragging up rotates the filmstrip toward the back. Dragging down rotates the filmstrip toward the front. Dragging left rotates it to the left, and dragging right rotates it to the right. Each time you release the mouse button and drag again with the 3D Rotation tool, you are rotating the rotated item, not the original item. If you want to start over, you can choose Edit > Undo or use the copy of the filmstrip you placed on the pasteboard.*

5) Switch to the Pointer tool and then move the filmstrip below the film canister, so the canister appears to be sitting on the filmstrip. If your filmstrip is too large or too small, double-click it to display the transform handles and then use the handles to scale the filmstrip.

Since the filmstrip is on its own layer that is beneath the other objects on the page, you can move the filmstrip so it appears to be underneath the film canister.

6) Save your file.

CHANGING THE LAYER COLOR

You may have noticed a blue color chip next to each layer on the Layers panel. That color corresponds to the color used to highlight the points and paths of the items on that layer. When you select an item on your drawing, you can easily glance at the Layers panel to see the assigned layer. But if you have a more complex drawing, you may have difficulty figuring out which objects are on which layers. To help you see which objects are on the same layer, you can change the layer color for key layers. Then all you need to do is select an item and check the color of its points or paths to see which layer it is on.

In the next steps, you will select a color from the Crayon color library and use that color for the film layer.

1) Choose Crayon from the Swatches panel Options menu.

You may need to scroll down the list of options in the menu to see the color libraries. The list has several color libraries that you can use in your drawings. PANTONE® colors are used for print, and web-safe colors are used when you are creating graphics to be used on a web page. The Crayon color library contains colors you might recognize from your childhood.

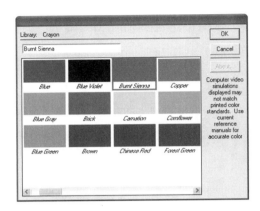

2) Select Burnt Sienna from the color swatches and click OK.

The color is added to the Swatches panel.

3) Drag the Burnt Sienna color chip from the Swatches panel and drop it on the blue color chip next to the film layer on the Layers panel.

The layer color changes. To see the color change, select the filmstrip on the page. You should see brown handles around the bounding box of the object. Select the canister; it has blue handles because it is on a different layer with a layer color of blue.

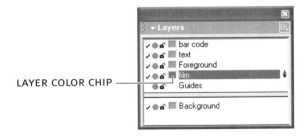

4) Save your file.

WHAT YOU HAVE LEARNED

In this lesson, you have:

- Used the Arrange commands to move objects above and below other objects (pages 104–105)

- Added layers to the Layers panel and moved objects to those layers (pages 105–108)

- Locked and hidden layers to manage the objects on those layers (pages 108–109)

- Used the Align panel to align and distribute objects (pages 109–113)

- Used the 3D Rotation tool to distort an object in 3D space (pages 114–117)

- Changed the color of a layer (pages 117–118)

using points and paths

In this lesson, you will create an advertisement for the Action Photos web site. You will draw a bicycle on a layer, using a template to guide you. Once the bike is complete, you will add other layers and use them to draw a cyclist on the bike. You will use the Pen tool and the Bezigon tool while learning about **points** and **paths**.

To make full use of all of FreeHand's capabilities, you need to understand points and paths. Every object you draw in FreeHand is composed of points and paths. Continuous lines are called paths. Every path is made up of two or more points. Paths can be open or closed. An arc is an example of an open path; a rectangle is an example of a closed path.

A point has **control handles** that you can use to control the curve of the line segment between adjacent points. You'll use these control handles to draw the cyclist's back as well as the curved road.

In this lesson, you will draw a bicycle using the Bezigon tool and draw the rider and the background with the Pen tool. You will place the different elements of this drawing on separate layers.

To see the completed image for this lesson, open the road_ad.fh11 file in the Completed folder within the Lesson05 folder.

WHAT YOU WILL LEARN

In this lesson, you will:

- Use the Bezigon tool to draw shapes with straight line segments
- Use commands to combine several shapes into one shape
- Add PANTONE® colors to the Swatches panel
- Change the view mode so you can more easily select objects
- Add a dashed line and then customize the dash spacing
- Add multiple equally spaced guides to a page
- Use the Pen tool to draw objects with curved and straight line segments
- Change a curved point to a connector point as you draw with the Pen tool
- Use the control handles to change the shape of a curved line segment
- Use the Object panel to retract or extract control handles on a point
- Export a color library for use in another document
- Use the Freeform tool to change the shape of a path
- Use the Pencil tool to draw freeform shapes

APPROXIMATE TIME

This lesson takes approximately 3 hours to complete.

LESSON FILES

Media Files:

Lesson05\Media\bike_template.tif
Lesson05\Media\bike_and_rider.tif
Lesson05\Media\road_ad.tif

Starting Files:

Lesson05\Start\learn_pen_tool.fh11
Lesson05\Start\pen_practice.ft11
Lesson05\Start\curved line segment.tif

Completed Projects:

Lesson05\Completed\road_ad.fh11
Lesson05\Completed\cyclist.fh11

USING THE BEZIGON TOOL

In the previous lessons, you used the basic drawing tools to draw rectangles, circles, polygons, and lines. When you want to create shapes other than those, you need to use either the Pen tool or the Bezigon tool. Although the two tools share the same cursor (the pen cursor), they are quite different in the way they place points on the path.

As a child, you may have created drawings by following a series of numbered dots. The Bezigon tool works great for that type of drawing: shapes with straight line segments. With the Bezigon tool, you click to place a point. You can move the point by dragging it before you add the next point. You can also create curves with the tool, but these are harder to control. If you are familiar with pen tools in other applications, you may find the Bezigon tool awkward because it doesn't behave like a pen tool. If you are new to pen tools, then this tool is a great way to start.

The frame of the bike you are going to draw in this lesson contains mostly straight line segments, so the Bezigon tool will work well. Later you will use the Pen tool to create the curved line segments of the drawing.

1) Create a new document and save your file as *cyclist.fh11* in the Projects folder. From the Layers panel Option menu, choose New (Windows) or New Layer (Mac OS). Name the layer *bike_BG* and drag it below the Background layer. Change the name of the Background layer to *rider_and_bike_BG*. Select the bike_BG layer.

You are going to import an image of a bike and use it as a guide for the bike you will draw. After the bike is complete, you will import another image of a bike and rider and use it to draw the rider. The bike and rider are separated so you can more easily focus on the bike as you learn to use the Bezigon tool. The letters *BG* were added to the layer name to identify it as a background layer.

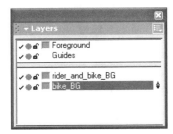

2) Choose File > Import and select the bike_template.tif file from the Lesson05 Media folder. Click to place the image in the middle of the page on the bike_BG layer. Lock the bike_BG layer.

The image is screened back because it is on a background layer. This will make it easier to use as a guide for drawing the bike. You'll notice a crosshairs at the top left of the image. Later you will use the crosshairs to help you align the two background images. Locking the layer ensures that it stays in place as you draw over it.

_____ SCREENED IMAGE ON
BIKE_BG LAYER

3) Change the Foreground layer name to *bicycle*.

You will be adding several layers to your image, and it is helpful to have the layers named with the items they contain.

4) On the Tools panel, hold down the mouse button on the Pen tool. Choose the Bezigon tool from the tool pop-up menu.

The pointer changes to a pen. You'll use this tool to draw the bike frame in the next step. You may want to zoom in on the bike so you can more easily draw over the image.

NOTE *The Pen tool displays the same cursor as the Bezigon tool. The only way to identify which tool you are using is to glance at the Tools panel.*

5) On the Object panel, change the stroke width to *0.5* point.

Changing the stroke size (or any other stroke property) before you begin to draw changes it for all of the objects you draw until you change the stroke property again.

6) Click the left side of the seat post under the saddle to place the first point. Move to the bottom of that line (toward the pedal) and click again. Continue to click to form a thin rectangle for the seat post and the seat tube.

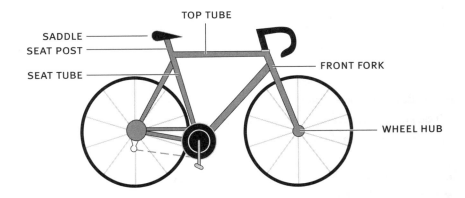

When you are over the first point, FreeHand adds a small square to the pointer to indicate that you are about to create a closed path.

You may have noticed that parts of the frame are connected. For example, the part you just drew (the seat post and the seat tube) is connected to the top tube and the front fork. You will combine these in a later step.

You can use the objects in your drawing to hide other objects. For example, the saddle is a solid black color and covers the top end of the seat post. Knowing this, you can draw your frame so that it overlaps the saddle. This approach is easier than trying to make the top of the seat post match exactly.

7) Press Tab to deselect any selections. Click the left side of the top tube, hold down Shift, and then click the right side of the top tube. Release Shift and click the middle of the front wheel. Continue to click around the corners of the frame until you return to the starting point.

When drawing with the Bezigon tool, you can move the point before you release the mouse button. After you release the mouse button, the next click creates a new point.

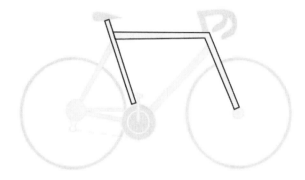

◎ POWER TIP *You can move a point even after you release the mouse button as you are drawing with this tool. Hold down Ctrl (Windows) or Command (Mac OS). The pointer changes to an arrow. Drag any point on the path to move it. When you release the modifier key (Ctrl or Command), the pointer returns to the pen, the last point is selected, and you can continue to add new points.*

USING THE COMBINE COMMANDS

You can create an object of any shape using the Pen and Bezigon tools. You can draw rectangles and circles, polygons and stars. Of course, FreeHand provides you with tools for drawing these basic shapes, and you can create them more quickly using those tools than by drawing them manually. Some shapes are really a combination of those basics shapes. For example, look at the following examples and see if you can identify the basic shapes that were used to create them. You could draw these shapes freehand with the Pen tool, but you can draw them much more easily by using the **Combine commands**.

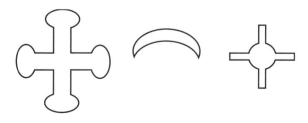

The Combine commands work on two or more overlapping objects. Your choices on the Modify > Combine menu are Union, Divide, Intersect, Punch, and Crop.

NOTE *You'll use some of these commands in the following task on the bike you just drew. If you want to experiment with them before the next task, draw some objects on the pasteboard and use the commands.*

- **Union** combines two or more overlapping shapes. The overlapping parts of each shape are discarded, leaving only the outline of the combined shapes.

SHAPES BEFORE AND AFTER UNION

- **Divide** cuts the selected shapes based on the overlapping areas.

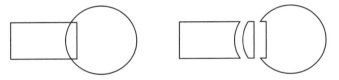

SHAPES BEFORE AND AFTER DIVIDE

- **Intersect** creates a shape based on the common areas of the selected shapes.

SHAPES BEFORE AND AFTER INTERSECT

- **Punch** removes the part of the topmost shape that overlaps the other objects.

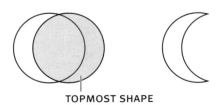

TOPMOST SHAPE

SHAPES BEFORE AND AFTER PUNCH

126

- **Crop** keeps just the area in which the shapes overlap.

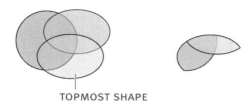

TOPMOST SHAPE

SHAPES BEFORE AND AFTER CROP

In this task, you will combine the two shapes of the bike frame. Then you will add a circle for the hub of the front wheel and combine it with the frame. First, you need to adjust your objects so they overlap one another. If your shapes already overlap, you can skip to step 3.

1) Use the Pointer tool to select the top left point of the last shape you created: the top tube of the bike.

When selecting points, you click once to select the path and then click the point to select it. The point is selected when you see a hollow square.

SELECT TOP LEFT POINT

2) Use the arrow keys to move the point to the left to overlap the seat tube. Repeat this action for the bottom point.

It doesn't matter how much the two shapes overlap.

TIP *You could also select the first point and then hold down Shift and select the second point. Then you can use the arrow keys to move both points at the same time.*

127

3) Hold down Shift and select both objects.

If you are continuing from step 2 and the top tube shape is still selected, then hold down Shift and simply select the other shape.

4) Choose Modify > Combine > Union.

The two shapes are combined into one to form the frame of the bike.

Next you will draw the hubs (the center part of each wheel) of the bicycle. As you learned in Lesson 1, "FreeHand Basics," you will drag guides from the ruler to help you place the hubs.

5) Drag horizontal and vertical guides to the intersection of the wheel hubs. Select the Ellipse tool. Hold down Alt+Shift (Windows) or Option+Shift (Mac OS) as you draw a circle for the front hub. Select both the frame and the hub and combine them as you did in step 4.

Holding down Alt or Option while pressing Shift allows you to draw from the center point of the guides. You want the circle to overlap the fork. You may need to adjust the points on the fork to make the fork long enough to cover the hub before you combine the two shapes.

128

6) Draw the remaining red shapes of the bike frame using the methods you just learned.

Just draw the red shapes of the frame for now. You can overlap the remaining shapes. When you fill the frame with color, you can adjust the shapes so they look more realistic.

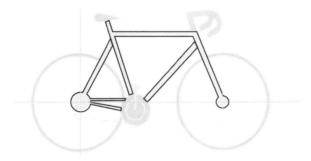

ADDING PANTONE® COLORS

FreeHand comes with a number of spot and process color libraries that are commercially available color-matching systems. The PANTONE® Color Matching System (PMS for short) is a common color system used by most commercial print houses in the United States. By choosing a color from the color library, you are assured that your colors print correctly. Picking a color by viewing it on your screen is not recommended if you are outputting your document for print. You should purchase a color book and choose your colors from there. Once you pick your color from the color book, you can select that color from the FreeHand color library. In this exercise, however, you will select colors without regard to how they will appear when printed.

NOTE *Visit www.pantone.com to read more about the PANTONE® Color Matching System and to purchase PMS color guides.*

1) From the Swatches panel Options menu, choose PANTONE® Solid Uncoated.

You can choose from Coated and Uncoated libraries. Coated (shiny) and uncoated (matte) refer to the types of paper stock you use to print your document.

2) Hold down Ctrl (Windows) or Command (Mac OS) and select PANTONE® Yellow U, PANTONE® Warm Red U, PANTONE® Orange 021 U, PANTONE® Blue 072 U, and PANTONE® 148 U from the dialog box. Click OK.

Holding down Ctrl (Windows) or Command (Mac OS) allows you to select multiple colors. Use the scroll arrow to find the last color. You'll use some of these colors later when you draw the cyclist.

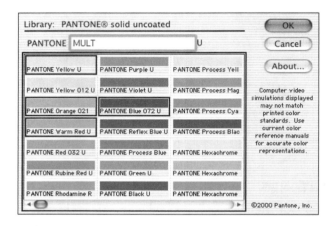

NOTE *You'll see a U after each of the color names on the Swatches panel. The U is added to the color name to indicate that you picked that color from the Uncoated color library. Coated colors display a C after the color name.*

3) Select all of the parts of the frame. Drag the Warm Red color chip on the Swatches panel to the fill color icon on the panel.

The bike frame is filled with red.

This is another way to fill a selected item or items with color. Next to the fill color icon is the stroke color icon. The third icon is for applying color to both the fill and stroke; if you want both the fill and the stroke to be the same color, you drop the same color chip on the third icon. The first item on the Swatches panel is None; if you want to remove a fill or stroke, you drop the None chip (a square with an X) on the icon for the fill color, stroke color, or both fill and stroke color.

FILL COLOR ———
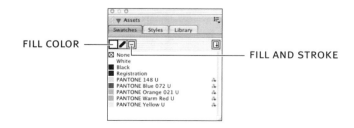
——— FILL AND STROKE

4) Select the top frame of the bike and then choose Modify > Arrange > Bring to Front.

This action should hide any overlapping areas of the other parts of the bike.

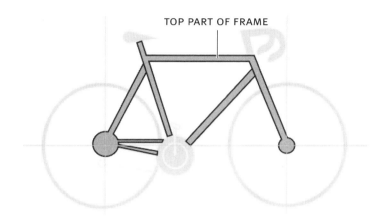

TOP PART OF FRAME

5) Save your file.

CHANGING THE VIEW MODE

FreeHand offers four modes for viewing your document on your monitor: Preview, Fast Preview, Keyline, and Fast Keyline. To access these modes, you use the View pop-up menu located on the Status toolbar (Windows) or at the bottom of the document window (Mac OS).

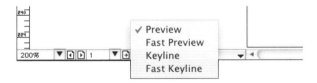

The default view is Preview, which is the one you've been using. This view displays the highest-quality drawing, showing you gradients, fills, and effects; it displays the document as it will print. Fast Preview cuts some corners in what it displays; it doesn't display all of the steps in a blend, and text is greeked (dimmed on the screen). Keyline displays only a black hairline path on objects; you don't see any fills or strokes. Fast Keyline displays blends with reduced steps, and the text is greeked.

There are advantages and disadvantages to each of these views. Preview is your best option, but you may have to wait to display complex images on slower computers. Keyline redraws your document quickly, but you won't see the fills. Keyline view makes it easy to select points or objects, especially if they are behind filled objects.

131

You'll find yourself switching back and forth between Preview and Keyline views as you create more complex drawings.

TIP *Ctrl-K (Windows) or Command-K (Mac OS) is the keyboard shortcut to toggle between Preview and Keyline views.*

You can also change the views for each layer, to display a particular layer in a Preview or Keyline view. The advantage to switching views on a layer is that the view for only that layer changes. When you use the View pop-up menu, you change the view for the entire document.

1) From the View pop-up menu, choose Keyline.
In Keyline view, you see only the outlines of the bicycle parts you've drawn. Notice that the background image disappears.

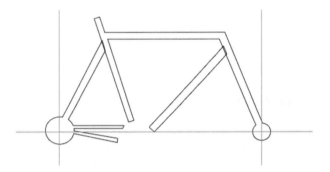

2) From the View pop-up menu, choose Preview.
Your drawing displays the background and the red bicycle frame.

3) On the Layers panel, click the keyline icon (the filled circle) on the bicycle layer.
You see the outlines of the bike, but the background image remains. Click the icon again (now a hollow circle) to return the layer to Preview mode. You may want to

132

leave your layer in Keyline view for the next task you do on your own. Just remember that when you fill an object on this layer, you will not see any fills until you restore Preview mode on the layer. It can be very frustrating if you forget you are in Keyline view as you add fills to your objects.

KEYLINE VIEW ON LAYER ——————

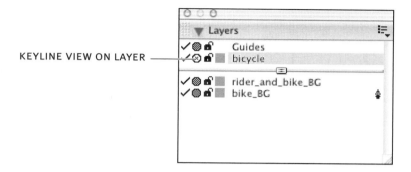

ON YOUR OWN

Draw the remaining parts of the bike, except for the handlebars and the chain. The pedal consists of rounded rectangles. The derailleur (the part below the hub of the rear wheel) is a rectangle and circle combined. Once those shapes are combined, select the top points and use the arrow keys to move them slightly apart to flare the ends. The saddle is a triangle and a circle combined. To get the skinny saddle look, scale the triangle. Remember that you can rotate or scale any of the shapes by double-clicking them and using the transform handles. You may need to use the Arrange menu to move objects in front of or behind other objects. Fill the objects as needed. For the pedal, create a 20-percent black color and add that color to the Swatches panel. The chainrings (the pedal is attached to the chainring) are represented by two circles. The inner circle of the chainring has a stroke of white.

DRAWING DASHED LINES

FreeHand contains several dashed lines that you can use in your drawings. Changing a line to a dashed line is not difficult as long as you know where to look. The Dash pop-up menu is on the Object panel. You select a line, select the Stroke property on the Object panel, and then choose one of the dash patterns from the pop-up menu. If you need to, you can edit the dash patterns. You will modify one of the dash patterns in this exercise to create the bike chain.

1) Use the Bezigon tool to draw a line for the chain. Change the stroke width to 1 point. On the Object panel, select the Stroke property and then select the first dash pattern from the Dash pop-up menu.

The line you drew changes to the selected dashed pattern.

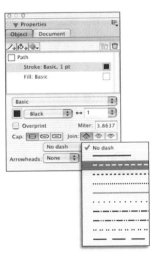

2) Hold down Alt (Windows) or Option (Mac OS) and select the dash pattern again from the pop-up menu.

The Dash Editor appears displaying the setting for the current dash pattern.

NOTE *The Dash Editor dialog box appears after you release the mouse button.*

3) Change the first On value to 5 and the first Off value to 3. Click OK.

Your line changes to reflect those settings. You have not changed the pattern in the pop-up menu; you just changed the dash pattern for your line.

4) Save your file.

You can close this file for now. You will use it again in the section "Using the Pen Tool."

ADDING MULTIPLE GUIDES

In this task, you will add multiple guides to a page to help you as you learn to use the Pen tool. When you use the Pen tool, you drag to create a curve. The amount and direction you drag controls the shape of the curve. You'll use the intersections of the guides as target points for dragging as you learn to use the Pen tool.

In Lesson 1, "FreeHand Basics," you learned how to drag guides onto the page to help you draw or position objects. Here, you will add multiple guides to a page, letting FreeHand do the work of equally spacing the guides on the page.

1) Open the learn_pen_tool.fh11 file in the Start folder within the Lesson05 folder. Make sure your measurement units are set to Points.

This file has some sample shapes on a background layer. The values you are instructed to enter in this task are given in points.

2) Choose View > Guides > Edit.

The Guides dialog box displays a list of the guides on all of the pages in your document. You can add, delete, or release guides on your pages. Releasing a guide converts it to a line.

3) Click Add. Select Horizontal and Increment and then type *88* in the Increment text box. Click Add.

You have the choice of entering a set number of guides or an increment value for spacing the guides. If you specify the number of guides, the distance between the guides is determined by the page size and the number of guides requested.

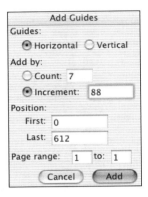

4) Click Add again. This time select Vertical and Increment and type *66* in the Increment text box. Click Add and then click OK.

The vertical guides are added along with the horizontal guides created in the previous step. The guides should be over the circle points on the document.

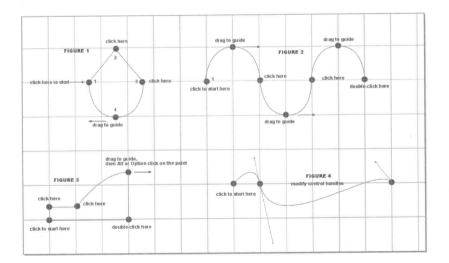

USING THE PEN TOOL

To really appreciate the power of FreeHand, you need to master (or at least get comfortable with) the Pen tool. As with any new artistic medium, you need to practice using the tool to get the feel of it. In the next task, you will practice using the Pen tool by drawing some simple shapes. The guides you placed on the page will help you place points as you draw the shapes. Once you get the feel of the Pen tool, you can advance to drawing the handlebars and the cyclist.

Although the Pen tool works differently than the Bezigon tool, you could have just as easily drawn the bicycle frame with the Pen tool, clicking to place each point as you did with the Bezigon tool. Where the Pen tool shines is in drawing curved paths. You'll find that using the Pen tool is a two-handed operation: one hand drives the mouse, and the other presses the modifier keys, such as Alt or Option, on the keyboard. If using both hands is not possible or is uncomfortable, you can use the tool with one hand; it is just faster with two hands.

1) From the Tools panel, select the Pen tool.

Since you used the Bezigon tool last, hold down the mouse on that tool; select the Pen tool from the menu.

TIP *If you have Snap to Guides turned on, the pointer jumps to the intersection when you move close to the guides. To turn on the snapping option, or to check whether it is on, choose View > Guides > Snap to Guides. A check mark next to the command indicates that the option is on. This option is helpful in this task, but it may be annoying when drawing other shapes.*

2) Locate Figure 1. Click the starting point. Move to point 2 and then click again. Move to point 3 and click.

You should see an upward-pointing angle. Each time you click to place a new point, you are adding a straight line segment between the points just as you did with the Bezigon tool. The background layer of this document is locked so you should be placing your points on the Foreground layer.

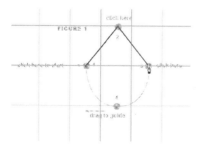

3) Move to point 4 and drag to the left. Release the mouse button when your curve matches the curve in Figure 1.

When you drag with the Pen tool, you create a curved point and extend the control handles. You use the control handles to change the shape of the curve. You will modify a curve with the control handles later in the lesson. For now, just note the position of the handles.

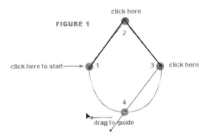

4) Move back to the starting point and click.

The pen cursor adds a small square when you are directly over the starting point. By clicking the starting point, you create a closed path, releasing the Pen tool from the path. You can now click to start a new path.

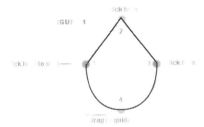

5) Locate Figure 2 (the S curve shape). Click the starting point and follow the instructions in the document to either click or drag a point.

You can hold down Shift when you drag a point to constrain the control handles. Double-click the last point to end the drawing of the path.

If you feel you need more practice, delete your paths and draw them again.

ADDING CONNECTOR POINTS

Paths can have three types of points: **corner**, **curve**, and **connector**. When you click to place a point with the Pen tool, you add a corner point. When you drag with the Pen tool, you add a curve point. A corner point appears as a square when selected; a curve point appears as a circle. A connector point creates a transition between a curve and a corner point. For example, suppose you are drawing a curved line using the intersection of the guides to place your points as you did in the previous task. You click to place the first point and then drag to place the second point, creating a curved path. Now you want a straight line for the next line segment. If you click for the next point, the line is curved. That is not what you want. To achieve your goal, you need a connector point.

In this task, you will practice changing a curve point to a connector point.

1) With the Pen tool, click the starting point in Figure 3. Hold down Shift and click the next two points going clockwise.

Holding Shift constrains the line segment between any two points to 90 degrees.

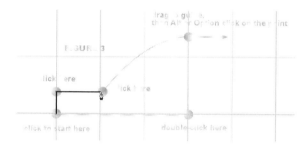

2) At the fourth point, drag to get a curved line.

The next line segment in the figure is a straight line. If you move (don't click yet) the pointer to the next point, you'll see the curved line that would be created. Instead, you want to change the fourth point to a connector point: a point that connects a curved line segment to a straight line segment.

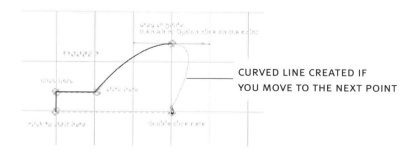

CURVED LINE CREATED IF
YOU MOVE TO THE NEXT POINT

139

3) Hold down Alt (Windows) or Option (Mac OS) and click the fourth point.

You click the last point again to change it to a connector point. You'll see the control handle on the right disappear when the point is converted.

4) Hold down Shift and click the next two points.

The last click closes the path and releases the Pen tool.

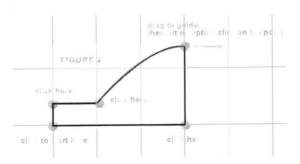

MANIPULATING CONTROL HANDLES

Once you get the hang of dragging to create a curve, you can use the **control handles** to change the shape of the curve. This skill may be a bit harder to master, but you need to learn it to get the most out of drawing in FreeHand.

Each point has two handles, though you may not always see them. For example, the handles of a corner point are retracted by default, but you can pull them out if you need them. When you select a curve point, you see its handles, plus you may see handles on the surrounding points. The handles you see, either on the selected point or other points, control the shape. For example, the left handle controls the curve to the left of the point, and the right handle controls the curve to the right of the point. If the handle to the left of the point is also displayed, then that handle also helps to control the curve.

The easiest way to see what this all means is to draw a curve and manipulate the handles. You will get some practice in this next task.

1) Click or drag on the points in Figure 4 to draw a curved line.

As you drag to create the curve point, try to match the curvature of the line segment. Don't worry if you can't get your curves or handles to match the example; you will modify them in the next step.

2) Switch to the Pointer tool and select the second point.

You see both handles on the point, plus a handle on the following point.

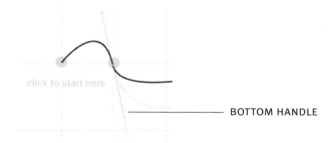

BOTTOM HANDLE

3) Drag the bottom handle to match the handle in Figure 4.

The curve of the line should start to match the curve in the example. Notice that you can move the handle left or right, in toward the point or away from the point. Each movement changes the curvature of the line.

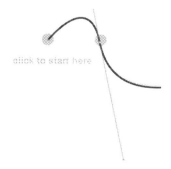

4) Drag the handle of the third point until it matches the example.

This handle is not on the selected point, but it controls the curve between the two points.

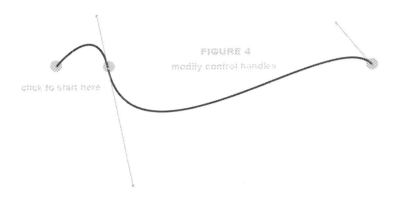

FIGURE 4
modify control handles

click to start here

RETRACTING AND EXTRACTING HANDLES

As you've seen, the handles control the curvature of the line between two points. But what if you change your mind and want a straight line segment instead? To retract a handle, you drag it inside its attached point. You can also use the Object panel to accomplish this. Using the Object panel is easier, and you are assured that the point is completely retracted.

If a point you are working with doesn't display handles when it is selected, you can pull out the handles.

In this next task, you will practice retracting and extracting handles.

1) Select the second point on the path you created in Figure 4.

The Object panel displays information about the selected point: its location and type and buttons to retract the handles. Don't forget: to select a point, you click once to select the path and then click again to select the point.

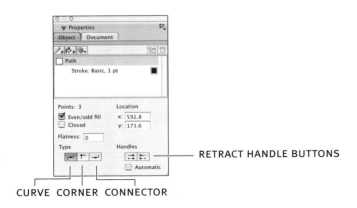

RETRACT HANDLE BUTTONS

CURVE CORNER CONNECTOR

2) Click the left retract button.

The handle retracts into the point, and the curve in the left line segment is removed.

3) Click the right retract button.

The handle retracts into the point, and the curve in the right line segment is removed. After the handles are retracted, you can pull them out again if you need to change the curve. In the next step, you will extract the handles.

4) Hold down Alt (Windows) or Option (Mac OS) and drag down from the point. Repeat this process, dragging up from the point.

The handle appears as you drag. Move the handle to match the Figure 4 example.

TIP *You can quickly switch point types by selecting the point and then clicking the new point type on the Object panel.*

ON YOUR OWN

If you would like more practice using the Pen tool, open the pen_practice.ft11 file in the Start folder within the Lesson05 folder. Use the intersection of the guides to help you place your points as you draw around the D shape in the file.

After you complete drawing the D shape, you can tackle the handlebars on the bike in your cyclist.fh11 file. Draw the handlebars on the bicycle layer. Once you complete the right (front) handlebar, make a copy of it and cut it with the Knife tool to create the smaller portion of the left (back) handlebar. Move this piece behind the right handlebar. You will need to move the left handle of the handlebar once you draw the arms of the rider, but for now you want to make sure the bike looks correct.

ADDING THE RIDER

Now you are ready to get back to your project. Your next step is to add the rider to the bicycle. You first need to import an image that contains the bicycle and the rider. You'll use the crosshairs to help you place the new image in the exact same position as the first image. To create the rider, you need to draw objects for each body part that is a different color. If you look at the final image, you'll notice that some of the objects are behind other objects. For example, the left leg and arm of the rider are behind the bicycle. You'll need to use layers and the Arrange commands to position the various parts properly.

1) Select the rider_and_bike_BG layer. Import the bike_and_rider.tif file from the Lesson05 Media folder and place it on that layer.

ALIGN CROSSHAIRS

Use the crosshairs on the two background images to align the images to each other. Once the two background images are aligned, lock the new layer. You can then hide the bike_BG layer.

NOTE *The crosshairs are to the top left of the rider. You may want to increase the magnification to align the two images. Use the arrow keys to move the image a pixel at a time.*

POWER TIP *To quickly scroll back to the rider, press the spacebar and drag; the pointer changes to a hand. You can also select the Hand tool on the Tools panel, but the spacebar shortcut is faster. When you release the spacebar, the pointer returns to the last-selected tool.*

2) Create another new layer and name it *rider*.

You will use this layer for the head and body of the rider, the right arm, and the right leg. Since the left leg and left arm are behind the bike, you will need to create other layers for those parts.

3) Click the left part of the jersey (the yellow shirt) with the Pen tool and then drag the next point at the neck. Hold down Alt (Windows) or Option (Mac OS) and click the last point to change the curve point to a connector point. Continue to click around the yellow section to complete the object.

When you see a curved section of the jersey, drag to create a curved line. To close the path, click the starting point. The pointer adds a small circle to the pen cursor to indicate that you are over the starting point. Switch to the Pointer tool and use the control handles of your points to make any adjustments to the curved sections.

DRAW JERSEY ———————

4) Continue drawing the remainder of the rider body, the head and helmet, the right leg, and the right arm.

Remember that each shape you draw needs to be a closed path so you can fill it with color.

5) Once you are satisfied with your results, add color to each part. You can use the colors you added earlier to the Swatches panel, or you can add or mix your own colors.

146

6) Create a new layer and name it *left leg*. Move this layer below the bicycle layer. Draw the left leg on this layer.

As you draw, you may find it helpful to hide the other layers so you can concentrate on just the leg. For the left foot and shoe, you can make a copy of the right foot and shoe, group those parts, and then rotate them slightly for the left side.

LEFT LEG LAYER VISIBLE

7) Create a new layer and name it *left arm*. Move this layer below the bicycle layer. Select the left portion of the handlebar and move it to this layer. Make a copy of the right arm you drew and move it to this layer as well.

You will need to move the left arm to offset it from the right arm.

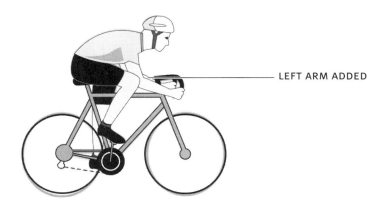

LEFT ARM ADDED

147

8) Press the Tab key to deselect any selected object. Unlock the bike_BG layer and then select the layer. From the Layers panel Options menu, choose Remove. Click Yes (Windows) or OK (Mac OS) to dismiss the alert dialog box. Repeat this process for the bike_and_rider_BG layer.

FreeHand alerts you when you are deleting a layer that contains data.

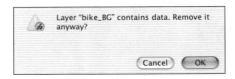

Once you are satisfied with your drawing, you no longer need the background images you used as guides. You can hide those layers, but the images will still be part of your document. If you import the cyclist into another document, as you will do later in this lesson, those background images will be imported as well, even though the layer is hidden.

EXPORTING COLOR LIBRARIES

In the section "Adding PANTONE® Colors" earlier in this lesson, you added several colors or tints of colors to your Swatches panel for use in this document. If you want to reuse those colors in other documents, you can export them as a color library and then import the library in the other documents. This saves you time and, more important, ensures that you use the same colors. If you are printing your drawings, it could be an expensive mistake if you inadvertently use two similar, but different, blue colors. For example, suppose you create two drawings for use in a newsletter that will print in two colors: black and blue. For one image, you use PANTONE® Blue, and for the other image, you use PANTONE® Reflex Blue. When you add the two images to your newsletter, the page layout program sees that there are two blue colors plus black. When you output the job to the printer, instead of a two-color job, you now have a three-color job. That extra color can significantly increase the printing cost.

Of course, with only one color, it is not difficult to create that same color in your new document. But when you have several colors, as you do in your cyclist drawing, exporting the colors makes your job easier.

1) From the Swatches panel Options menu, choose Export.

The Export Colors dialog box displays a list of all of the colors and tints of colors.

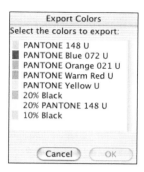

2) Hold down Shift, select the first color in the list, and then select the last color in the list. Click OK.

Holding down Shift lets you select all of the colors at once. If you want to export only some of the colors, you can hold down Ctrl (Windows) or Command (Mac OS) and click the colors you want.

NOTE *In Mac OS, you can also use the Shift key to select individual colors from the list.*

3) Type *cyclist* as the color library name and change the file name to *cyclist.bcf*. Click Save.

You now have a color library that you can use whenever you want. You'll import this color library into another document later in this lesson.

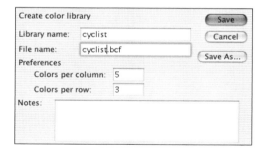

NOTE *Color libraries that appear on the Swatches panel are stored in the Macromedia/FreeHand/11/English/Settings/Colors folder within your user-specific Application Data (Windows) or Application Support (Mac OS) folder. The location of the user-specific Application Data or Application Support folder varies depending upon your operating system.*

4) Save your file.

USING THE FREEFORM TOOL

Now that you've completed the cyclist, you will add your image to another document to create an ad page. You could have drawn all of the elements in one document, but by creating separate documents, you can easily add the cyclist to other pages if needed.

Hopefully, by now you are getting the hang of using the Pen tool. Don't worry if you still feel awkward using the tool—it takes lots of practice. In this task, you will use the Pen tool to draw the mountains, but then you will switch to the Freeform tool to modify the curves instead of using the control handles as you did previously. The Freeform tool lets you modify a path by pushing, pulling, or reshaping. As you use the tool, points are automatically added or deleted on the path.

Push/Pull mode lets you adjust a selected path by pushing the pointer across a path segment or by pulling the segment directly. Pulling is similar to dragging a segment using the Subselect tool. Pushing reshapes only that part of the path that the pointer touches.

Reshape mode functions similar to pushing, except that the effect weakens as you drag the pointer. Reshaping is a powerful way to create naturalistic shapes, such as tentacles or tree branches.

1) **Create a new document and save your file as** *road_ad.fh11* **in the Projects folder. Choose Window > Document or click the Document tab in the Properties panel group. Select Letter as the page size and Landscape as the page orientation.**

LANDSCAPE PAGE ORIENTATION

2) **Select the Background layer and then import the road_ad.tif file from the Lesson05 Media folder. Place the image on the background and then lock the layer.** You will use this image to help you draw the road and mountains for the ad page. The image is the same size as the page. Before you lock the background layer, you can check the Object panel to verify that the image is centered on the page. With the object selected, the X and Y coordinates in the Object panel should be equal to zero.

If they are not, enter zero in each text box and then press Enter (Windows) or Return (Mac OS) to apply your changes. The image should now be centered.

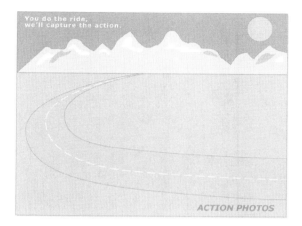

3) Create a new layer and name it *mountains*. Draw a rectangle for the sky area. Use the Pen tool to roughly draw the shape of the mountain.

Don't try to create the curved lines—you will use the Freeform tool in the next step to shape the mountains. Just click around the area to form jagged straight-line segments. Remember that you can hold down Shift as you click to create the horizontal line segment at the bottom of the mountain range.

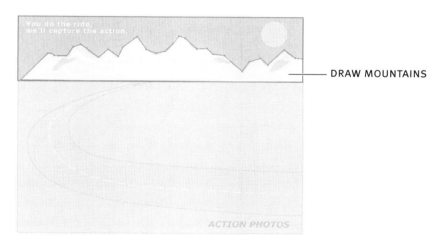

DRAW MOUNTAINS

151

4) Double-click the Freeform tool to open the Freeform Tool dialog box. In the dialog box, select Push/Pull. Change the push size to 20 and then click OK.

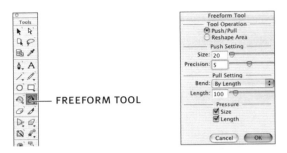

— FREEFORM TOOL

The Freeform tool offers these options:

Push Size: Enter a value from 1 to 1000 in the Size box or adjust the slider.

Push Precision: Enter a value from 1 to 10 in the Precision box or adjust the slider. Lower numbers mean lower precision and fewer points added to the path.

For the pull settings, you can select a Bend option from the pop-up menu:

By Length: Use this option to specify the length of the segment that will be affected; you can specify from 1 to 1000 pixels.

Between Points: Select this option to affect all of a path segment between its end points. A small *s* appears beside the pull pointer when this option is active.

If you are using a pressure-sensitive drawing tablet, you can set the Pressure options:

Size: This option activates the tablet's pressure-sensitive size adjustment capability.

Length: This option activates the tablet's pressure-sensitive length adjustment capability.

5) With the Freeform tool, click within the mountain area. Hold down the mouse button and gently push an area of the mountain path.

When you hold down the mouse button, the pointer changes to a circle cursor. The size of the circle is the size you set in the previous step. As you push with the tool, the path changes based on where you push and the size of the circle. You can push the path outward or inward with the tool.

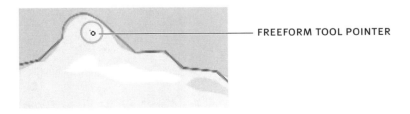

— FREEFORM TOOL POINTER

You can change the size of the circle while you are using the Freeform tool. Use the left arrow key to decrease the circle size, and the right arrow key to increase the circle size. You can change the size with the arrow keys only when you are holding down the mouse button and the circle cursor is visible.

6) Move the pointer close to the path of the mountain and drag the path.

The pointer adds a small *s* to the cursor to indicate that you are in Pull mode.

Continue to push or pull the path with the Freeform tool to shape the mountain to your liking. You don't have to match the background image.

USING THE PENCIL TOOL

You can use the Pencil tool to draw freeform shapes. Instead of clicking or dragging as you do with the Pen tool, you simply drag with the Pencil tool. You use it as you would use a pencil on a piece of paper. You don't have as much control as you draw with the tool, but you can always alter the path later. For areas of your drawing where you are not as concerned with precise curves and corners, the Pencil tool offers a fast way to create shapes. The highlight areas in the mountains provide a perfect opportunity to use this tool.

1) Double-click the Pencil tool to open the Pencil Tool dialog box. Enter *5* in the Precision text box. Select Draw dotted line and then click OK.

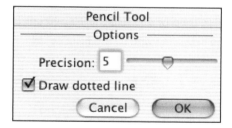

You can enter a value from 1 to 10 in the Precision text box, or you can adjust the slider. A high value shows minor variations as you draw; a low value smoothes minor variations as you draw. You can draw paths more quickly by displaying a dotted line as you draw; the final path will still be solid.

2) Draw around the highlight areas on the mountain.

Again, don't try to match the background image exactly. Use the Freeform tool to modify the shape of an area if necessary.

3) From the Swatches panel Options menu, choose Import and locate the cyclist.bcf file you created earlier. Click Open (Windows) or Choose (Mac OS). Hold down Shift and select all of the colors in the library. Click OK.

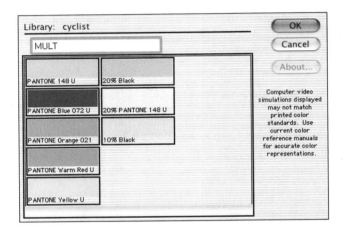

The colors are added to the Swatches panel for this document.

4) Create 70 and 20 percent tints of the blue color and add these to your Swatches panel. Fill the mountains with the 20 percent color and use the 70 percent color and white for the highlight areas. Change the sky rectangle to the blue color.

NOTE *Check the Object panel to make sure your highlight areas are closed paths. Remember: you can't fill a path with color unless it is closed.*

ON YOUR OWN

Add a new layer for the ground and the road. Draw a rectangle for the ground area and use the Pen tool to draw the road. Add a brown or tan color from the PANTONE® color library for the ground color. Add the sun and the text.

ADDING THE BIKE AND RIDER

The last piece you need to add to your drawing is the cyclist you created earlier. Remember that the cyclist file contains several layers. You will import all of those layers into this document along with the objects on the layers. You drew many elements for the bike and the cyclist, and they are not grouped. When you first import the file, all of the elements are selected, making it easy for you to immediately group them. If you were using the bike and rider in numerous other documents, you might want to group all of the elements in the cyclist file. Since you are using them only in this document, however, you will group them once they are imported.

1) Choose File > Import and locate your cyclist.fh11 file. Move it off to the side to the pasteboard and then click to place the file.

Placing the image on the pasteboard instead of on the page makes it easier to select all of the parts of the bike and rider if you inadvertently deselect the elements. You'll move the image back to the page after you group all of the elements.

2) Choose Modify > Group.

All of the elements are grouped as one. The group appears on only one layer. Before you move the rider to the page, you need to change the order of the layers.

3) Drag the road and mountain layers below all of the layers for the bike and rider. Move the cyclist group to the page and position it on the road.

Depending on the curvature of your road, you may need to rotate your cyclist. If necessary, double-click the group and use the transform arrows to rotate the cyclist. You want the wheels of the bike to align with the stripe in the road.

4) Save your file.

Take a break. You deserve it after this lesson.

WHAT YOU HAVE LEARNED

In this lesson, you have:

- Used the Bezigon tool to draw shapes with straight line segments (pages 122–125)
- Used the Combine command to combine several shapes into one shape (pages 125–129)
- Added PANTONE® colors to the Swatches panel and filled objects with those colors (pages 129–131)
- Changed to Keyline mode so you could more easily select objects (pages 131–133)
- Customized a dashed line for a drawing (pages 134–135)
- Added multiple guides to the page (pages 135–136)
- Used the Pen tool to draw objects with curved and straight line segments (pages 136–138)
- Changed a curve point to a connector point while drawing with the Pen tool (pages 139–140)
- Used the control handles of a point to change the shape of a curved line segment (pages 140–142)
- Retracted and extracted control handles on a point (pages 142–143)
- Exported a color library for use in another document (pages 148–149)
- Used the Freeform tool to change the shape of a path (pages 150–153)
- Used the Pencil tool to draw freeform shapes (pages 153–154)
- Imported a color library into a new document (page 154)

adding
special effects

In this lesson, you will explore some of the special effects you can use in FreeHand to add realism and dimensionality to your objects. Some of the effects you will use in this lesson change the appearance of the object, but don't actually modify it; if you are unhappy with the results after applying an effect, you can easily remove the effect, returning the object to its original state. You will also attach text to a path so that the text flows along the path, convert the text to a graphic, and then modify the character shapes of the text.

The magnifying glass is one object you will draw in this lesson. It contains a lens fill that you can set to magnify objects that appear under the lens.

WHAT YOU WILL LEARN

In this lesson, you will:

- Use the lens fill to magnify and add transparency

- Make text flow on a path

- Convert text to a graphic

- Create a composite path and then paste a bitmap image inside the path

- Use the Extrude tool to create a 3D object

- Change the profile of an extruded object

- Distort an object by using an envelope effect

- Add vector and bitmap live effects to an object

APPROXIMATE TIME

This lesson takes approximately 2 hours to complete.

LESSON FILES

Media Files:

Lesson06\Media\clouds.tif
Lesson06\Media\location.fh11
Lesson06\Media\distort_shape.fh11

Starting Files:

Lesson06\Start\camera.fh11

Completed Projects:

Lesson06\Completed\lens.fh11
Lesson06\Completed\action.fh11
Lesson06\Completed\text_effects.fh11

USING THE LENS FILL

A **lens fill** attribute transforms a fill into any one of six special-effect lenses that modify the appearance of objects underneath the lens. FreeHand lets you invert colors or change the transparency, color, lightness, darkness, or magnification of the object. The lens fill offers a variety of creative possibilities that you may want to experiment with when you complete this task.

NOTE *Repeatedly applying lens fills to objects that already contain lens fills can increase the file size and cause printing problems. You cannot apply a lens fill to text unless the text has been converted to paths.*

DRAWING THE MAGNIFYING GLASS

In this task, you will draw a magnifying glass and use a lens fill to magnify objects underneath. You will also use the transparency lens fill to add a highlight to the magnifying glass.

1) Create a new document and name it *lens.fh11*. Save the file in the Projects folder. Then draw a circle about 150 pixels in diameter at the top middle of the page.
Remember to hold down Shift as you draw with the Ellipse tool to get a circle. The circle should have a stroke and no fill.

2) Choose Window > Transform to open the Transform panel and click Scale.

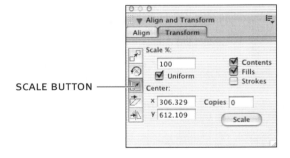

SCALE BUTTON

The Scale panel allows you to make a copy of an object and then scale it in one step.

3) For the Scaling option, be sure Uniform is selected, and type *85* in the Scale % text box. Deselect the Strokes option. Type *1* in the Copies text box. Then click Scale.

You now have another circle within the first circle. This second circle is 85 percent the size of the original circle. In addition to applying uniform scaling, you can scale the stroke, fill, and contents of an object proportionally as you make the copy. For example, if the stroke of an object is 1 point and you scale the object and its stroke 85 percent, the stroke size of the copy would be 0.85 point. For this example, you want the stroke of both circles to be the same, so you deselect the Stroke option.

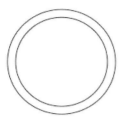

4) Use the Alt-drag or Option-drag method to make a copy of the smaller circle and move it to one side. Alt-drag or Option-drag this copy and offset the new copy down and to the right of the first circle.

You should see two crescent shapes where the circles overlap.

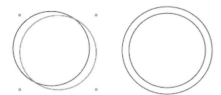

5) Select the two overlapping circles and then choose Modify > Combine > Punch. Fill the resulting shape with 30 percent black and remove the stroke.

You now have a single crescent shape. You'll use the shape later in this task to create a highlight area for the magnifying glass. The fill you added will help you place the shape later in this task.

6) Select the two concentric circles and then choose Modify > Combine > Punch. Fill the shape with black.

The Punch command creates a ring shape with a hole the size of the smaller circle. This ring will be the band around the magnifying glass.

7) Hold down Alt (Windows) or Option (Mac OS) and select the inner circle. Choose Edit > Clone.

You could also have used the Subselect tool to select the inner circle, but the shortcut is faster. The clone is the shape you will use for the magnify lens fill. The clone is filled with black, but you will change that in the next step.

8) On the Object panel, select the Fill attribute. From the Fill Type pop-up menu, choose Lens. If the Lens Warning dialog box opens, click OK.

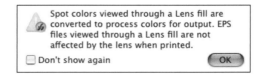

The warning message informs you that spot colors displayed beneath a lens fill are converted to process colors. This change will affect your work if you are printing your document. You can select the option not to show the warning message again, but this is one instance where the message is a helpful reminder.

9) From the Lens Type pop-up menu, choose Magnify. Change the magnification level to 2x by either dragging the slider or entering the value in the Magnify text box.

The black fill is removed. You won't see the effect of the magnify lens until you move the magnifying glass over another object.

FreeHand provides six lens types for you to choose among:

- **Transparency** makes objects appear partially or completely transparent. You select a screen for the transparency using the color box or the pop-up menu. You adjust the degree of transparency by dragging the slider. The values range from 0 to 100. A value of 0 makes the effect completely transparent; a value of 100 makes the effect completely opaque.

- **Magnify** enlarges objects under the lens. You can either enter a number from 1 to 100 or drag the slider from 1 to 20 to set the degree of magnification for objects under the lens.

- **Invert** reverses colors to their complementary CMYK colors (their opposites on the color wheel) for a reverse-color effect.

- **Lighten** lightens the colors of the objects beneath the lens. You adjust the effect by dragging the slider. A setting of 0 has no effect on the lightness, and a setting of 100 makes the area under the lens completely white.

- **Darken** darkens the colors of the objects beneath the lens. You adjust the effect by dragging the slider. A setting of 0 has no effect on the darkness, and a setting of 100 makes the area under the lens completely black.

- **Monochrome** displays colors underneath the lens as monochrome tints of the selected color. The intrinsic lightness of the original color determines the tint value.

FreeHand also provides three options you can use for the lens fill:

- Select **Centerpoint** to display a handle at the center of a selected lens. To reposition the center point anywhere in a document, drag the center point using the Pointer tool. Shift-click the center point to return it to the center of the lens. The center point disappears when you deselect the object.

- Select **Objects Only** to apply the lens effect to objects, not empty areas, under the lens.

- Select **Snapshot** to capture the current contents of the lens, so that the lens can be moved anywhere in the Document without changing the lens contents.

10) Select the crescent shape you created earlier. Choose Modify > Arrange > Bring to Front.

The crescent shape is the highlight area for the magnifying glass and needs to be in front of the lens shape.

11) Move the crescent shape on top of the lens shape. Double-click the crescent and use the transform handles to make the crescent smaller.

Resize the crescent shape until it appears as a highlight on the glass of the lens.

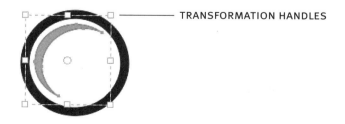

TRANSFORMATION HANDLES

12) Select all of the objects and then choose Modify > Group. Create a new layer, name it *lens*, and move the group to that layer. Create another new layer and name it *map*. Move the map layer below the lens layer.

The map layer will hold the object you want to magnify with your magnifying glass and needs to be beneath the layer that contains the lens fill.

13) Choose File > Import and import the location.fh11 file from the Media folder within the Lesson06 folder. Move the imported graphic to the map layer.

The graphic is a location map.

14) Move the magnifying glass over the red star on the map.

You should now see the part of the map below the lens magnified twice its size. The fill in the crescent shape is opaque and covers the area of the map beneath it. In the next step, you will change the fill on the crescent to a lens fill, but you will use transparency instead of the magnify option as you did for the glass.

15) Hold down Alt (Windows) or Option (Mac OS) and select the crescent shape.

The shape is part of a group. Using the modifier key allows you to select an object within a group.

16) Select the Fill property in the Object panel and change the fill type to Lens. Change the lens type to Transparency. Drag the opacity slider to 50 percent or type the value in the Opacity text box.

The transparency attribute of the lens fill uses the original color of the object: 30 percent black in this case. You can change the color by using the color pop-up menu or the color box. If you change the color of the transparency, you may need to change the opacity amount. For this example, you want the crescent shape to be visible, but not so dark that you can't see the map area.

17) Save your file.

ON YOUR OWN

The remaining part of the magnifying glass is the handle. On the lens layer, draw a rectangle with rounded corners for the handle. Mix a brown color and fill the handle with a gradient using the brown color and black. Rotate the handle and then move it so that it appears attached to the glass object you just created. You may need to send the handle to the back so that the top of the handle is partially hidden by the band around the glass. Group the handle with the lens and then save your file.

167

ADDING TEXT TO A PATH

FreeHand has tremendous text handling abilities. In Lesson 7, "Page Layout and Printing," you will explore some of the ways you can flow text on a page. Sometimes though, you may want to manipulate your text to add some pizzazz to your document or drawing. One popular feature in FreeHand lets you make text flow along a path. This means that instead of sitting on a straight baseline, text can follow a curve or circle—and you can even still edit or format the text. In the next task, you will add text to a circle and to a curved path.

1) Create a new document. Save the file as *action.fh11* in your Projects folder. Type the text *capturing the action one frame at a time*. Format the text as Arial Black, 18 points.

The text will be attached to a circle you draw in the next step.

2) Draw a circle on the page. Make the circle about 325 points in diameter.

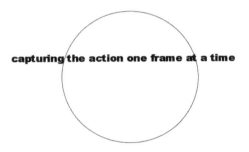

3) Select both the text and the circle. Choose Text > Attach to Path.

The text flows around the top of the circle.

NOTE *The initial alignment of text on a path is center alignment.*

Note that when you deselect the circle, the path disappears. This is the default behavior, but you can change that option if you need to. You'll do that in the next step.

4) In the document window, select the text on the path. On the Object panel, select the Text on a path property and then select Show path.

When you select the text, you see the outline of the circle. When you select Show Path, the path of the circle is displayed.

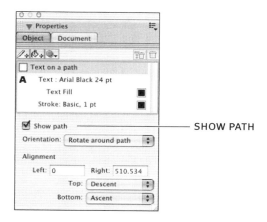

SHOW PATH

The placement of the text on the path is controlled by the text alignment and begins at the first point of the path. If your text is left aligned, then the text on the path begins at the left point of the circle. If your text is center aligned, then the text is centered between the left and right points of the path. If your text is right aligned, then the text on the path is right aligned to the right point.

LEFT ALIGNED   CENTER ALIGNED   RIGHT ALIGNED

NOTE *All paths have a beginning point and ending point. If a path is closed, the first point and the last point are the same point. If you ungroup your circle, you'll see the four points (top, bottom, left, and right) that define the shape of the circle. The point on the left is the first point.*

5) On the Object panel, select the Text property and then click the Center alignment button if you changed the alignment from its default setting.

The text on the path is centered on the circle. There are other options you can change for the text on the path, but first you will change the placement of the text. Notice that the text flows in one continuous path. You can split the text so that part flows along the top of the circle, and the remaining text flows along the bottom of the circle. You'll do that in the next step.

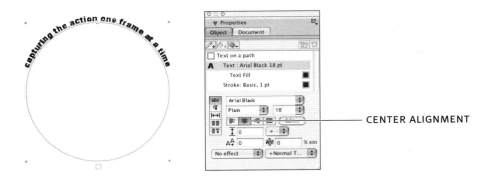

CENTER ALIGNMENT

6) With the Text tool, click before the word *one* in your text. Press Enter (Windows) or Return (Mac OS).

Adding a Return character forces the second paragraph of text to flow around the bottom of the circle.

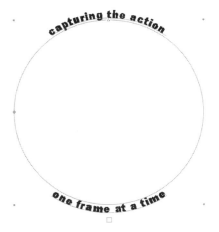

NOTE *For proper alignment for centered text, you would also need to delete the space character after the word action. This is not needed for this task.*

7) Import the camera.fh11 file you created in Lesson 1 and place it in the middle of the circle.

If you no longer have the file, you can use the camera.fh11 file located in the Start folder within the Lesson06 folder. Resize the camera if needed to fit within the circle.

8) Select the path of the circle. Then, on the Object panel, select the Text on a path property. Drag the small triangle handle that appears on the path.

As you drag the triangle either left or right, the text moves around the circle. The text dims (changes to gray rectangles) as you move the mouse. If you want to see the characters of the text as you move them, hold down Alt (Windows) or Option (Mac OS) as you rotate the text. The location of the triangle handle depends on the alignment of the text.

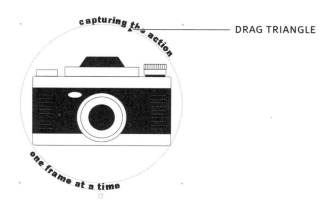

DRAG TRIANGLE

The amount you rotate the text is displayed in the Alignment text boxes on the Object panel. (Select the Text on a path property to view this setting.) You could also type values in the text boxes if you need to align the text precisely.

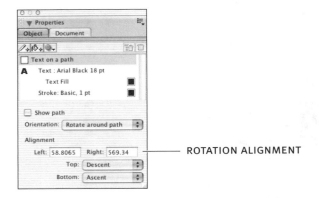

ROTATION ALIGNMENT

9) Drag one of the corner handles of the selected circle and reshape the circle to an ellipse.

You can still reshape the path even though you have already attached text. The text reflows along the new shape.

NOTE *You may need to move the ellipse to keep the camera within it.*

10) On the Object panel, select the Text on a path property and then select Vertical from the Orientation pop-up menu.

In addition to showing the path as you did in step 4, you can change the orientation of the text on the circle. To see these settings, you need to select the Text on a path property on the Object panel. You may want to experiment with the other settings for the orientation as well.

FreeHand provides four choices for changing the orientation:

- Rotate Around Path (the default)
- Vertical
- Skew Horizontal
- Skew Vertical

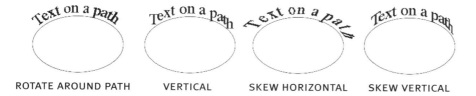

ROTATE AROUND PATH   VERTICAL   SKEW HORIZONTAL   SKEW VERTICAL

You can also change the way the baseline of the text attaches to the path. Again, these settings are on the Object panel when you select the Text on a path property. Your options are Baseline, Ascent, and Descent. You can also choose None, but that makes your text disappear. There are separate controls for text that is split on the top and bottom of a path.

If you choose **Baseline**, the baseline of the text sits on the path; descenders (the bottom part of the *g* below the baseline, for example) are below the path, if you show the path. If you choose **Ascent**, the ascenders (the top of a capital *T*, for example) of the text touch the path; this setting moves the text below the path. If you choose **Descent**, the descenders of the text sit on the path, moving the text slightly above the path.

BASELINE   ASCENT   DESCENT

11) Deselect the Show path option on your ellipse and save your file.

In this example, the path of the ellipse does not add any interest to the drawing so you want to hide it from view. It does help to show the path as you experiment with the different orientation and alignment settings, however.

ON YOUR OWN

Experiment with adding text to other paths. For example, draw an *S* curve with the Pen tool and attach some text to that path. If you have a path with a sharp curve, the text on the path may overlap itself. Use the Text tool to kern (add spacing) between the letters.

capture the action one frame at a time

CONVERTING TEXT TO A GRAPHIC

Converting text to a path changes editable text to a graphic. This feature offers many possibilities for your projects. Say, for example, that you want to create a logo that consists mainly of type, and you want to embellish the characters to make them unique for the logo. You can type your text, convert the text to a graphic, and then manipulate the points on the path to your liking. Once you convert the text to a graphic, you can no longer edit the text, but you gain the ability to change the text characters. For example, you can add a gradient fill to the character shapes or edit the shape of each letter, as you'll see in this next task.

1) Create a new document and name it *text_effects.fh11*. Save the file in the Projects folder. Then type *ACTION PHOTOS* on the page and change the text to a big, bold font such as Arial Black, 65 points.

Before you convert the text to a graphic, be sure to make all of the formatting changes you want. For example, since this text is so large, you may want to tighten the spacing (adjust the range kerning) between the letters as you did in Lesson 2. When you want to tighten all of the letters in a text block, you can use a shortcut: just drag the left or right center handle on the text block. If you drag the right center handle to the left, you tighten the spacing; if you drag the right center handle to the right, you expand the spacing. Once the text is to your liking, you are ready to convert it to a graphic.

ACTION PHOTOS
ACTION PHOTOS —————— DRAG THE CENTER HANDLE

2) Choose Text > Convert to Paths.

The text block disappears, and selection handles appear on your text. All of the converted characters are grouped together. You can drag one of the handles to change the shape or size of the grouped characters. For example, you can drag up on one of the top handles to vertically stretch the text.

ACTION PHOTOS —————— DRAG THE HANDLE TO STRETCH

3) Choose Modify > Ungroup.

To work with the individual characters, you need to ungroup the paths. You'll see the individual points on the separate characters.

ACTION PHOTOS

4) Press Tab to deselect the text. Select the bottom two points on the *T* character in the word *ACTION*. Press the down arrow key about 10 times. Repeat for the other *T*, in the word *PHOTOS*.

Because each letter is now a graphic, not text, you can alter the points on the path to change the shape of each character.

◎ POWER TIP *Hold down Shift and press the down arrow key once to move the selected points ten units at a time. To change the default cursor distance, choose File > Document Settings > Cursor Distance and enter a new value.*

Cursor Distance	
Arrow Key Distance:	1
Shift+Arrow Key Distance:	10
	Cancel OK

NOTE *Another use of the Convert to Path feature is to preserve a unique typeface in your document when you send your file to a printer or to someone who may not have the font you are using. If you convert your text to a graphic, you don't need to worry about sending your fonts to the printer along with the document, because your text is now a graphic and will print as you've created it.*

5) Save your file.

USING COMPOSITE PATHS

A composite path consists of two or more closed paths that are joined. One advantage of creating composite paths is that you can create shapes with holes in them. Think back to the magnifying glass you created in this lesson. You drew two circles, one on top of the other, each with a black fill. When you applied the Punch command, the result was a ring shape with a hole in the middle. That shape was a composite path. When you converted your text to paths, the letters *A*, *P*, and *O* were converted to composite paths. Any letter with a "hole" you can see through is a composite path. If you place an object underneath any of these letters, you will be able to see through the hole in the letter.

In this task, you will experiment with joining and splitting paths to get a better understanding of composite paths. Then you will create a composite path from the text you converted. Later, you will fill the letters with a photographic image.

1) Draw two circles on the page. Make the second circle smaller and place it within the first circle. Fill both circles with black.

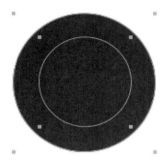

You are filling the shapes with black so you can see the hole when you join them in the next step.

2) Select both shapes and then choose Modify > Join.

The shapes are converted to a composite path. Instead of two objects, you now have one. If you drag the object over the ACTION PHOTOS characters, you'll be able to see the characters through the middle of the shape.

NOTE *In this step you could have also used the Punch command (Modify > Combine > Punch) to create the composite path for the two circles. Although Punch does not always replicate the Join command, it does in this instance.*

3) Choose Modify > Split.

The shapes are disconnected, and the hole disappears. Did you notice that the Ungroup command was not available for the composite path? Composite paths look as if they are grouped elements, but they're not. If you are unsure about an object, check the Object panel to determine whether an object is a group or a composite path.

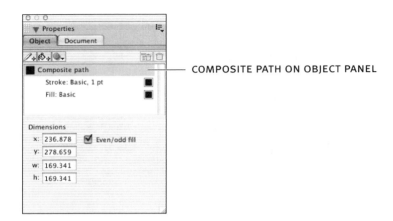

COMPOSITE PATH ON OBJECT PANEL

NOTE *When you ungrouped the converted text, you may have noticed that the A, P, and O letters each appeared to be individually grouped. They appear this way because they are composite paths. If you wanted to modify those letters, you would either select each letter and use the Split command as you did here, or you could Alt-click or Option-click to select a single path within the letters.*

4) Delete the two circles.

The circles were created so you could see how composite paths work. You don't need them for the remainder of this lesson.

5) Select all of the characters in the ACTION PHOTOS text. Choose Modify > Join.

The characters are now joined as a composite path. In the next task, you will paste a photograph within the outlines of the letters, and you will need all of the letters combined as one unit.

6) Save your file.

PASTING CONTENTS INSIDE A PATH

Have you ever tried to fit a square peg in a round hole? Sure, it fits when the peg is smaller than the hole, but what if the peg is larger? In FreeHand, you can paste a larger object within a smaller object. The larger object then fits within the path of the smaller object. *Masking*, *clipping paths*, and *paste inside* are terms you may have encountered in working with other applications that offer ways to use the path of one object as the frame or container for another object.

In this task, you will paste a photograph within the path of the text you converted in the preceding task.

1) Choose File > Import and select clouds.tif from the Media folder in the Lesson06 folder. Click to place the photograph on top of the ACTION PHOTOS character object. Choose Modify > Arrange > Send to Back.

You want the character object to fit within the picture area. If the character object is too large, drag one of the corner handles to resize it.

NOTE *Since the imported image is a bitmap, you don't want to change its size in FreeHand. Instead, use an application such as Macromedia Fireworks or Adobe Photoshop to resize the image. The clouds.tif image for this task is low resolution and intended for demonstration only, not for printing.*

2) Select the photograph and choose Edit > Cut. Select the character object and then choose Edit > Paste Contents (Windows) or Edit > Paste Inside (Mac OS).

The cloud image is pasted within the path of the text.

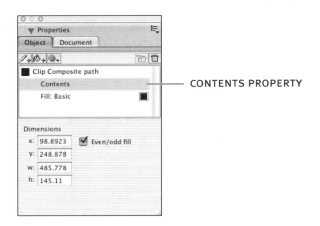

NOTE *If the Paste Contents command is not available, then your text object is not a composite path. Make sure you use the Join command, not the Group command.*

The position of the text object on the picture determines the position of the picture when it is pasted within the path of the text. You can still move the picture once it is pasted within the object. In the next step, you will move the picture to change its placement.

3) From the Object panel, choose the Contents property.

You should see a small blue star handle within the text object. The star is the handle for the content (the photograph in this instance). Drag the star to move the photograph within the text area. You'll see a blue outline of the photograph as you drag. The small star handle is easy to miss as you try to move it. If the text outline moves instead of the clouds, try to drag the star again.

DRAG THE STAR HANDLE TO REPOSITION THE CONTENTS

NOTE *The entire photograph you pasted inside the text is still contained within your document, even though you don't see all of it once you paste it in the text. This is important to keep in mind when exporting or printing your document because the photograph increases the file size and may slow down the printing time. Exporting and printing are covered in Lesson 7, "Page Layout and Printing."*

4) Save your file.

USING THE EXTRUDE TOOL

With the Extrude tool, you can simulate three-dimensional (3D) objects. Extruded objects have the appearance of 3D objects, but you can still edit the original 2D objects you used to create the extrusion. You can set the extrusion amount, control the light from two light sources, and change the shading, among other settings. You set the extrude amount by dragging the object with the Extrude tool. If you drag a square with the tool, a box shape appears; if you drag a circle, the shape becomes a cylinder.

In this task, you will use the Extrude tool to add a 3D effect to some text. Later you will use the Extrude tool on a star and then twist the extruded area to create a special effect.

1) Create a new page in the text_effects.fh11 document. Type *ACTION* on the new page. Change the font to a big, bold font such as Arial Black, 36 points. In another text block, type *PHOTOS* and set the font and size the same as for the first text. Change the color of both text blocks to a light color, such as a light blue or yellow.
Make sure that you have two separate text blocks, not one text block with the text separated by a space character; the effect you are going to apply to the text requires two blocks of text. The 3D effect you are going to use on the text uses a darker shade of the text color to create the shading. If you use a dark color or black for the text, you will not be able to see the shading.

2) Choose Window > Align to open the Align panel. Select both text blocks and then double-click the bottom section of the preview pane to align the text blocks along their bottom edges.

You could also choose Modify > Align > Bottom to align the text blocks.

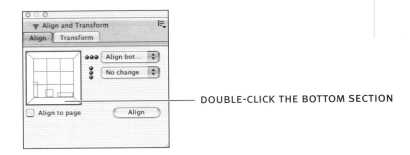

DOUBLE-CLICK THE BOTTOM SECTION

3) Hold down Shift and click one of the text blocks to deselect it. From the Tools panel, select the Extrude tool. From the middle of the text block, drag down and to the right.

As you drag, you'll see a 3D box outline and the extruded text. The distance you drag away from the text determines the length of the extrusion. The angle (left or right) you drag determines the vanishing point of the 3D effect.

CIRCLE CONTROLLING THE DEPTH

CENTER POINT   VANISHING POINT

Several handles appear on an object when you select the Extrude tool. The small circle controls the depth of the extrusion. The small star controls the vanishing point. The X in the middle of the text block is the object's center point. You can change the position of the object and leave the vanishing point in its current position by dragging the object's center point.

4) Select the other text block and drag with the Extrude tool as you did for the first text block.

You can select the text block with the Extrude tool; you don't have to switch to the Pointer tool. Try to match the same distance and angle you used for the first text block. Don't worry if the two blocks are not exactly the same; you will adjust the extrusion in the next step.

5) Using either the Extrude tool or the Pointer tool, select the first text block. On the Object panel, select the Extrude property. Note the value in the Length text box. Then select the other text block and change the Length value on the Object panel to match that of the first text block.

The settings for the extrusion appear on the Object panel. Three buttons display controls for editing different attributes of the extruded object. The first button displays controls for editing the extrusion, the second button displays controls for setting the surface values, and the third button displays controls for changing the profile of the object. We will explore each of these types of attributes in the following steps, starting with the extrusion itself.

You can adjust several attributes of the extrusion:

- **Length** sets the distance of the extrusion end to end, in points. The maximum length of an extrusion is 32,000 points.

- **Vanishing Point** sets the X and Y coordinates of the vanishing point, relative to the active page. Objects appear smaller as they move away from the eye. When you draw objects with the proper perspective, the side of the object farther away from the eye appears smaller. The lines of the object appear to converge at a single point (the vanishing point).

- **Position** sets the X, Y, and Z coordinates of the object, relative to the active page.

- **Rotation** sets the X, Y, and Z rotation angles, relative to the 3D center of the extruded object.

6) Select both objects with the Pointer tool. Choose Modify > Extrude > Share Vanishing Points. Drag below the two text blocks to place the point and move it to a new location.

The vanishing points of the two text objects are combined into one. Changing the vanishing point of an object changes the direction of the extruded part of the object. When objects share the same vanishing point, as your text objects now do, they appear to be located in the same 3D space.

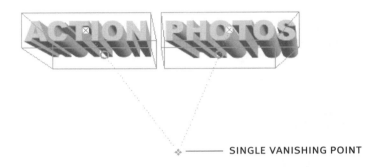

SINGLE VANISHING POINT

NOTE *If you simply click to place the shared vanishing point instead of dragging it, you don't get the opportunity to change the point. If you need to change it, repeat step 6 and create a new vanishing point. You can edit one of the points and not affect the vanishing point of the other object, but the vanishing points can then no longer be shared.*

In addition to Share Vanishing Points, you can use these other commands on extruded objects:

- **To convert a selected extruded object to a group of flat objects:**
  Select Modify > Extrude > Release Extrude. Extruded objects consist of a set of polygons. When you release the extruded objects, you can ungroup the object to get access to the individual polygons.

- **To remove extrusion from a selected object:**
  Select Modify > Extrude > Remove Extrude. The object is restored to its original state.

- **To reset a selected extruded object to its original settings:**
  Select Modify > Extrude > Reset Extrude.

Now let's look at some surface attributes.

7) Using the Extrude tool, select one of the text objects. On the Object panel, click the Surface button. Change the Ambient setting to 50 percent by dragging the slider or typing the value in the Ambient text box.

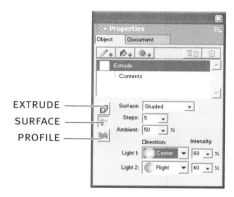

EXTRUDE

SURFACE

PROFILE

The **Ambient** setting controls the amount of light on the extruded object. Lower numbers produce darker images; higher numbers produce lighter images.

To see other settings that you can apply to the surface of your image, use the Surface pop-up menu:

- **Flat** produces extruded sides using the same fill color as the extruded object.

- **Shaded** produces a realistic, smoothly shaded extrusion. This is the default setting.

- **Wireframe** uses a grid pattern instead of a fill to display the surface.

- **Mesh** produces extruded sides using polygons that have strokes but no fills.

- **Hidden Mesh** produces extruded sides using polygons that have strokes and fills.

The **Steps** text field controls the amount of detail included in drawing the surface of the extruded object. Higher values produce smoother shading, but take longer to render and print. You can either type a value or drag the slider to set the number of steps. For this task, the default number of 5 works well because the extruded part of the text is not large. If you create a shape such as a circle, you may need to increase the number of steps to produce a smooth surface.

TIP *To speed redrawing of an extruded object as you draw, set Steps to a low number while drawing and then increase the Steps setting when you are done.*

You can also control two light sources on the extruded object. The light source direction and intensity change the shading on the object.

8) Experiment with the surface settings on your objects. If you make a change to one text block, make the same change to the other one as well.

CHANGING THE PROFILE OF AN EXTRUSION

Normally extrusions extend in straight lines toward the vanishing point. The Profile button on the Object panel lets you customize an extrusion by altering its angle, twisting the extrusion as it approaches the vanishing point, or altering the shape (the profile) of the extrusion.

To see the effects you can create from the Profile button, in the following task you will draw a path and use the path to alter the shape of the extrusion.

1) Draw a star on the page. Add a fill and stroke of the same color. On the Object panel, type *6* for the corner radii of the vertices. Drag with the Extrude tool to create a 3D object from the star.

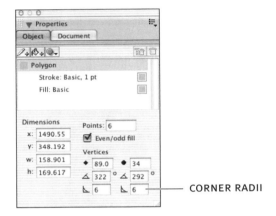

CORNER RADII

Typing a value for the corner radii of the vertices of the star curves both the points of the star and the angle between the points. The left column of controls affect the vertices that display with diamond handles—the points on the star in this example. The right column affects those with the round handles—the angle between the points on the star in this example.

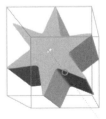

2) Using the Extrude tool, double-click the star. Drag to rotate the extruded star.

A circle surrounds the star that you use to rotate the object in 3D space. Drag within the circle to rotate the star on its X or Y axis. Drag outside the circle to rotate the star on the Z axis. The small triangle on the outside of the circle shows the position of the Z axis as you drag around the circle.

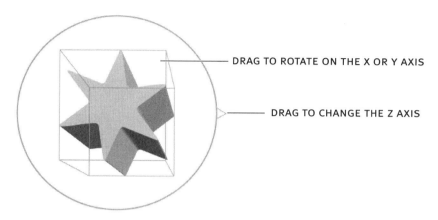

DRAG TO ROTATE ON THE X OR Y AXIS

DRAG TO CHANGE THE Z AXIS

NOTE *Double-click to release the rotation circle. In the next step, you will select another tool, which also releases the rotation circle.*

3) Using the Pencil tool, draw a semicircle.

Don't worry if the curve of the circle is not smooth; you'll fix that in the next step. You'll use the path to shape the profile of the extruded star.

4) Choose Modify > Alter Path > Simplify. Type *10* in the Amount text box and then click OK. Choose Edit > Copy.

When you draw with the Pencil tool, you can't always control the number of points on the path. The Simplify command removes some of the points and smoothes the path. Of course, you could have used other methods to draw the semicircle. For example, you could have used the Pen tool, or you could have drawn an ellipse and then used the Knife tool to cut the ellipse.

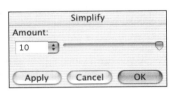
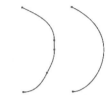

SEMICIRCLE BEFORE AND AFTER SIMPLIFY

5) Using the Extrude tool, select the extruded star and then click the Profile button on the Object panel. From the Profile pop-up menu, choose Static; then click Paste In.

The extrusion changes to match the shape of the semicircle. The smoothed shape of the semicircle appears in the Profile Preview box on the Object panel.

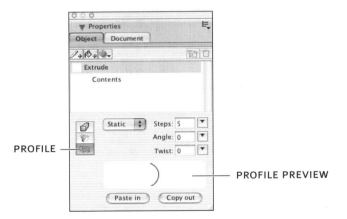

Your options in the Profile pop-up menu are None, Bevel, and Static. None creates a default extrusion and doesn't use a path for changing the shape of the profile. When None is selected, the Paste In button is dimmed. Bevel creates an extrusion by using the shape of the path around the outside of the extruded shape. Static creates an extrusion that follows the shape of the path.

6) Drag the Angle slider to change the angle of the path that is applied to the extrusion.

Experiment with the angle setting to find the value that works best for your star.

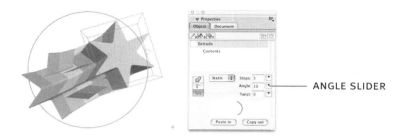

ANGLE SLIDER

7) Slowly drag the Steps slider to increase the detail used in rendering the surface of the star.

Look at the results after each small increment to the number of steps. The higher the number, the smoother the surface, but the longer the effect will take to render. If you increase the number of steps too much at one time, you may have to wait while your computer processes the steps before you can see the effect.

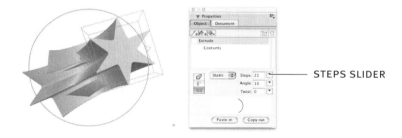

STEPS SLIDER

If you are not happy with the look of your extruded star, you can try rotating it again to change the star's appearance. Remember to double-click with the Extrude tool—not with the Pointer tool—to access the rotation circle.

NOTE *If you double-click the extruded star with the Pointer tool, the transform handles will appear as they do for other shapes. Once you rotate (or scale) with the transform handles, you can't modify the extrude properties. You'll then need to choose Modify > Extrude > Reset Extrude to remove the transformation. If you need to reset the extrusion, select the object with the Pointer tool—not the Extrude tool—before choosing the Reset command.*

8) Save your file.

ON YOUR OWN

Experiment with the Extrude tool on various shapes. For example, draw a circle and add a light color to both the fill and stroke of the circle. Drag with the Extrude tool to create a cylinder. Draw a curved path and use the path as the profile of the extruded shape to create a vase shape. Note: you need to use Bevel for the Profile type to create the vase shape.

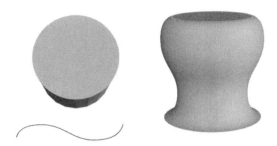

EXTRUDED CIRCLE AND PROFILE SHAPE   SHAPE AFTER APPLYING PROFILE

USING THE ENVELOPE EFFECTS

Envelopes are effects that you can add to objects or text blocks to change their shape. Actually, the envelope is a closed path that attaches to your object. When you modify the points of the envelope, the shape of the object distorts to match the changes in the envelope. FreeHand provides 21 envelopes you can use, or you can create your own.

Envelopes are fun to use, and you can use them to create shapes that would be difficult to draw manually. To see how envelope effects work, you will apply several effects to some objects and then modify the envelope points to distort the shape even more.

1) Create a new page in the text_effects.fh11 document. From the Lesson06 Media folder, import the distort_shape.fh11 file. Choose Window > Toolbars > Envelope to display the Envelope toolbar.

The imported file has two shapes that you can use to experiment with the envelope effects, or you can create your own shape and use it to apply envelope effects.

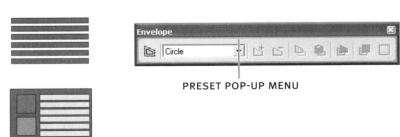

PRESET POP-UP MENU

2) Select the first shape—the six grouped rectangles—and from the Preset pop-up menu on the Envelope toolbar, choose Circle. Click Create.

The circle envelope is applied to the group of rectangles, and points are added to the shape. You can change the distortion by moving the points or change the shape of the path by adjusting the control handles on the points.

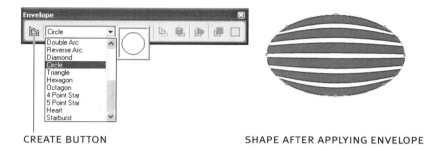

CREATE BUTTON   SHAPE AFTER APPLYING ENVELOPE

3) Select the point at the bottom of the oval shape. Drag down to move the point.

The shape within the envelope changes to match the new path of the envelope.

DRAG BOTTOM POINT DOWN

Editing a point on the envelope changes not only the point, but also the surface of the shape of the envelope. To see the surface, you can add a map, as you will do in the next step.

4) Click Show Map on the Envelope toolbar.

A grid, or map, appears on the object. You may find this map helpful when modifying points, especially if you are trying to retain some uniformity when applying an envelope. For example, on a circle envelope, the map resembles the latitude and longitude lines on a globe. When you move the points on the envelope, you can view the map to make sure that your modifications to the envelope don't bend the map in a manner you didn't anticipate.

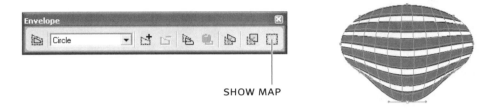

SHOW MAP

5) Select the second shape—the green rectangle filled with several smaller rectangles—and from the Preset pop-up menu on the Envelope toolbar, choose Rectangle. Click Create.

The rectangle envelope is applied to the grouping of rectangles.

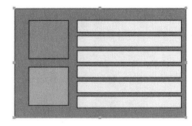

6) Drag with the Pointer tool around the left side of the group of rectangles.

The three points on the left side of the group are selected.

SELECTED POINTS ON LEFT

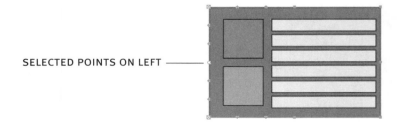

7) Drag any one of the three selected points up and to the right.

The left side of the rectangle group moves, and the contents distort to match the shape.

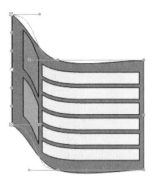

8) Repeat steps 6 and 7, this time selecting the right points and dragging up and to the left.

The right side contents change to conform to the distorted shape. You can move any of the points on the path to change the look of the object.

You can save the envelope you created on this object for use on other objects. You'll do that in the next step.

9) On the Envelope toolbar, click Save as Preset. Type *sides up* in the Name text box in the New Envelope dialog box. Click OK.

SAVE AS PRESET

The envelope is added to the list of preset envelopes. You can choose it from the Preset pop-up menu just as you did the circle and rectangle envelopes.

You can also release or remove the envelope from the object. *Releasing* the envelope retains the changes to the object's shape but deletes the envelope; once the envelope is deleted, you can edit the object normally. If you *remove* the envelope, the object returns to its original shape, with any changes to the object removed. In the next steps, you'll remove the envelope and then reapply the envelope you saved in this step.

NOTE *To get the desired effect you want on an object, you may want to release the envelope and then make additional changes to the points on the object. If you make changes while the envelope is attached to the object, you will be changing the surface of the object (which could affect more than one area), not a single point.*

10) On the Envelope toolbar, click Remove.

The envelope is removed, and the object returns to its original shape.

REMOVE

11) With your shape still selected, choose Modify > Envelope > Create.

The sides up envelope you created earlier is applied to the object. The Envelope menu command contains the same options as the Envelope toolbar. However, the option to choose a preset envelope is not available from the Envelope menu. Instead, the last selected item from the Envelope toolbar (the sides up preset in this example) is used if you use the menu instead of the toolbar. If you want to select another envelope effect, you will need to use the Envelope toolbar and select the envelope as you did in steps 2 and 5

12) Save your file.

ADDING LIVE EFFECTS

Live effects are properties you can apply to your objects to change their shapes or to add special effects. One advantage of live effects is that the object is not modified. Because the effects are *live*, if you decide later to remove an effect, you just delete the property from the Object panel, and the object returns to its original state.

You can add vector and raster live effects to your objects. Live vector effects produce vector graphics. Therefore, vector effects are independent of display or printer resolution and scale smoothly to any size. Raster effects, like vector effects, act as properties of the object they are applied to and do not modify the object itself. Live raster effects applied to vector graphics produce raster, or bitmap, graphics. For example, if you apply a drop shadow effect to a rectangle, the rectangle is converted to a bitmap graphic. Therefore, raster effects look best when rendered at the correct resolution for the final output device, whether a computer monitor or a hard-copy printer.

NOTE *Raster effects are composed of pixels. Vector effects are composed of mathematical lines and therefore can be moved and reshaped or even deleted.*

In the next steps, you will add a Bend effect to the rectangle. Then you will draw a star and add a Duet vector effect and an Inner Bevel raster effect.

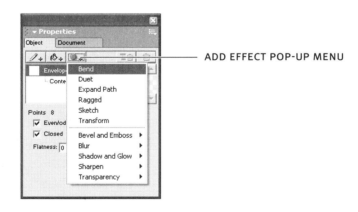

ADD EFFECT POP-UP MENU

1) Draw a rectangle and fill it with a light gray color. From the Add Effect pop-up menu on the Object panel, choose Bend.

The Bend effect distorts a shape by pulling the points on the perimeter toward or away from the center point. You can adjust the amount of distortion and move the center point to alter the appearance of the effect.

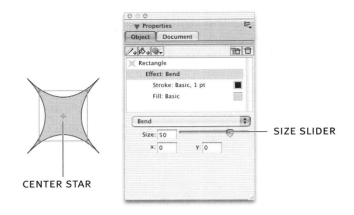

CENTER STAR

SIZE SLIDER

2) Drag the Size slider to increase or decrease the value.

The Size value determines how far from the center point the points on the shape are moved. A positive number moves the points away from the center; a negative number moves the points toward the center. The small blue star within the selected objects marks the center point.

BEND SIZE EFFECT ON RECTANGLE

NOTE *If you don't see the center star within your rectangle, select the rectangle with the Pointer tool and then select the Bend property on the Object panel.*

3) Drag the center point (the blue star) down to change its position.

You can also enter values in the X and Y text boxes to change the center point position.

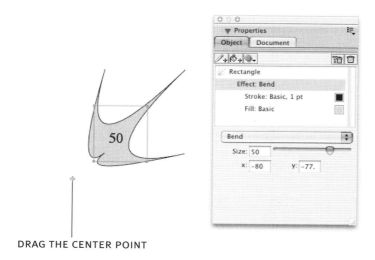

DRAG THE CENTER POINT

If you no longer want the effect added to the object, select the effect property on the Object panel and then click the trash icon.

You can add multiple effects to an object. Each new effect is added at the top of the properties list.

4) Draw a five-pointed star on the page. Add a light yellow fill color. From the Add Effects pop-up menu, choose Duet.

The Duet effect creates one or more copies of a shape and combines the copies with the original to create a single, complex shape. The default option for this effect creates a single mirror image of the object. You can define the number of copies to create and determine whether the copies are to be rotated or reflected from the original shape. You can also define the center point around which the copies are rotated or reflected.

NOTE *You can get different results depending on what attribute on the Object panel is selected before you add the effect. For example, if you select the stroke property on the Object panel, the Duet effect is applied to the stroke and not the fill of the star. If you select the fill property, the effect is applied to the fill and not the stroke. If you select the Polygon property, the effect is applied to both the fill and stroke.*

STROKE SELECTED   FILL SELECTED

5) Select Rotate and then type 4 in the Copies text box. Press Enter (Windows) or Return (Mac OS) to apply your changes to the effect.

The following options are available for the Duet effect:

- Select **Reflect** to create a single mirror image of the original.

- Select **Rotate** to create duplicates rotated around a center point. Drag the center point (the small blue star) or edit the **X** and **Y** coordinates to change the angle and orientation of the copied shapes.

- Enter a number in the **Copies** text box to set the number of copies to be rotated.

- Select **Joined** to automatically connect the original shape with its copies.

- Select **Closed** to close either the cloned shapes (if Joined is deselected) or the entire new path (if Joined is selected).

- Select **Even/Odd Fill** to make overlapping areas of a fill alternate between filled and transparent.

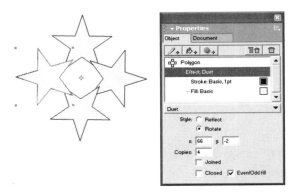

6) With the star still selected, choose Bevel and Emboss > Inner Bevel from the Add Effects pop-up menu.

A bevel effect is added to the edges of the stars. Any attribute on the Object panel that appears below the bevel effect is rasterized.

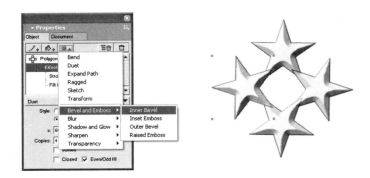

You can set several options to control the appearance of the bevel:

- Enter a **Width** value to define the emboss depth on the object.

- Enter a **Contrast** value to define the brightness and darkness of the highlights and shadows.

- Enter a **Softness** value to affect the smoothness without affecting the width of the bevel.

- Enter an **Angle** value or use the pop-up dial to set the angle of the light source.

- Choose an **Edge Shape** shape from the pop-up menu.

- Choose a **Button Preset** highlighting effect from the pop-up menu.

> **NOTE** *If you use raster effects with spot colors, the colors are converted to RGB for display on the screen and then converted to CMYK process color for printing. PostScript fills do not print correctly when combined with raster effects.*

7) Save your file.

ON YOUR OWN

Experiment with the other effects on the pop-up menu. You can add them to the stars or draw other shapes and then add the effects. Remember that to change the attributes of an effect, you must select the effect property on the Object panel.

WHAT YOU HAVE LEARNED

In this lesson, you have:

- Used the lens fill to create a magnifying glass and to add transparency (pages 160–167)

- Made text flow along the top and bottom of a circular path (pages 168–174)

- Converted text to a graphic and then modified the points on the path of the graphic (pages 174–176)

- Created a composite path and then pasted a bitmap graphic inside the path (pages 178–181)

- Used the Extrude tool to create a 3D object (pages 181–185)

- Changed the profile of an extruded object (pages 186–189)

- Added an envelope effect to distort an object (pages 190–194)

- Added a vector and a bitmap live effect to an object (pages 195–199)

page layout and printing

LESSON 7

In this lesson, you will create an advertising page for Action Photos. In the process, you will learn to use FreeHand's text editing tools as you work with imported text and create multicolumn text blocks. You will wrap the text around a graphic, check the spelling, and create text styles. Then you will learn how to set up your page for printing.

Although not designed to be a page layout application, FreeHand excels at creating one-page graphic-intensive documents. The ability to create multiple pages, each with a different page size, is a powerful feature of FreeHand, as you will learn in this lesson.

In this lesson, you will add a page to the corp_identity.fh11 file you created in Lesson 2 and design a data sheet for Action Photos. You will import text and add the camera logo and the film canister objects you created in previous lessons.

WHAT YOU WILL LEARN

In this lesson, you will:

- Align objects to the page

- Import text saved as RTF and ASCII files

- Use the Text Editor

- Create multicolumn text blocks

- Check the spelling in a document

- Wrap text around graphics

- Create and edit styles for text

- Export your document as a PDF file

- Check imported images

- Prepare files for output

- Print your document

APPROXIMATE TIME

This lesson takes approximately 2 hours to complete.

LESSON FILES

Media Files:

Lesson07\Media\datasheet.rtf

Lesson07\Media\phonenumber.txt

Lesson07\Media\film_canister.fh11

Lesson07\Media\camera.fh11

Lesson07\Media\big_air.tif

Starting Files:

Lesson07\Start\corp_identity_start.fh11

Completed Projects:

Lesson07\Completed\corp_identity.fh11

ALIGNING TEXT TO THE PAGE

In Lesson 2, you created a document containing a postcard, a business card, and an envelope. You placed some headline text on the postcard without regard to its placement on the page. You've used the Align panel to align objects to each other, but you can also use it to align objects to the page. Perhaps you noticed the Align to Page check box on the Align panel. You'll use the Align panel to align the text on the postcard in the next task.

1) Open your corp_identity.fh11 file. Select the headline text on the postcard page.

If you no longer have your file, you can use the corp_identity_start.fh11 file in the Start folder within the Lesson07 folder and save the file as corp_identity.fh11 in your Projects folder.

2) Choose Window > Align to open the Align panel. From the Vertical Alignment pop-up menu, choose Align Center, select the Align to Page check box, and then click Apply (Windows) or Align (Mac OS).

The text block is centered on the page.

ALIGN TO PAGE

3) Select the phone number and web address on the business card and repeat step 2 to align the text blocks to each other and to the page.

4) Save your file.

IMPORTING TEXT

FreeHand can import either **ASCII** text files or Rich Text Format (**RTF**) files. ASCII text files are imported as plain text with no formatting. If you save a file from Microsoft Word as text only, you are saving your file as an ASCII file. RTF files are imported with the formatting intact. RTF files are actually text-only files, but they contain text codes that describe the formatting. You can also drag text from other applications if the other application supports the drag-and-drop text feature.

In the next task, you will add a new page to the corp_identity.fh11 file and then import some text saved as an RTF file and some text saved as an ASCII file.

203

1) Add a new letter-size page to your document. Change the measuring units to inches and add vertical ruler guides on the page at 1 and 7.5 inches. Add horizontal ruler guides on the page at 0.5, 6.25, 9, and 10 inches.

The vertical guides will serve as the left and right margins for this page, and the horizontal guides will help you position the text blocks on the page.

NOTE *These guide positions are only suggestions. Once you place the text, you may want to adjust the guides to suit your changes to the design of the page.*

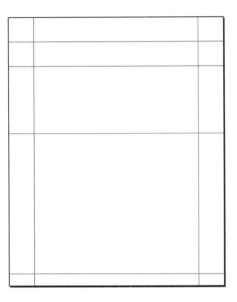

NOTE *Remember that to place guides precisely, you can choose View > Guides > Edit and add the guides in the Guides dialog box instead of dragging them onto the page.*

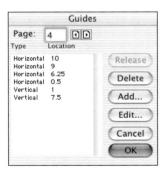

The horizontal guide at 10 inches is located toward the top of the page. If that seems backwards to you, look at the zero point of the rulers on the page. The **zero point** is the intersection of the zero measurement of both the horizontal and vertical rulers. In FreeHand, the default location of the zero point is the lower left corner of the page.

You can move the zero point by dragging the zero-point marker located at the upper left corner of the document window. The marker is visible only when the page rulers are visible. To return the zero-point marker to its default position, double-click the zero-point marker.

ZERO POINT MARKER

Moving the zero point is handy when you want to position objects on the page relative to another object on the page rather than to the page itself. For example, if you want an object 2 inches away from another object, you can move the zero-point marker to the side of the first object and then use the Object panel to position the second object exactly 2 inches away from the first.

For this task, you want the zero point at its default position. If you experimented with moving the marker, double-click it to return it to its default position.

2) Choose File › Import. From the Media folder within the Lesson07 folder, select the datasheet.rtf file; then click Open.
When you import a file, whether it is text or a graphic, the pointer changes to the corner cursor.

205

3) Move the pointer to the top guide on the page and drag to draw a small rectangle about 1 inch wide and 0.5 inch high.

——— DRAG TO DRAW A RECTANGLE

When you release the mouse button, a portion of the imported text appears in the text block. The Link box contains a small circle, indicating that there is more text. You will link to another text block in the next step. Resize this text block so you see only the company name (Action Photos) and the tag line ("We capture the action, one frame at a time"). In the next step, you will link this text block to a new text block.

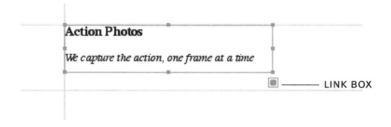

——— LINK BOX

4) Select the Text tool and drag to draw another rectangle below the first text block, using the 9-inch horizontal guide to place the top of the text block and the left and right guides to set the width of the text block. Make the height of the text block about 2 inches.

When you drag with the Text tool, FreeHand creates a non-expanding text block with the width and height you specified by dragging.

5) Hold down the Shift key and select the first text block so that both text blocks are selected. Drag from the Link box of the first text block to the empty text block you just created.

As you drag from the Link box, a blue link line emerges from the box. Release the mouse button when the link line is within the second text block.

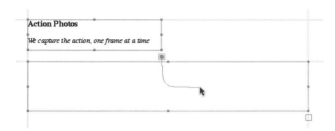

N O T E *You are selecting both text blocks so you can more easily see what's happening as you drag from the Link box to the empty text block. You could just drag from the Link box of the first text block to the location of the second text block. If you are not over the second text block when you release the mouse button, though, the text will not be linked, and you'll need to drag from the Link box again.*

6) Draw another text block using the 6.25-inch guide to place the top of the text block and the left and right guides to set the width of the text block. Repeat step 5 to link this third text block to the second one.

You now have three linked text blocks on the page.

N O T E *To unlink text blocks, drag the Link box to an empty part of the page.*

7) Resize the second text block so you can see only the text in italics. Resize the third text block until you see the remainder of the text.

Make sure that you drag a corner handle to resize the text block. Remember that the bottom handle adjusts the leading.

NOTE *When all of the text is visible within the text block, the circle disappears from the Link box.*

You now should have the company name and tag line in the first text block, the introductory paragraph in the second text block, and the remaining body text in the third text block.

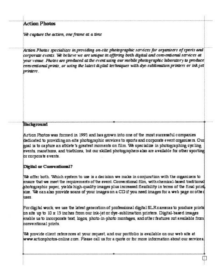

NOTE *If you see a blank line at the end of the text, delete it. FreeHand may have inserted an extra return character that is not needed for the next task.*

Now you will import an ASCII file containing the company phone number and use the bottom guide to place the text.

8) From the Media folder within the Lesson07 folder, import the phonenumber.txt file. Click to place the text at the bottom of the page.

This ASCII file contains a phone number and a web address. The original formatting of the text was lost when the file was saved as a text-only file in Microsoft Word. The text is formatted with the default FreeHand text style.

9) Change the phone number text block to Arial Black, 12 points. Use the guide at the bottom of the page to position this text block. Save your file.

You can use any font and size for this task. Arial Black is only a suggestion in this step.

CREATING MULTICOLUMN TEXT BLOCKS

For this document, you want two columns for the body of the text. You could resize the body text block and draw another text block next to it. Then you could link the text blocks by dragging the Link box to the new text block as you did in the previous task. You could also create a two-column text block within the current text block. The method you choose depends on the text and the design of the page. For example, if you want the two columns of text to be staggered vertically, you will need to create two separate text blocks so you can position the text columns independently. If you want both columns aligned at the top, then creating a multicolumn text block is the quicker and easier approach.

In this task, you will add another column to the existing text block and experiment with flowing the text.

1) Select the third text block.

This text block contains the body of the text that you want to divide into columns.

2) On the Object panel, select the Text property and then click the Rows and Columns button.

This panel displays options that let you create columns, rows, and tables.

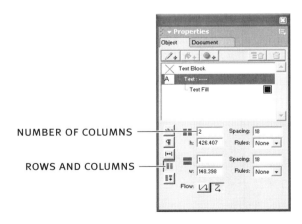

NUMBER OF COLUMNS

ROWS AND COLUMNS

3) In the Columns text box, type *2* and then press Enter (Windows) or Return (Mac OS) to apply the setting to the text block.

Your text block is divided into two columns, and the text flows to the second column. You could have just as easily created a three- or four-column text block.

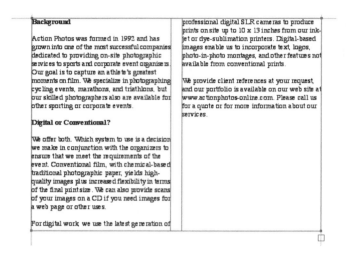

The spacing between the columns (the gutter) is set to 0.25 inch. You can change that setting by entering a new number in the Spacing text box. For this example, the default setting should work fine.

4) In the Height text box, type *5* and then press Enter (Windows) or Return (Mac OS) to apply the setting.

Previously you adjusted the height of the text block by dragging a corner handle and viewing the results on the page. If you need a specific value, you enter it here.

Notice that the text fills the left column, and the remaining text flows to the right column; the text is not distributed equally. To balance the text columns, you could drag a corner handle of the text block until the length of the text is equal (or nearly equal) in both columns. FreeHand also has an option to balance the text columns automatically. You will select that option in the next step.

5) On the Object panel, click the Adjust Columns button. Select Balance.

The text is balanced between the two columns as closely as possible.

You can also manually control the column balance, if you prefer, as you do in the next step.

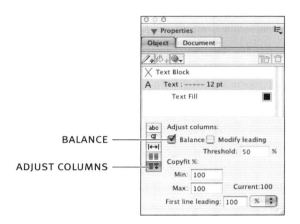

NOTE *If a blank line appears at the end of your text, Balance may not work properly. Delete the blank line and the text will reflow.*

6) Deselect the Balance option. Using the Text tool, place the insertion point before the subhead "Digital or Conventional?" Choose Text > Special Characters > End of Column.

Inserting an end-of-column character at this point forces the text that follows it to move to the next linked text block or next column.

Background

Action Photos was formed in 1992 and has grown into one of the most successful companies dedicated to providing on-site photographic services to sports and corporate event organisers. Our goal is to capture an athlete's greatest moments on film. We specialize in photographing cycling events, marathons, and triathlons, but our skilled photographers also are available for other sporting or corporate events.

Digital or Conventional?

We offer both. Which system to use is a decision we make in conjunction with the organizers to ensure that we meet the requirements of the event. Conventional film, with chemical-based traditional photographic paper, yields high-quality images plus increased flexibility in terms of the final print size. We can also provide scans of your images on a CD if you need images for a web page or other uses.

For digital work, we use the latest generation of professional digital SLR cameras to produce prints on site up to 10 x 13 inches from our ink-jet or dye-sublimation printers. Digital-based images enable us to incorporate text, logos, photo-in-photo montages, and other features not available from conventional prints.

We provide client references at your request, and our portfolio is available on our web site at www.actionphotos-online.com. Please call us for a quote or for more information about our services.

7) Make a copy of the camera logo from your postcard page in this document and paste it on this page.

Position the camera at the top right of the page and resize it as needed. You can import the camera.fh11 file from the Media folder within the Lesson07 folder if you no longer have your camera logo.

8) Save your file.

USING THE TEXT EDITOR

The Text tool in FreeHand allows you to type text directly on the page and edit and format the text. Sometimes when you are entering text, you may want to see the hidden characters not normally visible. For example, you may want to see the end-of-column character you just inserted, or you may want to see the paragraph marks in the text. If you need or want to see these special characters, you can use the Text Editor.

In the previous task, you inserted the end-of-column character before the "Digital or Conventional?" subheading. Later you may decide to delete the character, or maybe you forget that you inserted it and want to determine why the text jumps to the next column. You can use the Text Editor to view the text and either delete the invisible character or verify its existence.

In this task, you will use the Text Editor to view the invisible characters in your text and delete any extra paragraph marks.

TIP *You will also find the Text Editor helpful when you have several pages that contain linked text. Instead of having to jump from page to page to edit the text, you can open the Text Editor and see all of the text, no matter where it appears.*

1) Select any text block with the Pointer tool.

Since all your text is linked, you can select any one of the text blocks; all of the text will appear in the editor.

2) Choose Text > Editor.

The Text Editor window opens displaying all of your text. The Text Editor displays your text in the actual font and point size, but you will not see paragraph attributes such as leading, alignment, or spacing.

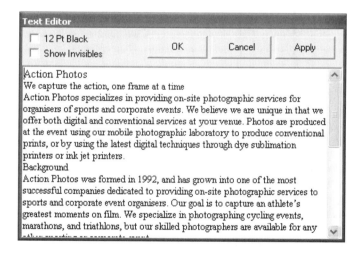

3) Select Show Invisibles.

You now should see all of the paragraph marks, indicated by a backwards *P*, and the end-of-column character, indicated by an upward-pointing arrow.

Look for the end-of-column character in your text. It should be before the subheading "Digital or Conventional?"

END-OF-COLUMN
CHARACTER

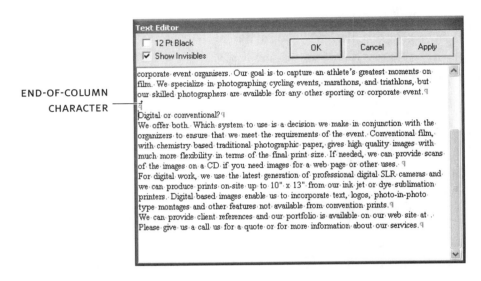

TIP *Notice that the Text Editor also has an option to display 12-point black text. If your text is white or is very small, you will not see it in the Text Editor. When you select this option, the text changes in the Text Editor only—it is not changed in the text block.*

4) Delete the end-of-column character, then click OK.

The end-of-column character created an awkward break in the text you don't like.

5) Select the Balance option again to flow the text between the columns.

In a later task, you will flow this text around a graphic. Using the automatic balance option gives you better results. Check to make sure that there is not an extra return character at the end of this text.

CHECKING THE SPELLING

It's late at night and you've been working all day to finish your project. Then you notice a misspelled a word on the page—or worse, all of the words on the page look misspelled to you! Here's where FreeHand's spell checker comes to the rescue. Although no spell checker can replace a good editor (thanks Judy and Joan), at least it can find those obvious errors.

The text you just imported contains some misspelled words, as you may have noticed when you imported the text. They were deliberately inserted so you can test the spell checker.

1) Select one of the text blocks containing the main body text.
You can use either the Text tool or the Pointer tool to select the text block.

TIP *If you select a text block, spelling is checked only in that block and any linked blocks. If no text block is selected, all text in the document is checked.*

2) Choose Text > Spelling. Click Setup and make any changes you want. When you are done, click OK.
The Preferences dialog box opens with the Spelling category selected. You can change the options here or leave them as they are. You can also pick the dictionary you want to use from the Dictionary pop-up menu.

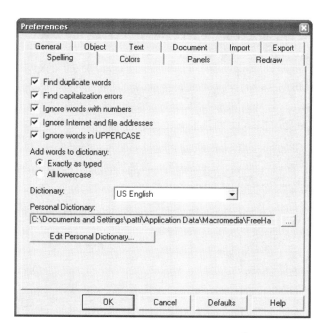

3) Click Start to begin checking the spelling.

FreeHand highlights the first suspicious word on the page and displays alternative words to pick from. In this example, the correct spelling of the word is selected. If you want to use one of the other words in a list of alternatives, select it before proceeding with the next step.

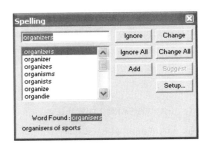

NOTE *The word* organizers *is spelled the British way:* organisers. *If you pick the British dictionary in the Preferences dialog box, that word is not flagged as misspelled.*

4) Click Change to change the spelling of the word or click Ignore if the spelling is correct.

If you click Change All, all occurrences of the misspelled word are changed. If you click Ignore All, any other occurrences of the word are skipped.

5) Continue to check the remainder of the text block. Click OK to close the Finished dialog box and then close the Spelling window.

FLOWING TEXT AROUND GRAPHICS

At this point, all of the text you've placed on the page is contained within the rectangular boundaries of the text block. Occasionally, though, you may want to flow text around a graphic for a more interesting design. You may be familiar with this concept (sometimes called run-around) from page layout programs. Like these programs, FreeHand lets you run text around graphics, as you will see in this next task.

1) Import the film_canister.fh11 file you modified in Lesson 4 and place it on the pasteboard. Group all of the objects in the film canister.

If you no longer have your file, you can use the file in the Media folder within the Lesson04 folder. You are placing the canister on the pasteboard initially so that you can group the objects in the file if they are not grouped already.

2) Move the grouped film canister object to the middle of the two-column text block.

When you flow text around a graphic, the graphic needs to be in front of the text block. Because the film canister was imported after you placed the text on the page, it is already in front. However, you can't flow text around a grouped object. But grouping the film canister makes it easier to manage if you need to move or resize it, so you don't want to ungroup it, plus there is not one object in the film canister that defines the shape around the outside of the canister. To work around this problem, in the next step you will draw a shape around the film canister so you can flow the text around it.

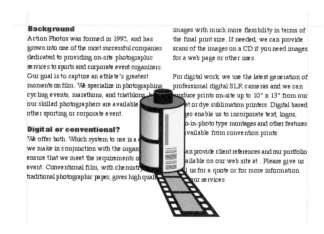

NOTE *If your graphic is not in front of the text, choose Modify > Arrange > Bring to Front.*

3) Select the Pen tool or the Bezigon tool and draw a path around the film canister. Stay about a pica (1/8 inch) from the outside edge of the canister. Be sure to close the path.

The shape around the film canister will define the area around which the text will flow.

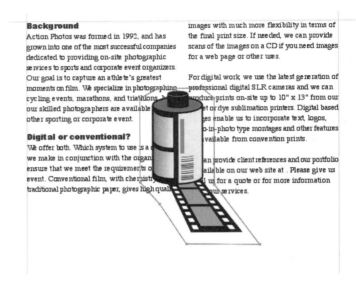

4) With the path selected, choose Text > Flow Around Selection. In the Flow Around Selection dialog box, click the flow-around icon (the right icon) and then click OK.

The text flows around the shape. Once you see how the text wraps, you may want to adjust the path. Drag a point on the path to change the shape, or click with the Pen tool to add a new point on the path.

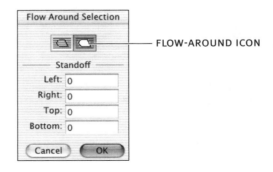

FLOW-AROUND ICON

NOTE *The left icon disallows text flow around the graphic.*

In this example, you can change the gap between the text and the film canister by adjusting the path. Because you can adjust the gap, you did not need to enter any values in the Standoff text boxes in the Flow Around Selection dialog box. If you were using a shape that wasn't grouped, then after you had applied Flow Around Selection to the shape, you would have to enter standoff values in the dialog box to adjust the gap.

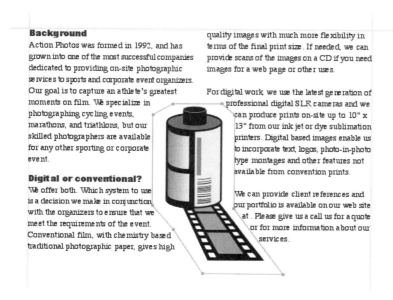

Once you are satisfied with the text flow, you need to remove the stroke on the path. You don't want the shape to show in the printed piece.

5) On the Object panel, select the Stroke property and then click the trash icon to remove the stroke on the path.

The flow-around path is now invisible.

TIP *If you need to edit or move the path later, switch to Keyline view. You'll be able to see the outline of the path so you can select it.*

Now you will add another graphic to the page and set the flow-around option on this graphic.

219

6) Import the big_air.tif file from the Media folder within the Lesson07 folder. Place the imported image to the left of the introductory paragraph (the second text block). Choose Text > Flow Around Selection.

Notice that you can flow text around this image without drawing another shape.

7) In the Flow Around Selection dialog box, click the flow-around icon. In the Right Standoff text box, type .25. Click OK.

The values you enter in the Standoff text boxes control the amount of spacing between the image and the text. In this example, the text appears only to the right of the image, so you need to enter standoff values only in the Right Standoff text box.

You can adjust the standoff amount and move the image around on the page to your liking. You may also need to adjust the height of the text block to display all the text in the paragraph.

Action Photos specializes in providing on-site photographic services for organisers of sports and corporate events. We believe we are unique in offering both digital and conventional services at your venue. Photos are produced at the event using our mobile photographic laboratory to produce conventional prints, or using the latest digital techniques with dye-sublimation printers or ink-jet printers.

SETTING RASTER EFFECTS RESOLUTION

In Lesson 6, "Adding Special Effects," you explored some of the live raster effects you can apply to objects on a page. In this document, you just imported a photograph saved as a TIFF file. You can apply any of the raster effects to this image as well. Remember that a raster effect produces a bitmap image and will look best when rendered at the correct resolution for the intended output device. The page you are creating in this lesson is to be printed. To ensure that both the bitmap and the live effect you are going to apply are rendered properly, you need to set the resolution either for the document or for the image itself.

NOTE *To speed rendering of raster effects while drawing for high-resolution devices, you can set the amount to 72 ppi while drawing and then increase the value before sending your file to the output device.*

1) Select the big_air.tif image and add a stroke and a drop-shadow effect.

You may want to experiment with the settings for the drop shadow. For example, you can increase the shadow amount and lighten the color of the shadow. Notice that even though the image is an imported bitmap, you can still add a vector stroke to it.

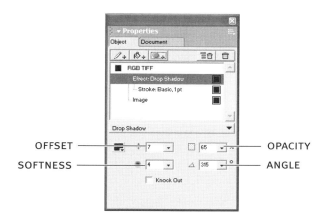

2) With the image still selected, choose Raster Effects Settings from the Object panel's Options menu. Deselect Use Document Raster Effects Resolution and then choose 300 ppi from the Resolution pop-up menu. Click OK to close the dialog box and click OK again if the warning dialog box appears.

Your resolution options are 72, 144, and 300 ppi. If you were exporting this page for use as a web page, you would choose 72 ppi. Since you are printing the document, you want a higher resolution, so you choose either 144 or 300. You can set the object's resolution as you did here, or you can set the resolution for the document. To change the effects resolution for the document, you would choose File > Document Settings > Raster Effects Settings. Then you would enter the resolution you want for the entire document.

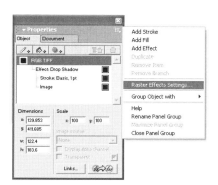 

3) Save your file.

WORKING WITH TEXT STYLES

When you look at the text in your document, you probably think about each paragraph as being some type of text. For example, in this document you have a headline (Action Photos), a tag line, an introductory paragraph, subheads, and body text. Each type of paragraph may have different formatting in your design.

Text styles are a means of storing the formatting attributes for each type of paragraph, making it easy to apply those attributes to other paragraphs in your document. Using text styles ensures that similar paragraphs are formatted exactly the same. You don't have to remember whether you used 12-point text or 11-point text for the body text. You simply save the text style and then apply it to other paragraphs with a single click. You'll appreciate text styles even more when you change your mind about your formatting. You can edit the style, and all of the text with that style applied will be reformatted automatically.

The easiest way to create a text style is to format a paragraph on the page using the Object panel. You can see the formatting as you apply it to the text and make any changes if you are not happy with the results. Then you can create a new style based on that paragraph.

In this task, you will format some text and create a style. Then you will apply the style to another paragraph on the page. In a later task, you will edit some styles to globally change the text.

1) Select the word _Background_ in the text. Change the font and the point size. For example, change the font to Arial Black, 12 points.
This text, along with the text "Digital or Conventional?," are subheads. You want both of them to be formatted the same.

2) Choose Window > Styles to open the Styles panel. From the Styles panel Options menu, choose Compact List View.
You could also click the Styles tab in the Assets panel group to access the Styles panel. The Compact list view and Large list view both display the name of your styles and are easier to use than the preview when working with text styles.

3) From the Styles panel Option menu, choose New.

A new style, Style-1, is added to the panel. The style contains the formatting for the selected text.

4) Double-click the Style-1 name on the panel and type *subhead* as the style name. Press Enter (Windows) or Return (Mac OS) to apply the name to the style.

It is always a good idea to rename your styles to indicate the type of paragraph each represents.

Once you have defined a text style, all you need to do is select it to apply it to other subheads in your document. In the next step, you'll apply your new style to the other subhead.

NOTE *FreeHand ships with numerous graphic styles installed. You can choose Remove Unused from the Styles panel Options menu to remove the excess styles.*

223

5) Select the text Digital or Conventional?. On the Styles panel, click the subhead style.

The formatting attributes are applied to this text.

TIP *When applying styles to paragraphs, you only need to place the insertion bar in the text; you don't need to highlight (and select) all of the words in the paragraph.*

ON YOUR OWN

Format the first paragraph after the "Background" subhead. Repeat from step 3 to create a new style and name the style *body*. Apply that style to the other body paragraphs in the text. Create styles for the other types of paragraphs: the headline, tag line, and introductory paragraph.

You may be wondering if it is worth the time to create styles for paragraphs that occur only once. For example, this page has only one headline; should you create a style for the headline? Perhaps not in this case, but what if you decide later to add another page to your document and you want the text to look the same as on this page? If you've created styles for everything, with just a few quick clicks you can change the text on that page to match this page. You don't have to jump back and forth between the pages making sure the formatting is the same.

EDITING TEXT STYLES

Once you create a style, you still can change the style's formatting—you are not locked into the original definition. The power of styles is apparent when you make a change to a style. You need only change the style, and then all paragraphs with that style applied are automatically updated.

You can change a style either by example or by specification. In the previous task, you created a style by example. In this task, you will change the body text style by specification and then you will change the subhead style by example.

1) Using the Text tool, click within one of the body paragraphs.

The body style is selected on the Styles panel.

224

2) From the Styles panel Options menu, choose Style Behavior.

The Edit Style Behavior (Windows) or Edit Style (Mac OS) dialog box opens.

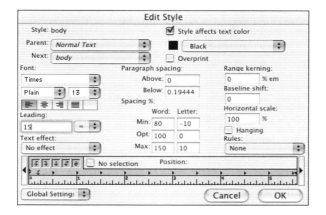

3) In the Edit Style dialog box, make a change to the paragraph definitions for the body style. For example, change the font size to 13 points. Make any other changes you want and then click OK.

All paragraphs with the body style are updated with your changes.

You have just changed a style by specification. Now you will change a style by example.

4) Select the word *Background,* which uses the subhead style, and make a formatting change.

For example, change the text to a blue color.

5) From the Styles panel Options menu, choose Redefine. Select subhead from the Redefine Style dialog box and then click OK.

FreeHand updates the style based on the character attributes you changed. All paragraphs defined with that style are updated as well.

6) Save your file.

Leave your document open; you will use this file in the next task.

EXPORTING AS A PDF FILE

Adobe's portable document format (**PDF**) is a popular solution for delivering cross-platform documents that preserve the design of your document. To view PDF files, you can download Adobe Acrobat Reader for free from the Adobe web site, and it also comes on most new computer systems. Rarely these days do you find someone who hasn't used PDF files. In fact, many service bureaus and commercial printers now accept PDF files for outputting your files. Your clients may not have FreeHand, but you can e-mail them PDF files from your FreeHand document during the approval stage instead sending them a printout; your clients can receive your design ideas in minutes rather than in days.

Note, though, that some effects won't export to PDF files:

• Custom and PostScript fills and strokes, arrowheads, and textured fills

• Alpha channel transparency

• EPS images

• Text effects

• Overprinting. Overprinting applied to objects is turned off when you export to PDF

In this task, you will create a PDF file from your FreeHand document.

1) Choose File > Export. From the Save as Type (Windows) or Format (Mac OS) pop-up menu, choose PDF. Save the file in your Projects folder and check the file name.
If you are using a Macintosh and added the file extension (.fh11) to your file name, FreeHand adds the .pdf extension to the end of the name, resulting in the name corp_identity.fh11.pdf. You probably don't want the fh11 added to the file name, so delete it. On Windows platforms, the file extension (fh11) is replaced by the .pdf extension for you.

2) Click Setup.

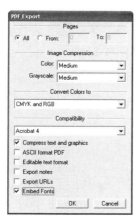

The PDF Export dialog box offers these options:

Select a **Color** or **Grayscale Image Compression** option to compress images and reduce the file size. A higher compression setting yields a smaller file size but may reduce image quality. For print, choose little or no compression. For onscreen display, choose higher levels of compression to create small files that are easier to transmit and download.

Select a **Convert Colors To** option to maintain color consistency across applications: CMYK for standard CMYK output and color separations, RGB for use in Macromedia Fireworks or Adobe Photoshop, or CMYK and RGB for print applications with a PostScript RIP such as Adobe Illustrator or Adobe Photoshop 4 or later.

A PostScript raster image processor, or RIP, is a piece of software that converts vector art to pixels for display in a software application.

For **Compatibility**, select an Acrobat version to determine which additional options are available:

- **Acrobat 4** converts gradients to PostScript 3 linear and radial gradients, and it converts envelopes as flattened vector graphics.

- **Acrobat 3** and **4** support compressed text and graphics, ASCII text format, notes, URLs, and editable text format.

- **Acrobat 2** supports ASCII format and editable text format.

- **Acrobat 1** supports no options.

227

Select additional options, depending on the Acrobat version you selected:

Compress Text and Graphics compresses text and graphic elements in the PDF document (using the PostScript language imaging model). If you selected a Color or Grayscale Image Compression option in step 2, bitmap images are compressed.

ASCII Format PDF exports documents as 7-bit files, to prevent problems when PDF files are shared on older networks and e-mail systems. Deselect this option to export ASCII documents as 8-bit files.

Editable Text Format exports editable text with the PDF file. Select this option only if you plan to edit the document in FreeHand or Illustrator. FreeHand text blocks from breaking into several text blocks during export. When selected, this option produces a larger document. Deselect this option if your goal is screen and print output.

Export Notes exports as PDF comments any notes you added in the Note text block on the Navigation panel.

Export URLs exports URLs as rectangular hyperlinks.

Embed Fonts embeds TrueType and Type 1 fonts in the document.

3) Select Embed Fonts and any other desired options for your document; then click OK.

For this document, you can use the default settings in the PDF Export dialog box for the page range, image compression, and color conversion. The option to embed fonts is one you may want to select whenever you create PDFs. Although embedding fonts increases the file size of your document, it ensures that your document looks the way you designed it. If you don't embed the fonts, your document may look drastically different to those people who don't have the fonts you used.

4) If you want to open the PDF file immediately after it is created, select Open in External Application. Locate your copy of Adobe Acrobat or Adobe Acrobat Reader in the next dialog box. Click Save (Windows) or Export (Mac OS).

A PDF version of your document is created. If you selected Open in External Application, then Acrobat or Acrobat Reader is launched, and the PDF file is opened. Otherwise, just open the PDF file in the usual way to verify that all is as you intended.

CHECKING YOUR LINKS

When you import a bitmap graphic, SWF movie, or EPD file, by default the graphic or movie is linked, not embedded in your FreeHand document. FreeHand displays a low-resolution preview of the graphic within your document, but when you print the document, FreeHand uses the linked high-resolution graphic instead of the preview. FreeHand thus needs to know the exact location of the graphic file. If you change the location of a linked file, FreeHand asks you to locate the file when you open the FreeHand document.

If you prefer, you can choose to embed (or store) the graphic within your FreeHand document. The advantage to doing this is that you don't have to keep track of the original file. If you transfer your files to a service bureau or someone else, you don't have to worry about sending the linked files as well. The disadvantage is that your FreeHand file size increases. If you embed a high-resolution image with a large file size, you may also see a slowdown in FreeHand's performance.

You can change your preferences to automatically embed imported images, or you can manually embed images. If you want to change your preferences, choose Edit > Preferences (Windows and Mac OS 9) or choose FreeHand MX > Preferences (Mac OS X) and click the Import tab (Windows) or select the Import category (Mac OS). Select the Embed images and EPS upon import option.

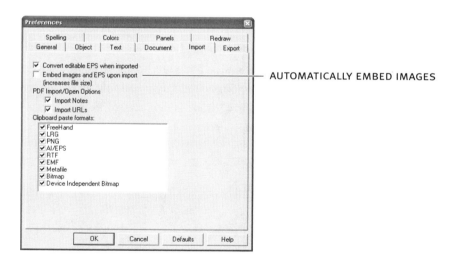

AUTOMATICALLY EMBED IMAGES

In this task, you will open the Links dialog box and manually embed the photograph you imported in your document.

229

1) Select the big_air.tif image. On the Object panel, click Links.

The Links dialog box opens displaying information about the linked file. You see the file name, the location of the file on your hard drive or network device, the file type (TIF, EPS, RBG, CMYK, and so on), the file size, and the page number where the file appears in your document.

You could also choose Edit > Links to display the same Links dialog box. The only difference is that when you use the Object panel, the file is selected in the dialog box.

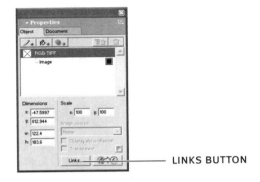

LINKS BUTTON

NOTE *If your image is on the pasteboard, the page number appears as a dash or bullet.*

2) Click Info and then click OK.

The Link Info dialog box opens showing you the complete path name of the file and the modification date. If you have a source file, you can click the folder icon and then locate that file. The source file is the original file. For example, if you have an imported JPEG image that you exported from Macromedia Fireworks, you would select the Fireworks PNG file as the source.

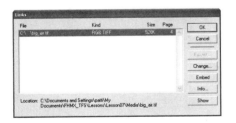
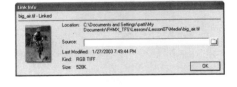

If you modify the linked image outside of FreeHand, the updated file is displayed in FreeHand when you reopen the FreeHand file. If you embed a file and then change it outside of FreeHand, you then need to click the Change button and relocate the updated image.

230

If you are waiting for a final image for your FreeHand document, you can create a for-position-only, or FPO, file with the same dimensions as the final image and use the FPO image in your drawing. Then, when you have the final image, you can click the Change button in the Links dialog box, locate the final image, and replace the FPO file.

3) Click Embed.

The big_air.tif image is now embedded in your FreeHand file.

4) Click OK to close the Links dialog box; then save your file.

COLLECTING FOR OUTPUT

The TIFF image you imported into your document is a linked image. As mentioned earlier, this means that a low-resolution preview of the image is imported into your FreeHand document. When you print your document, FreeHand sends the high-resolution image to the printer instead of the preview image. That works fine when you print from your computer, but if you use another computer to print your file, or if you send your file to a service bureau or a commercial printer, you need to remember to also send the external, linked file.

This document has only one linked file, so including this file would not be difficult. But what if you send your document to a printer a few months after you create it. Will you remember that it must include the linked file? Or what if your document contains several linked files that are stored in different locations on your hard drive or server? Will you remember to include those as well?

FreeHand offers two solutions for managing your linked files. In the previous task, you explored the Links dialog box. In this task, you will look at the Collect for Output feature. If you are familiar with page layout programs, you may have used a similar command before.

1) Choose File > Collect for Output.

If you haven't saved your file, FreeHand warns you and asks if you want to save the file. Click OK to save the file. You next will see an alert reminding you that fonts are copyrighted and that you should check your font license before sending copies of your fonts to service bureaus.

2) Click OK to close the font license alert dialog box.

The Document Report window appears. This is where you select the options you want to include in the report for this document. Notice that you can list all imported graphics, fonts, and colors. This information can be useful to your service bureau or commercial printer.

When you select a report category, the window displays the options available for that category.

3) In the Document Report window, leave the category set to Document and use the default Document options; then click OK (Windows) or Report (Mac OS).

A save dialog box appears asking for a location for all the files needed to output this FreeHand document. Typically, you select a disk or folder for the files.

4) Create a new folder within your Projects folder. Name the folder *Output*. Open that folder, type *Report* as the report name, and then click Save.

Collect for Output saves the report as a text file and makes a copy of your FreeHand document. Any fonts and linked graphics are copied and saved in the folder as well.

NOTE *If you just want to generate a report without collecting your files, choose File > Report.*

PRINTING YOUR DOCUMENT

Once you complete your document, you will want to print your work. You can print from the PDF file you created, or you can print directly from FreeHand. If you are sending your PDF file for output, you should first print the PDF file yourself to make sure it prints correctly. In fact, it is a good idea to print your PDF file from another computer, if possible. That way, you can verify that you've included everything in the PDF file. For example, if you have unique fonts on your machine and did not embed them in the PDF file, your file may not print correctly on another machine. You can then fix the problem before sending the file to a client or service bureau.

FreeHand is designed to take advantage of PostScript printers and high-resolution output devices, but you can print to just about any printer, even if it is not a PostScript printer. Depending on your printer, the choices and look of the Print dialog box may differ.

1) Choose File > Print to display the Print dialog box. From the Printer pop-up menu, choose your printer.

If you are using a Macintosh, you will need to choose FreeHand MX from the Print Options pop-up menu.

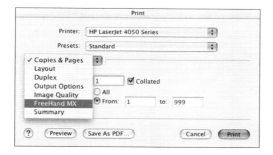

A variety of common print options are available. For example, you can choose to print one page or a range of pages if you have a multiple-page document.

NOTE *If your system is not configured to print to a PostScript printer, the Print dialog box will be different from the one shown here.*

2) From the Print Setting pop-up menu, choose a print quality.

If you're using a PostScript printer, choose Quality PS Level 2. If you don't have a PostScript printer, choose Normal instead.

PRINT SETTING POP-UP MENU

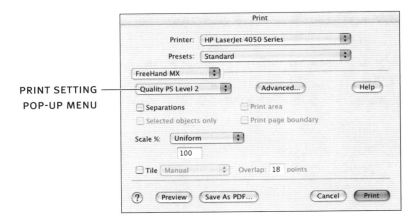

3) Click Advanced to display the Print Setup dialog box. Verify that Composite is selected.

Print Setup enables you to customize the settings for this print job. The preview window on the left shows you how your document will print with the current settings. On the right are three tabbed panels: Separations, Imaging, and Paper Setup.

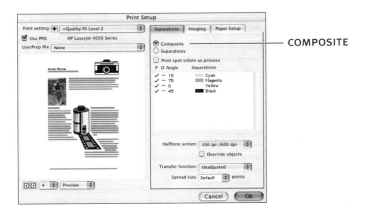

COMPOSITE

The Separations panel controls the way that colors are printed in your document. With a composite image, all colors print on the same page: if you print to a color printer, the document prints as you see it on the screen, depending on the quality of your printer; if you print to a black-and-white printer, your colors appear as grayscale values. Composite is the default selection in the dialog box. If you select Separations, each ink color in your document prints on a separate page. This is the setting used by commercial printers or service bureaus to create separate plates (or

234

film) for each ink color. Normally, a service bureau will select the options needed to print separations, so you don't need to set these.

TIP *Printing separations for your document prints a page for each ink used by the color defined in your document. If you are sending your files to a commercial printer, you can print separations to verify the number of colors in your document. For example, suppose you design a document with two spot colors—blue and black—but you inadvertently define two different colors of blue in your document. When you print your document with separations, three pages will print instead of the two you were expecting. By checking, you can fix your mistake before you send out your job.*

For this example, you will print the page with your postcard. If you don't have a PostScript printer, you can skip the remaining steps.

4) From the Page pop-up menu in the Print Setup dialog box, choose Page 1.
This is the page that contains your postcard. That page is smaller than a letter-sized page; so that you can see its edges, you will display crop marks in the next step.

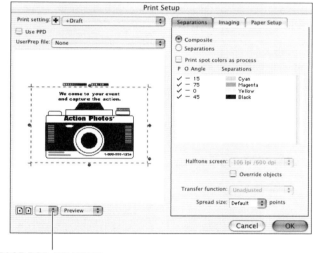

PAGE POP-UP MENU

5) Click the Imaging tab; then in the Labels and Marks area, select Crop Marks. Deselect the other options in this area if they are selected.

You should see dashed lines around the image in the preview panel, indicating the edges of the postcard page.

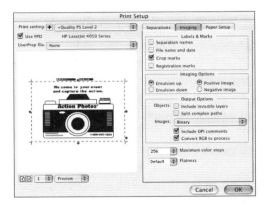

The Imaging tab also contains an option that allows you to include hidden layers in the printed output. In this document, you don't have any hidden layers, so it doesn't matter whether that option is selected or not.

6) Click the Paper Setup tab. From the Paper Size pop-up menu, choose the paper size, and for Orientation, select Automatic.

Here is where you select your paper size and page orientation. If you select Automatic for the orientation, FreeHand determines the optimum orientation based on the size of the pages in your document, the printer you select, and the paper size. If you deselect Automatic, you can choose either Tall or Wide as the page orientation.

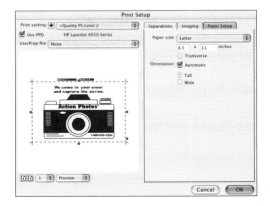

NOTE *The Paper Size pop-up menu may be dimmed depending on your printer driver. If it is dimmed, select Use PPD.*

236

7) Click OK to close the Print Setup dialog box. If you want to print this page, in the Print Range area, select Pages, and in the Pages text box, type *1*. Otherwise, click Cancel to close the dialog box.

You could also select All as the Print Range to print all of the pages in this document.

8) Save your file.

WHAT YOU HAVE LEARNED

In this lesson, you have:

- Aligned objects to the page (pages 202–203)
- Imported RTF and ASCII text files and placed them on the page (pages 203–209)
- Created a multicolumn text block for a two-column layout (pages 209–212)
- Used the Text Editor to display invisible characters (pages 212–214)
- Checked the spelling in the document (pages 215–216)
- Flowed text around graphics (pages 217–220)
- Set the raster effects resolution for printing (pages 220–221)
- Created and edited text styles and applied them to paragraphs (pages 222–225)
- Exported a document as a PDF file (pages 226–228)
- Checked imported images in the Links dialog box (pages 229–231)
- Prepared files for output using Collect for Output (pages 231–232)
- Printed a document (pages 233–237)

symbols, brushes, and hoses

After the successful introduction of symbols in Macromedia Flash, Macromedia wisely added symbols to its FreeHand and Fireworks programs. Although symbols work slightly differently in each application, the underlying concept is basically the same: symbols streamline the use of repeating elements on your pages. Multiple instances of a symbol on a page consume much less memory than the same number of separate images, reducing file size. More important, when you make a change to a symbol, every instance of the symbol on the page is updated automatically.

Whenever you create a symbol, it is added to the Library panel. As you will see in this lesson, you can group your library items to make them more manageable. Also, if you import FreeHand files into Macromedia Flash, your FreeHand symbols are imported into the Macromedia Flash document library, saving you a step when creating animations.

In this lesson, you will use blending techniques to add shading to objects. Then you will convert your objects to symbols and use the symbols as brushes and graphic hoses.

In this lesson, you will create and edit some symbols and use them as brushes and in a graphic hose. The brush feature allows you to take any element in your document (even text) and convert it to a brush stroke that you can apply to a path. This feature offers you new creative possibilities and saves production time when you want multiple objects to follow a set path. The Graphic Hose tool allows you to store up to 10 graphic objects in a hose set. When you drag the tool pointer around the page, the graphic objects in the hose set are sprayed on the page. You can change the settings to spray in random order and alter the scaling, spacing, and rotation of the objects as they are placed on the page.

This lesson also introduces some blending techniques that you can use to add shading to objects.

WHAT YOU WILL LEARN

In this lesson, you will:

- Convert an object to a symbol
- Edit a symbol
- Use blends for shading
- Use the Roughen tool
- Add a contour gradient
- Import a brush
- Create a library group
- Create and edit a brush
- Create a graphic hose
- Export your symbols

APPROXIMATE TIME

This lesson takes approximately 2 hours to complete.

LESSON FILES

Media Files:
Lesson08\Media\Graphic Brushes.fh11

Starting Files:
None

Completed Projects:
Lesson08\Completed\flowers.fh11

CREATING SYMBOLS

A **symbol** is a graphic or group of elements you have created and saved in a library for future use. When you want to use a symbol, you simply go to the library, find the symbol you want to use, and drag the symbol into your document. The copy of the symbol that you place in your document is referred to as an **instance**. For example, the camera you created in Lesson 1, "FreeHand Basics," could be converted to a symbol. Then, when you want to use it in another page, you could just drag it from the Library panel. Of course, you could always import the camera and copy and paste it from one page to another as you did in Lesson 7, "Page Layout and Printing," but symbols give you more flexibility and control.

An advantage of symbols is that even if you use a symbol numerous times in a document, the multiple instances of the symbol will not significantly increase the file size. Another advantage of symbols is that any change you make to a symbol changes all instances of that symbol in your document. For example, suppose you create a symbol of the camera logo and place it on several pages in your document as you did in the corp_identity.fh11 file you modified in Lesson 7. If you later decide to change the design or color of the logo, you simply make your edits to the symbol, and when you are done, all instances of the logo are automatically updated in your document.

You can also export symbols and use them in other documents. Then you can import them into the library of the document, or you can send the symbol file to co-workers for use in their documents. And if you are a Flasher—that is, if you use Macromedia Flash— you can easily import the symbols you create in FreeHand into Macromedia Flash.

NOTE *In Flash, you would open the document library and then import the exported FreeHand library into the Flash library.*

In this task, you will create a graphic, convert it to a symbol, and place instances of the symbol on the page. Then you will edit the symbol to see how the instances are automatically updated.

1) Create a new file and name it *flowers.fh11*. Save it in your Projects folder.
You will create a leaf and petal for a flower and save both as symbols.

2) On the page, draw a circle about 150 points in diameter. Choose Modify > Ungroup.
The size of the circle is not critical; you can always change the size of the final leaf. You want to ungroup the circle so you can modify one of the points.

3) Select the top point of the circle. Hold down Shift and drag the point upward.

Holding Shift as you drag maintains the horizontal alignment of the point. You want the shape to resemble an elongated egg.

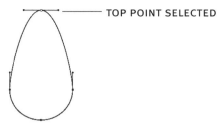

TOP POINT SELECTED

4) Drag the selection rectangle over the top and bottom points on the shape; then choose Modify > Split.

You now have two separate objects. In the next step, you will join the left side to create a closed path.

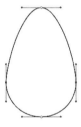

 NOTE *You can also Shift-click each point to select the points.*

5) Press Tab to deselect both objects and then select the left object. On the Object panel, select Closed. Delete the right object.

The left side is a closed object that you can fill with a gradient. Instead of manually creating the same fill for the right side, you will clone the left object and then use the Reflect tool to flip it to create the right side of the leaf.

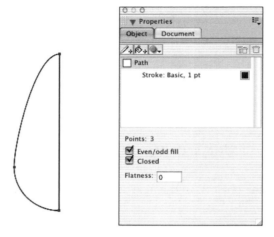

6) Add a green color to the Swatches panel; then add a 20 percent tint of that color to the Swatches panel. Using these two green colors, add a gradient fill to the left side of the leaf with the darker color on the left of the gradient ramp.

You could use Forest Green from the Crayon color list or mix your own color.

7) Change the angle of the gradient to 45 degrees.

Changing the angle of the gradient adds depth and shape to the leaf.

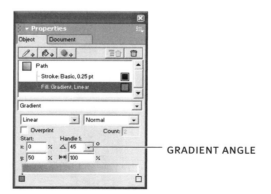

GRADIENT ANGLE

242

8) Choose Edit > Clone and then use the Reflect tool to create a mirror image of the clone.

Remember: To flip the clone, hold down Shift and drag down with the Reflect tool. The position of the Reflect pointer when you drag with the tool determines the reflection axis. If the right side of your leaf is not next to the left side, move the leaf halves together.

NOTE *If you position the Reflect pointer on the right edge of the object, the right flipped object should touch the left object.*

In the next step, you will convert your leaf to a symbol. Then you will make copies of the leaf symbol and rotate them to form a leaf circle. If you think that your leaf is too large, resize it after you group it.

9) With the leaf group still selected, choose Modify > Symbol > Convert to Symbol.

Your object is converted to a symbol and placed in the library, as you will see in the next step.

TIP *The shortcut for creating a symbol in FreeHand is F8. Conveniently, that is the same shortcut as in Macromedia Flash. You can also drag the object to the Library panel to create a new symbol of the object.*

NOTE *From the Modify > Symbol command, you can choose either Copy to Symbol or Convert to Symbol. If you choose Convert to Symbol, as you did in this step, you create a symbol, and the original object is converted to an instance of that symbol. If you choose Copy to Symbol, you create a symbol, but the original object remains as created. Choosing the Copy option saves you a step if you plan to modify the original object to create another symbol. If you do want to modify a symbol to create another symbol, you simply select an instance of the symbol and then choose Modify > Symbol > Release Instance. Then you can make any modifications and create a new symbol.*

10) Choose Window > Library or click the Library tab on the Assets panel.

The Library panel should list your new symbol with a generic name such as Graphic-01 and display a preview of the image. To make your symbols easier to work with, you should assign them names that indicate their use; you will do this in the next step.

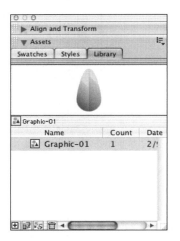

11) Double-click (Windows) or click (Mac OS) the generic symbol name on the Library panel and type *leaf* as the name. Press Enter (Windows) or Return (Mac OS) to apply the name to the symbol.

Now that your leaf is a symbol, you can easily use it to create a cluster of leaves on the page by using a power duplication method, creating a copy and rotating the copy in one step.

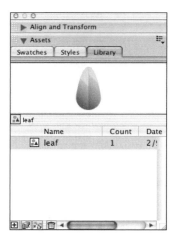

12) In Windows, either open the Info panel or use the Status toolbar bar that appears at the bottom of the document window. In Mac OS, open the Info panel.

You'll use the Status bar or Info panel as you rotate the leaf in the next step.

13) Clone the leaf. Select the Rotate tool and position the rotate pointer at the bottom of your leaf. Drag the mouse until you see 60 in the angle area of the Status bar (Windows only) or on the Info panel; then release the mouse button.

As you drag with the Rotate tool, a bounding box surrounds the object, and a line indicates the angle of rotation. If the object rotates too quickly, you can slow it down by moving the mouse pointer away from the center point of the rotation. The farther away from the center point you move the pointer, the more slowly the object rotates.

For this task, you want your leaves equally spaced as you rotate them. Since there are 360 degrees in a circle, using 60 degrees results in six leaves.

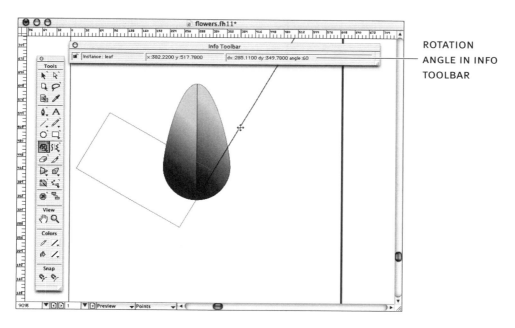

ROTATION ANGLE IN INFO TOOLBAR

14) Choose Edit > Duplicate.

A new copy of the leaf is created and rotated for you. When you clone an object and then perform a transformation such as a rotation, FreeHand remembers those steps and repeats them when you choose the Duplicate command.

15) Repeat the Duplicate command until you have a total of six leaves.

Each leaf in your cluster is an instance of the original symbol. In the next step, you will make a change to the symbol and see how FreeHand automatically updates all instances of the symbol on the page.

TIP *The shortcut for the Duplicate command is Ctrl+Alt+D (Windows) or Command+Option+D (Mac OS). When you are using power duplication, you'll want to use the shortcut instead of choosing the command from the menu.*

16) Save your file.

EDITING A SYMBOL

Once you place a symbol instance on the page, you can apply Transform (scaling, rotating, and skewing) and Arrange commands to it, but as long as it is a symbol instance, you cannot edit it in any other way as an individual object. Try to change one of the leaves on your page; you can't ungroup it, nor can you make any changes to its color or shape. You can, however, easily make changes to all instances of the leaf, by editing the symbol, as you will do in this task.

1) Select one of the leaves on the page and choose Modify > Symbol > Edit Symbol.

A new window opens where you can make changes to the leaf. Note the Auto-Update check box at the top left of the window. When this check box is selected (it is selected by default), any changes you make to the symbol are applied to all instances on the page.

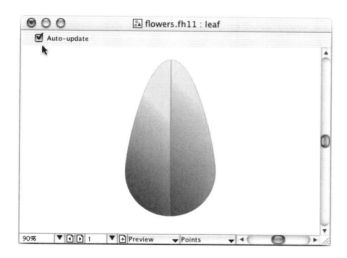

TIP *You can also double-click the symbol icon (to the left of the symbol name) on the Library panel to open the symbol-editing window.*

NOTE *The symbol-editing window is easy to confuse with the document window. The Auto-Update check box is your visual clue that you are in the symbol-editing window. Plus the symbol name, plus the document file name appears in the title bar of the symbol window.*

2) Make a change to your leaf. For example, change the gradient color or add a new color to the gradient ramp.

You might add a warm yellow color to the gradient to give an autumn tone to the leaf. The goal here is to make an obvious change to the symbol.

TIP *Use the Subselect tool to select an object in a group instead of ungrouping the object. To use the shortcut for the temporary Subselect tool, hold down Alt (Windows) or Option (Mac OS) and click one of the grouped objects.*

3) When you are done making changes to the symbol, close the symbol-editing window.

All instances of the leaf symbol on the page are updated with your changes. If there were instances of the symbol on multiple pages of your document, those would be updated as well.

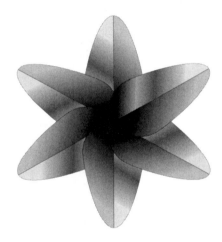

248

USING THE ROUGHEN TOOL

The Roughen tool changes smooth paths to irregular, ragged paths. It is a great tool for adding a hand-drawn effect to your artwork. The leaf you just created is a good example of a graphic with a smooth edge. Of course, Mother Nature is not that perfect, and you may want to alter your leaf to reflect the nonconforming edges in nature.

For this task, you will start with another instance of your leaf symbol and release it so you can roughen the edges.

1) Drag a new instance of your leaf symbol to the page. Choose Modify › Symbol › Release Instance.

This leaf is no longer a symbol, and any changes you make to this leaf do not affect the other leaves. Similarly, if you change the symbol, this leaf is not updated with those changes.

2) Double-click the Roughen tool to open the Roughen dialog box. Select Rough and drag the Amount slider to 6. Click OK.

You control the roughness of the edge by selecting either Rough or Smooth. Rough creates corner points and Smooth creates curved points. You use the Amount slider to control the number of segments that are added to the path when you use the tool.

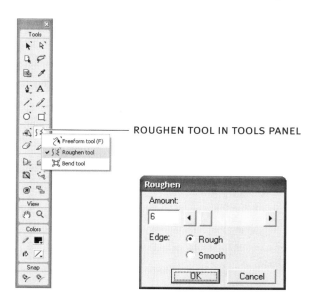

ROUGHEN TOOL IN TOOLS PANEL

249

3) Select the single leaf and drag with the Roughen tool.

The edges of the leaf change as you drag. The farther you drag, the greater the distortion. Notice that all edges of the leaf are distorted—even the middle edge where the two sides of the leaf meet. You may not like this look. In the next step, you will use the Punch command to smooth the inside edges.

4) Choose Modify > Ungroup. Move one side of the leaf away from the other.

You need to ungroup the leaf so you can separate the left and right sides.

NOTE *If you grouped your leaf before making it a symbol, you may need to perform the ungroup twice. Look in the Object panel to verify that the object is ungrouped.*

5) Draw a rectangle that overlaps the inside edges of each part of the leaf.

You will use the straight edge of the rectangle to cut though the roughened edges of the leaf parts. Make sure that the rectangle covers each side.

6) Select all three objects: the rectangle and both sides of the leaf. Choose Modify > Combine > Punch.

The inside edges of the leaf sides are sliced, resulting in straight lines.

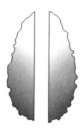

7) Move the leaf sides together and make the new leaf a symbol.

If you want to replace the leaves in your circle of leaves, drop your new leaf object on the leaf symbol on the library. Click Replace in the alert box to replace all instances of the leaf symbol with this new object.

The leaves are a good start, but the image needs petals to look like a flower. In the next task, you will create some petal designs, using blends instead of a gradient to create the shading.

USING BLENDS FOR SHADING

When the blend capability was first introduced for a competing product, marketing materials illustrated the feature by using the blend command to morph an S into a swan. That was pretty cool, but you probably won't be using blends in that way often. More frequently, you will use blends to create shading for objects.

Blending lets you create multiple paths that morph from one shape to another. If the paths contain different colors, the colors as well as the paths of the objects shift over the course of the steps in the blend.

In this task, you will use a blend to create the shading for a flower petal. To draw the flower, you will use a technique similar to the one you used to draw the leaves.

1) Draw a circle approximately 100 points in diameter and then ungroup it. Hold down the Shift key and drag the bottom point down to begin to create a flower petal.
The distance you drag the point determines the length of the petal. Experiment with the distance to get the shape you want for the petal.

2) Select the top point of the shape; on the Object panel, click both Retract Handle buttons.
When you retract the handles, the curved top of the petal changes to a point.

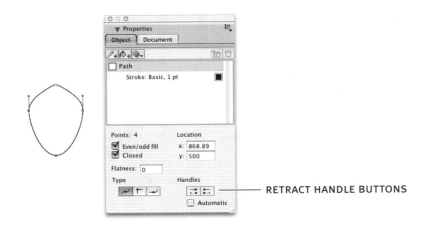

RETRACT HANDLE BUTTONS

3) Select the path of the petal.

In the previous step, you selected the top point. For the next step, you want just the path (not a point on the path) selected.

NOTE *If you see a hollow point on the path, that point is selected. Press Tab to deselect everything and then select the path again, making sure that you click the outline of the path, not the point.*

4) Choose Window > Transform to open the Transform panel. On the Transform panel, click the Scale button.

In the next step, you will create a scaled copy of the petal. The Transform panel allows you to make a copy and scale it all in one step.

SCALE BUTTON ———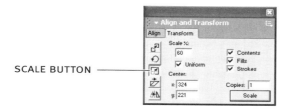

5) On the Transform panel, select Uniform and in the Scale percentage text box, type *60*. In the Copies text box, type *1;* then click Scale.

You now have a smaller copy of your petal.

Was the Strokes option on the Transform panel selected before you scaled the object? If so, the point size of the stroke on your petal was also scaled in the copy. For this task, the point size of the stroke is not a concern, as you will remove the stroke on both paths in the next step. Just remember to select the Strokes option if you need it when you use the panel for scaling other objects.

6) Fill the larger petal with a dark red color and choose a 10 percent tint of that color for the fill of the smaller petal. Remove the stroke on both petals.

In the next step, you will blend the two objects. You want a smooth transition from the smaller object to the larger one. If you leave the stroke on the petals, you will see the line of the stroke as part of the blend, which would not be desirable in this flower drawing.

7) Select the top point on both petals. Choose Xtras > Create > Blend.

The two shapes are blended together. FreeHand does a good job of guessing the number of steps needed for the blend, but you can alter that number if desired.

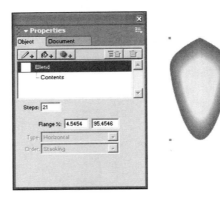

TIP *You can also choose Modify > Combine > Blend or click the Blend button on the Xtra Operations toolbar to create the blend.*

8) On the Object panel, in the Steps text box, type 4; then press Enter (Windows) or Return (Mac OS) to apply that number of steps.

When you use a small number of steps, you get a banding effect. If you don't see the banding effect, try entering a smaller number.

9) Now type *25* as the number of steps.

The more steps in a blend, the smoother the transition. Using a large number of steps can increase the time needed to print your document, however. Choose the number of steps that works best for your petal.

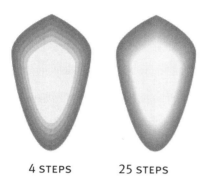

4 STEPS   25 STEPS

10) Save your file.

ON YOUR OWN

Once you have your petal to your liking, convert it to a symbol. Use the clone and duplicate method you used for the leaves to rotate the petals to form a circle of petals. Instead of rotating each petal 60 degrees as you did for the leaf cluster, try using 36 degrees to create 10 petals.

255

NOTE *You can also use the Scale command on the smaller petal to create a third petal as you did in step 5. Fill that shape with a third color, select the top points of the three shapes, and then execute the Blend command. This results in a three-color petal. Let your imagination go wild here.*

THREE-COLOR BLEND

You may want to experiment with other ways to use a blend. For example, draw a curved path using the Pen or Pencil tool and use the Alt-drag or Option-drag method to offset a copy slightly. Then use the Duplicate command as you did for the petal to make several more copies of the path. Use a different stroke color for each path. Select all of the paths and then apply the blend. The result is a colorful ribbon that blends from one color to the next.

BLENDED STROKES

ADDING A CONTOUR GRADIENT

To complete your flower, you just need to add the middle section (called the stamen). For that part, you'll draw a multifaceted star and add a contour gradient. A contour gradient is essentially a blend, similar to the blend you created for the petal and leaf of your flower. The difference is that FreeHand does all the work for you, plus it lets you control the amount of each color as the blend tapers from one color to another.

1) Double-click the Polygon tool to set the polygon options. Select Star as the shape of the polygon. Type *20* **as the number of sides and set Star Points to Manual. Drag the angle slider to preview the look of the star shape. When you are satisfied, click OK.**

You can change the number of points to match your flower. The number here is just a suggestion.

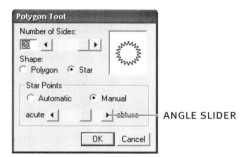

ANGLE SLIDER

2) Drag to create your star.

You want this shape in the middle of your flower. Release the mouse button when the star is the size you need.

TIP   *Once you create your star, you can modify the number of points by changing the number on the Object panel. Select the Polygon property on the Object panel and then type a new number for the points. You can also modify the angles and rotation of the star points. For example, type* 350 *for the rotation angle of the outer vertices to see the effect of the rotation.*

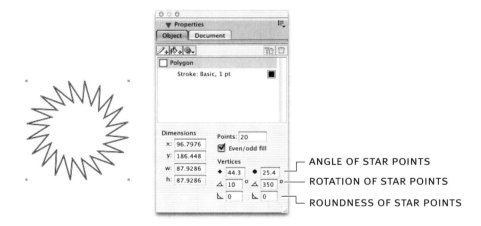

ANGLE OF STAR POINTS

ROTATION OF STAR POINTS

ROUNDNESS OF STAR POINTS

3) Add an orange fill to the star.

If you prefer, you can pick a different color, to match your flower.

4) On the Object panel, select the Fill property; from the Fill Type pop-up menu, choose Gradient; and from the Gradient Type pop-up menu, choose Contour.

The Object panel provides several settings that you can use to change the look of the gradient. When the Gradient property is selected on the Object panel, your object displays a start point (a small circle) and an end point (a small square.) You can drag the start point to reposition the gradient or drag the end point to adjust the length of the gradient.

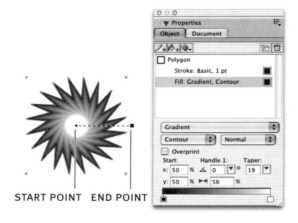

START POINT END POINT

The Object panel offers four gradient behaviors: Normal, Repeat, Reflect, and Auto Size. These behaviors affect the way that the gradient fills the object.

- **Normal:** The positions of the start and end points determine the length of the gradient.

- **Repeat:** The gradient repeats a specified number of times.

- **Reflect:** The colors transition from one end of the gradient ramp and then back, going through one transition for each Repeat count.

- **Auto Size:** The length of the gradient is set to the exact width and height of the object.

NOTE *When Auto Size is selected, the gradient start- and end-point handles do not appear on the selected object. To adjust gradient attributes when Auto Size is selected, use the Object panel.*

5) Adjust the contour settings to your liking and then save your file.

USING THE BRUSH FEATURE

What comes to mind when you think of a brush? If you have used a brush in a bitmap application such as Macromedia Fireworks or Adobe Photoshop, you may think of a brush as a tool for painting pixels. In FreeHand, you create a **brush** from symbols. Anything you can draw in FreeHand can be made into a brush that you can apply to a path. For example, suppose you want to create a circular border consisting of triangles. Sure, you can draw a triangle, clone it, and rotate it to form the circle. In fact, you did just that when you drew the petals and leaves for the flower. But what if you want to use that same effect to create a border in the shape of a square or a curved path? If you create a brush using a triangle, then all you have to do is apply the brush to a path, just as you change the stroke for a path. What could be easier?

In Lesson 5, "Using Points and Paths," you drew a bicycle and used a dashed line to represent the bike chain. The dashed line follows the curve of the path. Once you drew the path, changing it to a dashed line was just a matter of selecting the type of dashed line you wanted to use. What if you wanted to make a more realistic look for the bike chain? If you look at a bike chain, you'll see that it consists of links in the shape of figure eights. You could draw one link and then place copies of the link to form the chain. However, if you converted the link to a symbol and used the symbol to create a brush, all you would then need to do is draw the path and apply the chain brush to the path. If you alter the path, the chain brush will bend to follow the path automatically. On your bike drawing, you would just remove the dashed line on the path and then replace it with the chain brush.

FreeHand conveniently includes a chain brush that you will use in this task. Later, you will create your own brush.

In this task, you will examine some of the brushes that come with FreeHand. Then you will create your own brush.

1) Add a new page to your document. On this new page, draw a line using the Pen or Pencil tool. On the Object panel, select the Stroke property.

The Object panel displays the stroke attributes.

2) From the Stroke Type pop-up menu, choose Brush. Click the Options button (Windows) or Options pop-up menu (Mac OS) and choose Import. Select the Graphic Brushes file and click Import.

The open dialog box should open pointing to the Brushes folder within the Settings folder. If it doesn't, you need to navigate to that folder. If you do not have the Graphic Brushes file on your computer, you can use the Graphic Brushes.fh11 file in the Media folder within the Lesson08 folder.

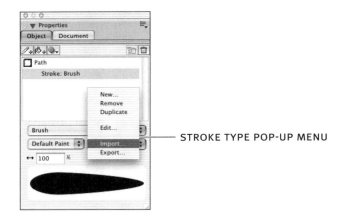

STROKE TYPE POP-UP MENU

NOTE *If you see a folder named Brush Tips in the Library panel, the Graphic Brushes file is already imported in your document. You can still follow these steps, you will just add a copy of the chain symbol to your document.*

260

NOTE *FreeHand stores symbols and brushes in the Macromedia/FreeHand MX/11/ English/Settings folder located in the user-specific Application Data (Windows) or Application Support (Mac OS) folder.*

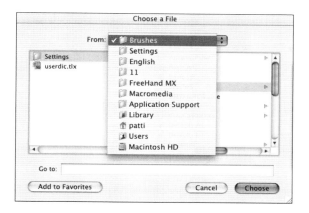

NOTE *You should have a default brush installed. If not, a dialog box opens before you have a chance to choose Import from the pop-up menu. Click Import in the dialog box and continue with the instructions for step 2.*

3) In the Import Brushes dialog box, select Chain from the list of included symbols and then click Import.

The selected symbol is placed in the library and added to your brushes list. The chain brush consists of two symbols: Link 1 and Link 2. You'll see when you create your own brush that you can use several symbols in a brush to add interesting effects.

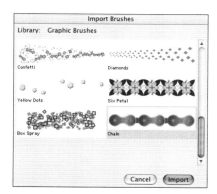

You should now have at least four symbols in your library: the symbols you just imported and the leaf and petal from the previous tasks. As you add more symbols to the library, you may want to organize them by grouping like items together. In the next step, you will create a group for the two brush symbols.

TIP *If you want to select multiple noncontiguous symbols in the Import Brushes dialog box, Ctrl-click (Windows) or Command-click (Mac OS) the images.*

4) From the Library panel Options menu, choose New Group.

A folder icon is added to the library list with a generic name such as Group-01. In the next step, you will rename the folder.

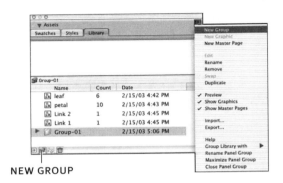

NEW GROUP

NOTE *You can also click the New Group icon at the bottom of the Library panel to add a library group.*

5) Double-click (Windows) or click (Mac OS) the default group name and then type *chain* as the new name. Press Enter (Windows) or Return (Mac OS) to apply the name to the group. Drag the Link 1 and Link 2 symbols to the Brushes group.

The symbols are added to this group. You can open and close the group on the panel to see or hide the contents. Click the plus sign (Window) or the right triangle (Mac OS) to open the folder; click the minus sign (Windows) or downward triangle (Mac OS) to close the group.

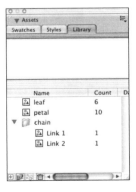

Once you add or import a brush, you can easily apply it to any path.

6) Using the Pen or Pencil tool, draw a curved path.

If you drag quickly with the Pencil tool, you should be able to create a smooth curve. Don't worry if it is not perfect.

7) On the Object panel, choose the Stroke property; from the Stroke Type pop-up menu, choose Brush; and from the Brush pop-up menu, choose Chain.

The Brush menu lists the chain brush you just imported plus any default brushes. When you select the chain brush, it is applied to the selected path.

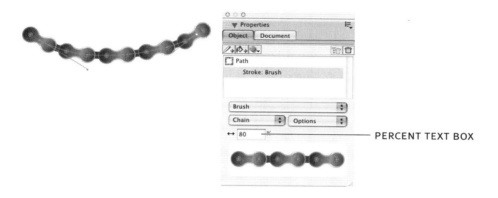

PERCENT TEXT BOX

8) In the Percent text box, type *80*; then press Enter (Windows) or Return (Mac OS) to apply that percentage amount.

The chain brush size changes based on the percentage you enter. Experiment by changing the points on the path to see how the brush adapts to the curves in the path. Try drawing other shapes and apply the brush to them as well. Remember the bicycle you drew in Lesson 5? You used a dashed line for the chain. Instead of the dashed line, you could use the chain brush for a more realistic look.

263

CREATING A BRUSH

You've seen how easy it is to apply an existing brush, but to really take advantage of this feature, you can create your own brushes. For instance, the chain brush consists of two simple objects that you could easily draw. Link 1 is a figure-eight object, and Link 2 is a square, and when they alternate and overlap, you get the chain appearance.

In this task, you will draw some simple objects and then use them to create your own brush.

1) Draw a triangle and a rectangle. Fill each with a different color.

These two objects will alternate to create your brush.

2) Select the triangle and press F8 to convert it to a symbol; then do the same for the rectangle. Give each symbol a meaningful name.

> **TIP** *You can also drag an object to the Library panel to convert it to a symbol.*

3) Select the triangle on the page (it is now an instance of the symbol) and choose Modify > Brush > Create Brush. In the Edit Brush dialog box, type *triangle* as the brush name.

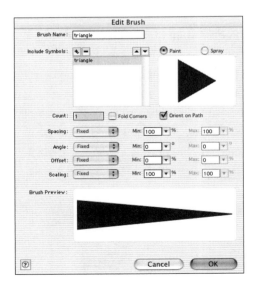

In the Edit Brush dialog box, you specify how you want the path altered when you apply the brush. You can either paint or spray the brush. Painting stretches the brush tip along the path. Spraying places the graphic along the path.

4) Select Paint and then click OK.

You will next apply the brush to a line to see the effect of the Paint option. Then you will edit the brush to add the rectangle and change the brush to use the Spray option.

5) Select the Line tool and draw a line. On the Object panel, select the Stroke property; from the Stroke Type pop-up menu, choose Brush; and from the Brush pop-up menu, choose triangle.

The brush stroke is applied to the line. The triangle shape is stretched along the path of the line.

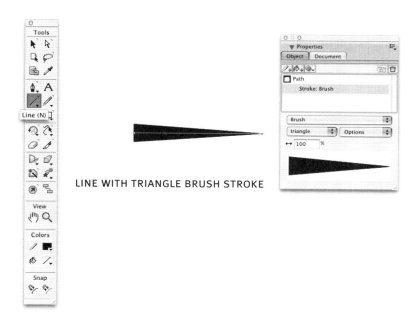

LINE WITH TRIANGLE BRUSH STROKE

◎ POWER TIP *You can change your preferences to apply the last stroke or fill to the next object you draw. Choose Edit > Preferences (Windows and Mac OS 9) or FreeHand MX > Preferences (Mac OS X) and click the Object tab (Windows) or the Object category (Mac OS). Select the option Changing Object Changes Defaults and then click OK. Now each time you draw a new object, it takes on the attributes of the last object drawn. This preference setting is helpful when you want to use the brush stroke on every object you draw. Remove the option when you want each object you draw to use the default attributes, not the last one used.*

Try drawing some different shapes. For example, draw a circle or an ellipse and apply the brush stroke. Use the Line tool and draw lines of different length with that brush applied.

LINE AND ELLIPSE WITH TRIANGLE BRUSH

EDITING A BRUSH

Once you create your brush, you have several options for changing its look. Remember that you created a symbol of the triangle. If you want to change the shape, color, or stroke of the triangle, you can double-click the symbol on the Library panel, make the change in the symbol-editing window, and then close that window. When you change the symbol, FreeHand updates the brush and all objects on the page that use that brush.

You can also edit the brush settings, changing the spacing, size, or rotation of the symbols that make up the brush. For instance, you will now add another symbol to your brush and change it to use the Spray option.

1) Select one of the paths with the triangle brush applied. On the Object panel, select the Stroke property; then click the Options button (Windows) or Options pop-up menu (Mac OS) and choose Edit.

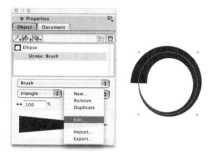

2) From the Plus pop-up menu, choose the rectangle symbol.

The symbol is added to the Include Symbols list for the brush. The order of the symbols will affect the look of the brush. You can use the up and down arrows to change the symbol order. Try moving each symbol to the top. As you move each symbol, look at the preview pane to see how your brush will appear. Then choose the look you like.

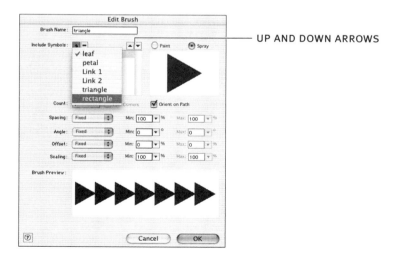

267

3) Select the triangle symbol and choose Spray. Select the rectangle symbol and choose Paint.

Each symbol in the list can use different options, giving you more flexibility for the look of your brush.

4) Select the triangle symbol and change the Minimum Spacing slider to 120 percent.

The Minimum Spacing option sets the distance between instances of that symbol on the path as a percentage of the symbol size. By default, the spacing option uses a fixed setting, but you can also choose either Random or Variable from the Spacing pop-up menu. When you choose Random or Variable, you then can set both minimum and maximum spacing percentages.

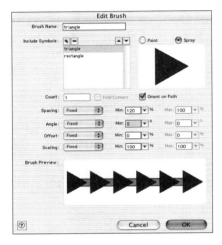

5) When you have the look you want for your brush, click OK. If the warning box alerting you that the brush is in use appears, click Change.

When you click Change, the brush attributes are changed, and any object that uses that brush is updated. If you click Create, FreeHand creates a new brush for you with a name such as Copy of Triangle.

ON YOUR OWN

By now, you are probably experimenting by creating all sorts of brushes. After all, this is fun! Hopefully, your creative mind is considering how you can use the brush feature in your drawings. The power of brushes is apparent when you need to use an object or effect repeatedly. If you just need two copies of an object, cloning the object is easier and quicker. If you want to use an object multiple times with varying lengths, then creating a brush may be the way to go. And because a brush is created from a symbol (or symbols), you are not drastically increasing your file size.

Here is something you can try. Convert some text to a symbol and then create a brush from the symbol. For the brush option, use Paint, and change the scaling to Flare. Change the minimum scaling to 30 percent and the maximum scaling to 200 percent. Experiment with these settings to create an appropriate look for your text. After you create the brush, draw a curved path and apply the brush. Pretty cool!

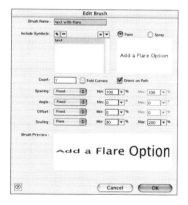

LINE AND CIRCLE WITH TEXT BRUSH

CREATING MORE SYMBOLS

If you want to place multiple instances of images on your page with varying sizes, rotation, and spacing, you can use the **Graphic Hose** tool. This may not be a feature that you will use often, but for certain drawing tasks, it can save you some time. Besides, it is fun to use.

To see how the Graphic Hose tool works, you'll draw a piece of candy, using what you learned earlier in this lesson to add some shading. You will create several symbols of the candy, each with a different color. Then you'll use those symbols to create a graphic hose.

1) Add a new page to your document. On this new page, draw a circle about 60 points in diameter. Fill the circle with a blue color. Make a copy of the circle and move it off to the side.

The circle is your candy. You will use the copy of the circle later to create a shadow for the candy.

2) Select the original circle and use the Transform panel to make one copy; scale the copy 80 percent. Fill the smaller copy with a 90 percent tint of the original color.

TIP *A quick way to add a color to the Tints panel is to use the Eyedropper tool. Select the Eyedropper tool and drag from the center of the circle to the color chip on the Tint panel. You should see a small square as you drag, indicating that you grabbed the color.*

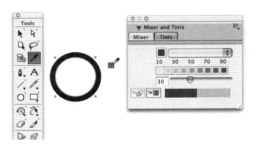

3) Select both circles, ungroup them, and remove the strokes.

You will create a blend from one circle to the other so you want to remove the strokes to get a smooth transition.

4) Select the top points of each circle and choose Xtras > Create > Blend. Change the number of steps for the blend to 5.

The blend should add some shading to your circle, giving it some dimension. You may want to zoom in on your circles to see if you have a smooth transition for your blend. If you don't, slightly increase the number of steps to make the transition smoother.

Next you will add a highlight to the candy.

5) Use the Pen tool to draw a curved path at the top right of your circles.

Adjust the path so that you have a smooth curved line. Don't worry about the stroke size or color of your path. In the next step, you will change the stroke to a shape that you can fill with color.

CURVED PATH FOR HIGHLIGHT

6) Choose Modify > Alter Path > Expand Stroke.

Expanding the stroke creates a single closed path that follows the outer edge of the stroke of the object.

7) For the stroke width, type 3, and for the Cap option, select the center icon. Click OK.

The Cap option determines the shape of the new path at its end points. The center icon rounds the end points of the new path.

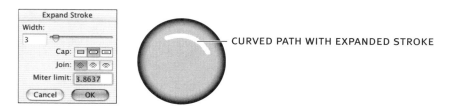

CURVED PATH WITH EXPANDED STROKE

8) Change the fill color of your new shape to white.

Next you will use the copy of the circle you moved aside to create a shadow for your candy.

> **TIP** *If you forgot to make a copy of the circle before you created the blend, hold down Alt or Option and click the outside edge of the blend to select the larger circle. Use the Alt-drag or Option-drag method to make a copy of this circle. Remember that you can also switch to Keyline view to see the outside circle.*

9) Use the Alt-drag or Option-drag method to make a copy of the circle you moved to the side of the page in step 1. Drag up and to the right.

You want a small crescent shape showing on the original circle when the two circles overlap. You want the shadow object to be opposite the highlight on the candy. Since you placed the highlight at the top right, you want the shadow at the lower left. By dragging the copy of the circle in the direction of the highlight, you should place the crescent in the correct position.

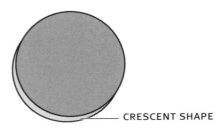

CRESCENT SHAPE

10) Select both circles and choose Modify > Combine > Punch. Fill the crescent shape with 80 percent black. Tuck the shadow under the candy.

Move the shadow so you don't see the pointed ends of the crescent shape. You may need to send the shadow back behind the candy.

The final touch for the candy is to add a label.

11) Type a letter for your label. A small *m* would be appropriate for this candy. Change the color to white and change the size so that the letter fits within your candy. Choose Text > Convert to Paths.

In the next step, you will convert your candy to a symbol. If you hadn't converted the text to a path, an error message indicating that the font could not be found might appear if you export this symbol for use on another computer.

12) Select all the objects in your candy and choose Modify > Group. Then choose Modify > Symbol > Copy to Symbol. On the Library panel, rename the symbol *blue candy*.

By using the Copy to Symbol command instead of pressing F8 (Convert to Symbol), you keep the original candy object intact. You will use that object to create several more symbols, each with a different color.

13) Save your file.

This might be a good time to take a chocolate break.

ON YOUR OWN

Remember that you blended two colored circles to create the main part of the candy and then you grouped all of the objects. To create a new color of candy, you need to change the color of the original two circles you created before you applied the blend. FreeHand will then create new colors for each step in the blend.

To change the color of the candy, first select the largest of the circles. If you created an eight-step blend, you will have eight circles. Use the Subselect tool, or (for an easier approach) hold down Alt (Windows) or Option (Mac OS) and click the outside edge of the circle; change the color of that circle. Select the Fill property on the Object panel, and you'll see a color chip with the color you just applied to the circle. Drag that color chip to the Tints panel. Now drag either the 80 or 90 percent color from the Tints panel to the middle of your candy. You should see a new candy color. Make as many different candy colors as you like. Convert each color to a new symbol. In the next task, you will use those candy symbols to create a graphic hose.

HOSING IT DOWN

The **Graphic Hose** is a tool you can use to spray objects on your page. With a garden hose, you spray water on your flowers. With the Graphic Hose tool, you can create flowers to spray on your page. The Graphic Hose tool allows you to place multiple copies of a graphic element on a page, randomly changing the size, rotation, or spacing between each object. Whereas brush objects are attached to paths, the Graphic Hose tool places individual elements on the page. Unlike with a brush, you do not need to use symbols when you create a graphic hose—symbols just make your task easier if you want to make changes. In addition, when you add symbols to a graphic hose and spray the page, you are placing instances instead of copies of the graphics, keeping the file size smaller.

1) Drag one instance of each candy symbol to the page.

Since all of your objects are now symbols, you first need to drag a copy of each one to the page.

To add an object to a graphic hose, you copy it and then paste it in the hose. To add multiple objects to the hose, as you will do here, you will select the instances one by one and paste them in the hose.

2) Select the first candy symbol and choose Edit > Copy. Double-click the Graphic Hose tool and choose Hose. From the Hose pop-up menu, choose New and for the hose name, type *candy*. Click Save.

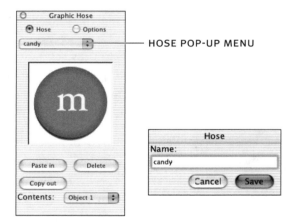

3) Click Paste In.

The first copy of your candy is added to the hose as Object 1.

You can add up to 10 objects in each graphic hose. Switch to the Pointer tool when adding multiple objects to the hose so you can select the other items to add to the hose instead of spraying with the hose.

4) Copy the next candy object and repeat step 3. Continue until you have added all of your colors of candy to the hose. To see a preview of an object in your hose, choose that object from the Contents pop-up menu.

Now you are ready to see the options for the hose.

5) Click Options. From the Order pop-up menu, choose Random. From the Spacing pop-up menu, also choose Random and drag the spacing slider to 74. From the Scaling pop-up menu, choose Random again and drag the scaling slider to 104. From the Rotate pop-up menu, choose Random and type *12* as the rotate angle.

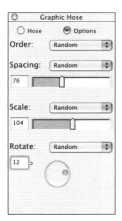

You can leave the Hose option window open as you try out your hose.

6) Drag the hose pointer around the page.

As you drag, your candy images are sprayed on the page. Experiment with the hose settings to see what effect each option has on the sprayed images.

ON YOUR OWN

Because you created your hose from symbols, you can change a symbol and update all instances of that symbol on the page. For example, edit one of your candy symbols and add a gaussian blur effect to the highlight object.

EXPORTING YOUR SYMBOLS

The brushes and symbols you create in a document appear only in that document. If you want to use your brushes or symbols in another document, you need to export them and then import them into the other document.

NOTE *If your symbols or brushes contain fonts or linked images, you need to send those elements along with the exported FreeHand file if you share your symbols with someone else or transfer them to another computer. Those elements are linked and are not included when you export.*

1) Select one of your candy symbols from the Library panel.

It doesn't matter which one you select; the Export option will display all of the symbols in your document.

2) From the Library panel Options menu, choose Export.

The Export Symbols dialog box displays all of the symbols currently stored in your document.

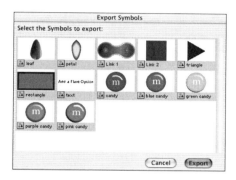

3) Select the candy symbols from the list and then click Export. In the Export Symbols (Windows) or Save (Mac OS) dialog box, type *mysymbols.fh11* and then click Save.

TIP *Ctrl-click (Windows) or Command-click to select multiple symbols in the list.*

You will use your candy symbols in another document in a later lesson and import them into that document as you did earlier in this lesson.

NOTE *If you make a change to an imported brush or symbol, that change is applied only in the current document. If you want to make a change to imported symbols in several documents, you need to make the modifications in each document.*

WHAT YOU HAVE LEARNED

In this lesson, you have:

- Converted an object to a symbol (pages 240–246)
- Edited the symbol (pages 247–248)
- Used the Roughen tool to distort the edges of an object (pages 249–251)
- Used blends to create realistic shading on an object (pages 252–256)
- Added a contour gradient to complete your flower design (pages 256–258)
- Imported a brush (pages 259–263)
- Created and edited a brush (pages 264–269)
- Created a symbol and used it in a graphic hose (pages 269–276)
- Exported a symbol for use in another document (pages 276–277)

creating animations and movies

Macromedia Flash movies are the hot ticket on the web. Flash movies look great when viewed on the screen, and they are generally small files that can be accessed even by those with dial-up access to the web. Many Flash designers have pushed the envelope of creativity to create projects that are interesting and fun to see and use. Flash uses vector graphics to create animations, but the drawing tools in Flash are not as sophisticated as those in FreeHand.

In this lesson, you will use FreeHand to create an aperture for a camera lens that would be almost impossible to draw in Flash. Then you will animate the opening and closing of the aperture. You'll use the multiple-page function in FreeHand to create a slide show presentation and add some simple scripting to buttons so that they take you to the pages in the slide show.

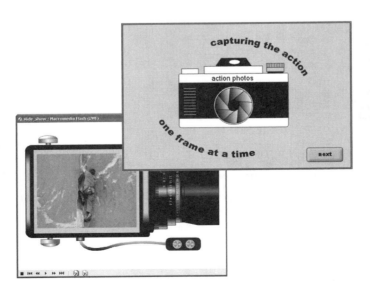

In this lesson, you will create an animation using the tools in FreeHand. Then you will create an interactive slide show to display your animation using the Flash player.

WHAT YOU WILL LEARN

In this lesson, you will:

- Assign a keyboard shortcut
- Create a drawing that you will animate
- Create a blend for an animation
- Release a blend to layers
- Export your file as a SWF movie
- Join a blend to a path
- Animate text
- Create a master page
- Use the Action tool
- Use the Navigation panel
- Edit a master page
- Add a path guide
- Use Macromedia Fireworks to optimize graphics
- Link to a Macromedia Flash movie from FreeHand and edit the movie in Flash
- Use Macromedia Flash to create a movie

APPROXIMATE TIME

This lesson takes approximately
3 hours to complete.

LESSON FILES

Media Files:

Lesson09\Media\climber.psd
Lesson09\Media\downhill2.psd
Lesson09\Media\downhill8.psd
Lesson09\Media\freeride1.psd
Lesson09\Media\medium_camera.fh11
Lesson09\Media\pic1.fla
Lesson09\Media\pic1.swf
Lesson09\Media\JPEGS

Starting Files:

Lesson09\Start\action.fh11

Completed Projects:

Lesson09\Completed\aperture.fh11
Lesson09\Completed\aperture.swf
Lesson09\Completed\aperture_opening.swf
Lesson09\Completed\slide_show.fh11
Lesson09\Completed\blend_animation.fh11
Lesson09\Completed\pic1.fla
Lesson09\Completed\pic1.swf
Lesson09\Completed\pic2.fla
Lesson09\Completed\pic2.swf
Lesson09\Completed\pic3.fla
Lesson09\Completed\pic3.swf
Lesson09\Completed\pic4.fla
Lesson09\Completed\pic4.swf

ASSIGNING KEYBOARD SHORTCUTS

Do you use keyboard shortcuts? Most people know the shortcuts common across applications. For example, many people use Ctrl+O (Windows) or Command+O (Mac OS) to open files, Ctrl+S or Command+S to save files, and Ctrl+P or Command+P to print files. One way to increase your productivity is to learn and use keyboard shortcuts. However, if you use applications from several vendors in creating your documents, you may be frustrated when applications use different commands for similar tasks. A good example of a tool used in other applications is the Hand tool, sometimes called the grabber hand. The Hand tool allows you to scroll through your document without using the scrollbars. In FreeHand, the spacebar is the shortcut for accessing the Hand tool when you are drawing on the page. If you are entering or editing text, the spacebar shortcut is disabled. Try using this shortcut as you complete the remaining projects in this book.

A useful feature in all Macromedia MX applications is the ability to redefine the keyboard shortcuts. You can change an existing shortcut, or if a shortcut is not assigned to a command, you can assign one. If you use several applications in your workflow, you may want to assign the same shortcut key to similar commands in all of the applications. For example, grouping and ungrouping is a common task in many graphics and page layout applications. If you are accustomed to using Ctrl+U (Windows) or Command+U (Mac OS) to ungroup objects, for example, you may want to change FreeHand to use that same shortcut key. FreeHand contains several shortcut command sets from other applications. You can use an existing set as a starting point and then modify it to suit your preferences. The standard Macromedia set contains shortcuts that are common across Macromedia products such as Flash and Fireworks.

In this task, you will assign a shortcut key to the Close Path option that appears on the Object panel when you select a path. Adding this shortcut now will make steps in the following task easier. You can change your keyboard shortcuts even if no file is open.

1) Choose Edit > Keyboard Shortcuts. Verify that Macromedia Standard is selected in the Keyboard Shortcuts Setting pop-up menu.

You'll add your shortcut for the Close Path option to the Macromedia standard shortcut set. (No, there is no assigned keyboard shortcut for the Keyboard Shortcuts command, although you could assign one.)

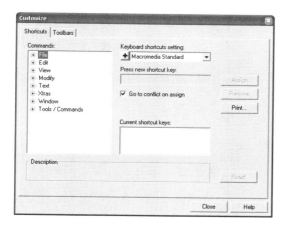

2) Click the plus sign (Windows) or the triangle (Mac OS) to the left of Tools/Commands to see the items within this section.

A list of tools and commands appears.

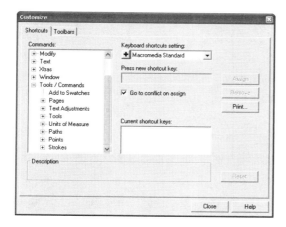

3) In the Tools/Commands list, click the plus sign (Windows) or the triangle (Mac OS) to the left of Paths.

You should see Close Path and Open Path listed.

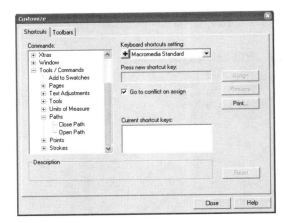

4) Select Close Path. Press Tab, hold down Ctrl+Alt+Shift+C (Windows) or Command+Option+Shift+C (Mac OS), and click Assign.

The keyboard combination is just a suggestion; you can use any combination you like. If a shortcut key or key combination is already assigned, the command with the conflict will be listed in the Customize dialog box.

NOTE *If you are going to make numerous changes to the keyboard shortcuts, you can make a new set instead of modifying an existing set. Click the plus button, enter a new name for your shortcut set, and then click Save.*

5) Close the Customize dialog box.

NOTE *FreeHand stores keyboard sets in the Macromedia/FreeHand MX/11/ English/Settings/Keyboard folder located in the user-specific Application Data (Windows) or Application Support (Mac OS) folder.*

If you want to remove a shortcut, select it in the Customize dialog box and then click Remove. If you want to print your shortcuts, click Print.

DRAWING THE APERTURE

In this task, you will draw an aperture for the camera logo you created in Lesson 1. The aperture is the part on a camera lens that opens and closes to control the amount of light hitting the film or the sensor on a digital camera. By varying the diameter of the aperture, you control the intensity of light passing through the lens into the camera to expose the film.

After you draw the aperture, you will learn a technique to animate the opening and closing of the aperture. You'll do all of the animation in FreeHand.

NOTE *Thanks to Ian Kelleigh for the idea for this project. Check out his web site at www.freehandsource.com for more FreeHand tips.*

1) Create a new file and name it *aperture.fh11*. Save the file in your Projects folder. Change the units of measure for the document to Pixels.

When you complete your drawing, you will export the file as a Flash movie and import it into another FreeHand file.

2) Choose Window > Document or click the Document tab in the Properties panel group. Click Landscape page orientation. From the Page Size pop-up menu, choose Custom and then type *400* as the X value and *300* as the Y value. Press Enter (Windows) or Return (Macintosh) to apply your settings.

You want the page size about the size of the finished drawing.

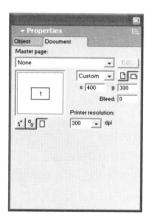

TIP *If the page size appears too small, you can quickly resize the page by pressing Ctrl+0 (Windows) or Command+0 to change the view to Fit Page.*

3) Draw a circle about 250 pixels in diameter. On the Transform panel, click the Scale button and type *20* in the Scale percent text box. Deselect the Strokes option, type *1* in the Copies text box, and click Scale.

A new circle 20 percent the size of the original circle appears on the page.

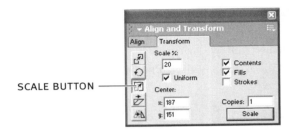

SCALE BUTTON

4) Select both circles and choose Modify > Ungroup. Then choose Xtras > Distort > Add Points.

The Add Points command adds a new point between each existing point on your circles without changing the shape of the circles. Your circles now each have 8 points.

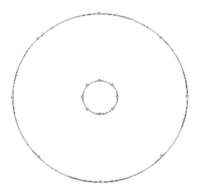

5) With the Pointer tool, drag around both circles to select all of the points on each circle. Choose Modify > Split. Press Tab to deselect both circles.

You now have eight arcs on each circle. In the next step, you will create new shapes from the arcs.

6) Select one arc on the larger circle. Shift-click the corresponding arc on the smaller circle. Choose Modify > Join.

The shortcut for the Join command is Ctrl+J (Windows) or Command+J (Mac OS). You'll be joining all of the arcs on the larger circle to their corresponding arcs on the smaller circle. Using the join shortcut will make this task much easier.

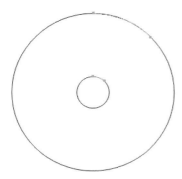

7) Use the keyboard shortcut you assigned to the Close Path command at the beginning of this lesson.

You could also click Close Path on the Object panel, but the shortcut is faster. Your path creates a shape that resembles a slice of pie.

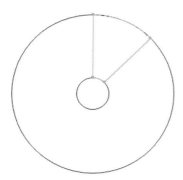

8) Repeat steps 6 and 7 for all of the remaining arcs.

Remember to close the last arc shape. Because closed paths surround it, you may not notice that it is not complete. You can check the Object panel to see whether the path is closed.

TIP *An easy way to verify that all of your arc shapes are closed paths is to drag a marquee around both circles with the Pointer tool. The Object panel should indicate that eight objects are selected.*

9) Using the Pointer tool, drag a marquee around the inner circle.

You want to select only the points on the inner circle. The selected points on the inner circle should be hollow.

10) On the Transform panel, click the Rotate button and type *50* in the Rotation Angle text box. Click Rotate.

The inner points rotate, distorting the pie shapes.

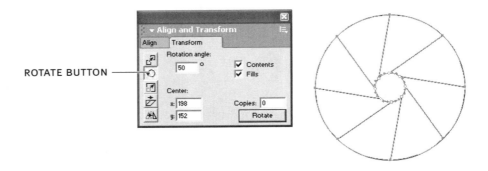

ROTATE BUTTON

11) Select all of the objects on the page and add a gradient fill. Group all of the objects.

You can use the default gradient fill from black to white for your aperture.

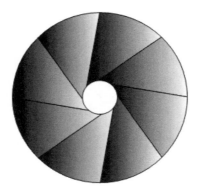

NOTE *If any of your objects fail to display the fill, you probably forgot to close that object. Select that object and use your keyboard shortcut or click Closed on the Object panel.*

CREATING A BLEND FOR ANIMATION

Your drawing should now look like the aperture of the camera. If you were creating a static image, your drawing would be complete. However, you want to animate the aperture, and you want to use this image as the starting image in the animation. You want the aperture to open, so you need to make another version of this image with a larger opening. Then you will use the Blend command to create the intermediate steps of the animation. You used the Blend command in Lesson 8, "Symbols, Brushes, and Hoses," to create subtle shading for objects. In this lesson, you will use the Blend command to morph a complex group (the aperture) into another group. Each step in the blend will increase the opening of the aperture.

1) Clone your grouped object and then create a new layer. On the Layers panel, select the new layer.

Your cloned object moves to the new layer. Normally, you would name your layer, but in this task, the layer is only temporary. By placing your clone on a layer, you retain the position of the object, but isolate it from the original object.

2) Click the checkmark next to the Foreground layer to hide that layer. Click the keyline icon on the new layer.

You need to select the points on the inner circle of the copy. In step 9 of the previous task, you used the Pointer tool and selected the inner points by dragging. Now your shape is filled and grouped, so that method won't work. If you drag within a filled object, instead of selecting the points on the object, you move the object.

Switching to Keyline mode on the layer displays only the outlines of the objects so you can use the drag selection method, as you will do in the next step.

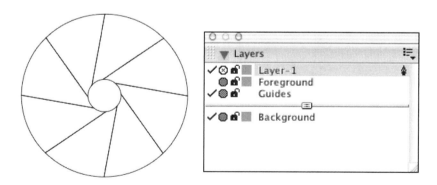

3) Make sure the new object is selected, hold down Alt (Windows) or Option (Mac OS) and drag around the points on the inner circle. In the Scale section of the Transform panel, type *180* in the Scale percentage text box. Deselect Fills and Strokes. Type *0* in the Copies text box and then click Scale.

You hold down Alt or Option to select points within a grouped item. You could also use the Subselect tool. The inner points move, making the inner circle larger.

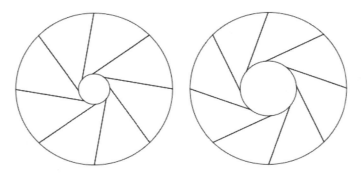

BEFORE AND AFTER SCALING INNER POINTS

NOTE *You may need to adjust the scale factor for your circle. You don't want any overlapping lines on your new inner circle. To check your object, zoom in on the page. You can always choose Edit > Undo and try a new number for the scale factor.*

4) Choose Merge Foreground Layers from the Layers panel Options menu.

Both objects are placed on the Foreground layer and the new layer is deleted.

5) Choose Xtras > Create > Blend.

FreeHand creates a blend with 25 steps. That number should work fine for this project.

6) Check your blend.

Look at the geometric shapes formed by the blend. You should still be in Keyline mode. If not, switch back so you can see the shapes within the blend. If your blend has a consistent geometric pattern, your blend is fine. If you see some inconsistency in the outlines, you can generally fix the problem by undoing the blend, selecting both shapes, and rotating the shapes 10 degrees. Then repeat the Blend command.

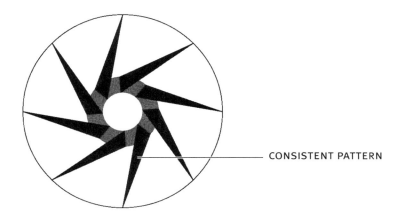

CONSISTENT PATTERN

7) Clone your blend. Add a new layer, name the layer *Reverse*, and then move the clone to the new layer.

You'll use that copy to reverse the animation of the aperture so that the aperture appears to be closing.

8) Save your file.

RELEASING TO LAYERS

FreeHand uses a frame-by-frame technique to create animations. You may be familiar with flip books, where each page of the book contains a slightly altered version of the image on the previous page. As you flip through the pages, the images seem to move. FreeHand can animate from one page to the next or from one layer to the next, creating motion in a manner similar to a flip book.

In this task, you will create your animation from layers. At this point, your blend is on one layer. To create the animation, you will use the Release to Layers command. Release to Layers places each step in your blend on a new, separate layer.

1) Select the blend on the Foreground layer and choose Xtras > Animate > Release to Layers.

The Release to Layers dialog box opens for you to set your options.

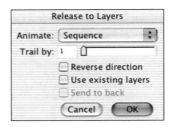

> **TIP** *The quick way to select objects on a layer is to hold Alt (Windows) or Option (Mac OS) and click the layer name on the Layers panel.*

> **NOTE** *Release to Layers works only on blends, groups, text blocks, text attached to a path, or blends attached to a path.*

2) From the Animate pop-up menu, choose Sequence and deselect Use Existing Layers. Click OK.

You want to add new layers and not use the Reverse layer you created. You should now have 27 layers (not counting the Guides, the Background layer, and your Reverse layer), each with a different step of the blend.

> **NOTE** *Your blend contained 25 steps plus the original 2 objects you used to create the blend, resulting in 27 total objects.*

FreeHand gives you four options for controlling the way objects are released to layers:

- **Sequence** releases objects in sequence to separate layers.

- **Build** creates a stacking effect as it creates the layers. For example, if you have a group of objects, the first object is placed on the first layer. The second layer contains a copy of the object on the first layer, plus the next object; the third layer contains a copy of all of the preceding objects, plus the next object; and so on.

- **Drop** copies objects to all layers, but drops one object in sequence from each layer. The object dropped is the object with the same number as the layer. For example, if a group contains three objects, objects 2 and 3 are placed on layer 1, objects 1 and 3 are placed on layer 2, and objects 1 and 2 are placed on layer 3.

- **Trail** copies and releases objects to the number of layers you specify. After you select Trail, you enter the number of layers on which objects will be copied in the Trail By text box. For example, if you enter 2 in the Trail By text box, and you have four objects, layer 1 contains object 1, layer 2 contains objects 1 and 2, layer 3 contains objects 1, 2, and 3, but layer 4 contains only objects 2, 3, and 4, dropping object 1. Since Trail = 2, you can have only three objects on a layer at a time: the current object and the previous two.

You can also select **Reverse Direction** to make an animation appear in reverse order.

The next step is to test your animation, which you can do in FreeHand.

3) Choose Window > Movie > Settings. In the Export Options section, for the Layers setting, select Animate, for the Movie Properties setting, select Autoplay; click OK.
You've moved each frame onto a different layer, and you want to animate the layers. If Animate is not selected, your movie will not play. Later, when you export your movie, you will examine the other movie settings.

4) Choose Window > Movie > Test.

Note that the shortcuts to test the movie are Ctrl+Enter (Windows) or Command+ Return (Macintosh). These are the same shortcuts as for testing a movie in Flash.

A Macromedia Flash SWF document window appears, showing the first object in your animation. Movie controls appear at the bottom left of the SWF document window; you can also control the movie by choosing Window > Movie and selecting commands.

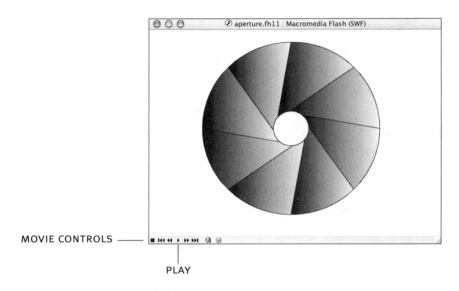

MOVIE CONTROLS

PLAY

NOTE *SWF is the format used by Flash when exporting files for playback in a browser.*

5) Click Play in the movie controls.

The aperture should look as though it is opening.

NOTE *You can play the movie aperture_opening.swf in the Completed folder within the Lesson09 folder to see an example of the aperture opening.*

6) Click the Close box on the Macromedia Flash SWF playback window and save your file.

You've completed the first part of the animation. The next task is to reverse the order of the animation so the aperture appears to close.

REVERSING THE ANIMATION

To reverse the animation, you will use the copy of the blend you placed on the Reverse layer. You will repeat the Release to Layers command, but this time selecting the option to reverse the direction of the animation.

1) Hold down Alt (Windows) or Option (Mac OS) and click the Reverse layer.

The blend on the layer is selected. You can check the Object panel to verify that only one object (the blend) is selected.

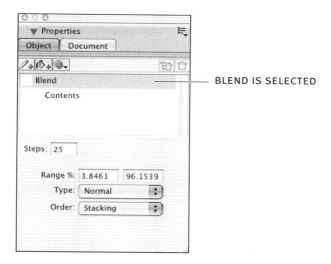

BLEND IS SELECTED

2) Choose Xtras > Animate > Release to Layers. Choose Sequence from the Animate pop-up menu, select Reverse Direction, and deselect Use Existing Layers. Click OK.

You should now have 54 animation layers.

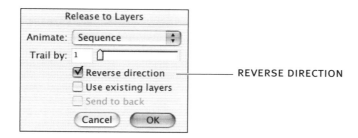

REVERSE DIRECTION

293

3) Press Ctrl+Enter (Windows) or Command+Return (Macintosh) to test your movie.

The aperture should appear to open and then to close.

When you are satisfied with your movie, you can export it and save it as a SWF file. You'll do that next. Leave the playback window open for the next task.

EXPORTING YOUR MOVIE

When you test your movie, FreeHand creates a temporary SWF file and plays it back in a Flash SWF playback window. The temporary file is deleted when you close the window. You can export the SWF file directly from the Flash SWF playback window, or you can choose File > Export in the FreeHand document window. Once you export your movie, you can place it on a web page, or you can import it into the Flash library as a movie.

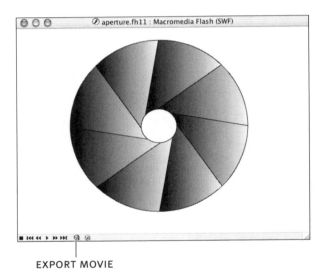

EXPORT MOVIE

1) Click Export Movie in the movie controls.

If you closed the playback window, you can choose File > Export. Either way, the same Export dialog box appears.

2) Choose Macromedia Flash (SWF) from the Save as Type (Windows) or Format (Mac OS) pop-up menu. Click Setup and then click OK.

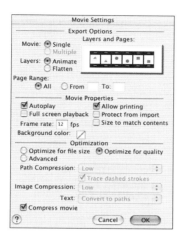

The Movie Settings dialog box opens. You used the Movie Settings dialog box earlier to set layers to animate. Before you export your SWF file, check all of the settings to verify that they are set properly.

Check the **Movie** settings:

• **Single** translates all of the pages to a single movie.

• **Multiple** translates each page to a separate movie.

Check the **Layers** settings:

• **Animate** translates each layer (per page) to a separate movie frame.

• **Flatten** translates all of the layers on a page to a single movie frame.

Page Range allows you to specify what pages you want to include in your movie.

Autoplay starts the movie automatically when the movie loads. If this option is not selected, the user must interact with the movie to start it.

Full Screen Playback plays the movie in full-screen mode in the player until you press the Escape key.

Allow Printing lets you print each frame of the movie from Macromedia Flash Player or the Flash Player plug-in.

Frame Rate controls the playback speed in frames per second (fps). You can enter frame rates from 0.01 fps to 120 fps. Use 12 fps for the smoothest animations.

295

Protect from Import locks the movie so that it can't be imported into another document.

Size to Match Contents sets the movie stage size based on the contents. If this option is not selected, the movie stage size is set to the first page size of the FreeHand document.

Optimize for File Size sets optimization automatically.

Optimize for Quality creates high-quality movie files.

Compress Movie reduces the file size of the exported movie.

Click **Advanced** if you want to manually control the optimization settings:

- **Path Compression** controls how precisely FreeHand paths are converted to Flash paths. None specifies no compression, the greatest number of points, and the highest quality; Maximum specifies the most compression, the fewest points, and the lowest quality.

- **Trace Dashed Strokes** converts dashed lines to multiple objects. Each dash segment is converted to a separate object, increasing export time and file size. If this option is not selected, dash strokes export as solid lines.

- **Image Compression** controls image quality and compression when converting bitmap images to JPEG format. None specifies the least compression and the highest quality; Maximum specifies the most compression and the lowest quality.

Select a **Text** option to control the export of text:

- **Maintain Blocks** keeps all of the text together in a FreeHand text block for editing in Flash 3 or later.

- **Convert to Paths** converts text to vector paths, so the text is no longer editable as text. Text attached to a path or text flowing inside a path is automatically converted to paths and therefore is not editable in Flash. (This option yields a smaller file size than Maintain Blocks.)

- **None** omits all text from the exported file.

3) Navigate to your Projects folder and click Save (Windows) or Export (Mac OS).

FreeHand adds the .swf extension to the end of your file name. If you are using a Macintosh and the name of your file is aperture.fh11, your exported SWF file is named aperature.fh11.swf.

4) Save your file.

JOINING A BLEND TO A PATH

To create animations in FreeHand as you've learned, you create a blend and then release the blend to layers. You can also group objects and then release the objects to layers to create an animation. For example, you could draw several objects in the order you want them to animate, group them, and then release them to layers. If you want objects in a blend to follow a path as they animate, you can join the blend to a path. In this task, you will draw a path and then create a blend that follows the path as it animates.

1) Create a new file and save it as *blend_animation.fh11* in your Projects folder. Change the document page size to Web.

The end result of this page is a SWF animation, so you want the page size to fit the final size of the animation.

2) Draw a rectangle 450 pixels wide and 300 pixels tall. On the Object panel, type *25* for the corner radius of the rectangle. Press Enter (Windows) or Return (Mac OS) to apply your settings.

The rounded rectangle is the path for your animation.

3) On the Align panel, select Align to Page and then double-click the center of the preview pane.

Your rectangle is centered on the page.

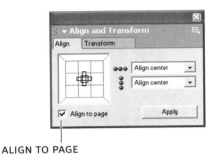

ALIGN TO PAGE

4) Draw a small circle and fill it with a bright color, such as red or blue. Place the circle at the top left of the page. Use the Alt-drag or Option-drag method to make a copy of your circle and move the copy to the top right of the page.

The placement of the circles is not important; you just want to space the circles apart. In the next step, you will create a blend from one circle to the other.

5) Select both circles and choose Modify > Combine > Blend.

This command is another way to create a blend. You could also choose Xtras > Create > Blend as you did previously. The resulting blend is the same. FreeHand creates 25 steps for the blend. Leave that number of steps set for now.

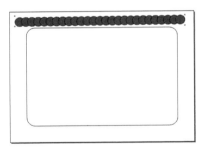

NOTE *Don't be concerned if you get fewer than 25 steps in your blend. If objects are close together, FreeHand creates fewer steps for the blend.*

6) Select both the blend and the rectangle. Choose Modify > Combine > Join Blend to Path.

The circles follow the path of the rectangle.

N O T E *You can modify the number of steps in the blend on the Object panel even though the blend is joined to the path.*

7) Choose Xtras > Animate > Release to Layers. Select Build from the Animate pop-up menu, deselect Reverse Direction, and click OK.

The Build option places each circle in the blend on a new layer. In addition, all of the circles from the previous layers are added to the new layer. For example, the first layer contains the first circle in the blend. Layer 2 contains the second circle and the first circle. Layer 3 contains the third circle plus the first and second circles, and so on.

If you had selected Sequence from the Animate pop-up menu, each circle in the blend would be placed on a separate layer.

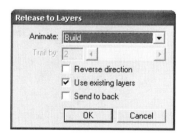

8) Press Ctrl+Enter (Windows) or Command+Return (Macintosh) to test your movie. Click Play in the movie controls to play the animation.

N O T E *The movie settings should be set correctly from the last task. If your animation doesn't work, close the movie window and check the settings by choosing Window > Movie > Settings. Make sure that layers are set to animate. Then test your animation again.*

The first circle of the blend appears on the page before you begin the animation. If you want the screen blank before the animation begins, you need to add a layer containing an empty object. You will add a new empty layer in the next step.

9) Close the animation window and press Tab to deselect any objects. Choose New (Windows) or New Layer (Mac OS) from the Layers panel Options menu. Drag the new layer below the Foreground layer.

The layer is added at the top of the layers list. You want this layer to be the first layer of the animation so it needs to be below the Foreground layer. The Foreground layer contains the first circle of the animation.

NEW LAYER MOVED

10) On the new layer, draw a circle, with no stroke or fill.

You need to put an invisible object on the layer. You can't just leave a layer blank.

11) Test your animation.

The animation window should be blank until you click the Play control.

ANIMATING TEXT

You can animate text so it appears one letter at a time. The process for animating text is similar to the process you just completed to animate the circles. You first need to convert your text to paths. In this task, you will add some text to a new layer, convert the text to paths, and then release the text to layers. In the resulting animation, the circle will move around the path of the rectangle and then the text will appear one letter at a time.

1) Create a new layer.

The text you add to this new layer will appear at the end of the current animation.

2) Type *ACTION PHOTOS* and place this text in the middle of the page. Format the text in a big, bold font.

The new layer you added should still be selected. When you add this text, it will be on the new layer.

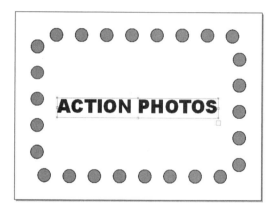

3) Choose Text > Convert to Paths.

The text is converted to a graphic element.

4) Choose Xtras > Animate > Release to Layers. From the Animate pop-up menu, select Build and click OK. Test your movie.

The circles move around the rectangle. When the circles have completed their circuit, the text appears one letter at a time. Because you added only the text on the new layer, after the circles, the circles surrounding the area do not appear when the text animates.

5) Save your file.

CREATING MASTER PAGES

The ability to create multiple pages in FreeHand gives you tremendous flexibility in the documents you create. You've seen that you can create an entire corporate identity in just one document. When you want to create several pages in a document containing a similar layout, you can define a master page for those pages. A **master page** contains text or graphics elements that you want to appear on several pages. For example, if you want your logo to have the same size and placement on several pages in your document, you can place it on a master page. Then when you create new pages, the logo will appear automatically; you don't need to import it or position it on each new page of your document. Also, if you later decide to change the color or the look of the logo, you just need to change the master page. All pages using that master page will automatically be updated with the new logo.

In the remainder of this lesson, you are going to be creating a slide show presentation, and you will create a master page for use with the slide show. In a subsequent task, you will create interactive buttons to move to the next page in the slide show, and you will place these on the master page as well.

1) Create a new file and save it as *slide_show.fh11* in your Projects folder. Change the document page size to Custom and type *600* pixels as the width and *400* pixels as the height. Change the page orientation to Landscape.

In the next steps, you will draw several objects that you want to appear on every page in your presentation. Then you will convert the elements on the page to a master page for your document.

2) Draw a rectangle the same size as the page. Use the Object panel to verify the size and placement of the rectangle. Fill the rectangle with a dark gray color and no stroke.

The Object panel should show zero for both X and Y, 600 for the width, 400 for the height. This rectangle forms the outside border of the background for the presentation.

You can type the needed values for your rectangle in the text boxes on the Object panel. This is faster than trying to manually position the rectangle.

3) Clone your rectangle. Choose Xtras > Path Operations > Inset Path. Type *12* in the Inset text box, and then click OK.

Inset Path either expands or contracts the selected path. If you entered a negative number in the Inset text box, the resulting rectangle would be larger than the original rectangle.

4) Fill the smaller rectangle with a light gray color.

This rectangle is the main content area of the presentation. Any objects on the page will be placed within this rectangle.

*You may have noticed the color boxes on the Tools panel. Click the fill color box to open a palette of **web-ready** colors (called color cubes). You can use the colors from this palette to pick the colors for this task. Web-ready colors consist of 216 colors that appear predictably on both Windows and Macintosh computers. You can also switch this palette to display colors from your Swatches panel. Use the right triangle on the palette to switch from color cubes to the Swatches panel colors.*

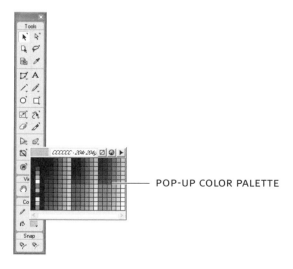

POP-UP COLOR PALETTE

5) Add a stroke to the smaller rectangle. Change the size of the stroke to 4 points and change the color to black. Add a new stroke to the same rectangle, make it 1 point, and change the color to white.

Notice that you're adding multiple attributes to the object. In this example, the white stroke is smaller and centered within the first black stroke, creating the appearance of a double line. You can add several different strokes to the same object. The order in which properties appear on the Object panel controls the final look on the object.

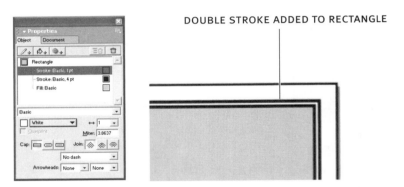

DOUBLE STROKE ADDED TO RECTANGLE

For example, drag the black stroke property below the fill property on the Object panel. Now, instead of two black lines, you get a black line on the outside and a white line on the inside.

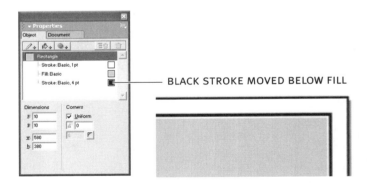

BLACK STROKE MOVED BELOW FILL

You can use either look for your rectangle. If you want the double lines, drag the black stroke property back to its position above the fill.

NOTE *If you add an effect to an object, you can change the look of the object by changing the position of the effect on the Object panel.*

The two rectangles on the page represent the objects that you want to appear on each page of your presentation. In the next step, you will convert these elements to a master page.

6) On the Properties panel, click the Document tab and from the Document panel Options menu, choose Convert to Master Page.

A master page, named Master Page–01, is created; the two rectangles are removed from page 1 and placed on the master page.

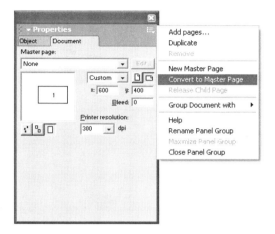

7) From the Document panel Options menu, choose Add Pages. Add one page, select Make Child of Master Page, and click OK.

If you have several master pages defined, you choose the master page you want to use from the Master Page pop-up menu. At this point, you have only one master page, and it is already selected in the pop-up menu.

Your new page (page 2) contains the two rectangles from the master page. You can add more pages that use the master page, or you can choose to add blank new pages.

NOTE *Remember that you can use the Page tool to move this new page closer to or below the first page.*

8) Choose File > Import and locate the action.fh11 file you created in Lesson 6, "Adding Special Effects." Place the file on page 1 of your document.

The file should be located in your Projects folder. If you no longer have that file, you can use the one in the Start folder within the Lesson09 folder.

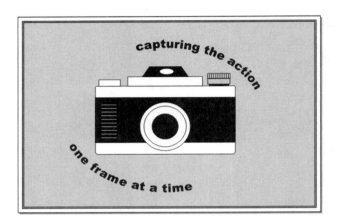

9) Import the aperture.swf file you created earlier in this lesson. Place it on the camera lens of the drawing you just imported. Scale the aperture.swf file to fit within the camera lens.

If you no longer have your aperture.swf file, you can use the one located in the Completed folder within the Lesson09 folder.

10) Save your file. Then test your movie.

At this point, you should see the aperture opening and closing. Soon, you will be placing objects on a second page. However, there is no way to get to that page in the slide show. In the next task, you will add a button so you can move to the next page.

USING THE ACTION TOOL

The **Action tool** allows you to assign a Flash action to an object so that the user can use the object to navigate to another page in your Flash movie. To use the tool, you drag from the navigation object to the page you want the object to jump to when the user clicks the object. FreeHand assigns a default action of Go to Page *X* and Stop. You can modify the action using the **Navigation panel**.

NOTE *The programming language in Flash is called ActionScript. A Flash action in FreeHand refers to the basic Flash scripting commands that you can add to your documents.*

In this task, you will add a button object to the first page and then use the Action tool to link the button to page 2 in your document.

1) Draw a small rectangle with rounded corners. Fill the rectangle with a color that complements the color of the background.

You can use the same color as the background or a contrasting color for the rectangle. In the next step, you will add a bevel to the rectangle to make your rectangle look like a button.

2) On the Object panel, from the Add Effect pop-up menu, choose Bevel and Emboss › Inner Bevel. From the Edge Shape pop-up menu, choose Smooth.

Your rectangle now has a smooth bevel. You can adjust other settings for your bevel.

- **Width**: Drag the width slider to change the width of the bevel.

- **Contrast**: Enter a value to define the brightness and darkness of the highlights and shadows in the bevel.

- **Softness**: Enter a value to change the smoothness of the bevel without affecting its width.

- **Angle**: Enter a value or use the pop-up dial to change the angle of the light source on the bevel.

In the next step, you will use the Action tool to add the Flash action to your button. Make sure that you can see both the button and part of page 2.

3) From the Tools panel, select the Action tool. Drag from the rectangle button to page 2.

When you release the mouse button, you'll see a blue line connecting the button to page 2. You'll also see a small arrow at the bottom right of your button, called the action proton.

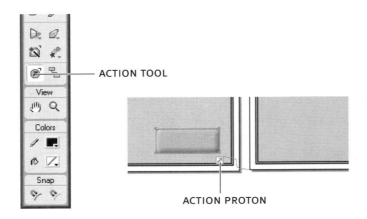

ACTION TOOL

ACTION PROTON

NOTE *To remove an action from a object, drag the object—in this case, the button—to the pasteboard with the Action tool.*

4) Double-click the action proton to open the Navigation panel.

You can use either the Action tool or the Pointer tool when you double-click the proton. You can also choose Window > Navigation to open the panel.

The Navigation panel displays the Go To and Stop action with the parameter of Page 2. The assigned event for the action is On (Press)—when the user presses the button, the movie will jump to page 2 of your document.

5) Use the Text tool to add some descriptive text to your button. For example, type *Next*. **Change the font, size, and color to fit your button. Group the text and the button.**

You can add text to your button after you add the action.

6) Save your file and then test your movie. Close the movie window after you test your button.

Click your button to check that clicking it moves you to the next page. Notice that the pointer changes to the hand pointer when you roll over the button.

Page 2 contains only the rectangles you created for the master page. Since you're going to be adding yet other pages to your presentation, you want the Next button to appear on this page as well. You could copy the button from the first page and paste it on this new page, but then you would need to do that for every page you add to your slide show. Instead, in the next task, you will add the button to the master page.

EDITING A MASTER PAGE

After you create a master page, you may want to make changes to it. You may have noticed that you can't select objects on the master page while you are working on a page in your document. This feature ensures that you don't accidentally move or delete objects on the master page while working on individual pages. To make changes to objects on a master page, you need to edit the master page.

1) Select the Next button and its text and choose Edit > Cut.

You are going to remove the button from the page and add it to the master page.

2) Click the Document tab in the Properties panel group. Click the Edit button.

The master page document window opens, ready for you to make changes.

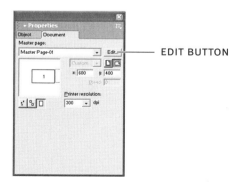

EDIT BUTTON

> **NOTE** *The pasteboard of the master page is gray, to help you remember that you are on a master page rather than a document page.*

3) Choose Edit > Paste.

Position the button where you want it to appear on the page. The position of the object is not retained when you cut or copy and then paste an object.

NOTE *Unfortunately, FreeHand does not have a "paste in place" feature. To be sure you paste an object in the same place as in its original location, you can note the object's X and Y coordinates on the Object panel before you cut or copy it and then enter those values when you paste the object on a new page.*

4) Press Tab to deselect all objects and then select the button. On the Navigation panel, from the Parameter pop-up menu, choose Next Scene.

The Action tool assigned Page 2 as the parameter, which was fine when the button was on page 1. Now that the button is on the master page, you need to reassign the action to jump to the next page in your document, regardless of the page number.

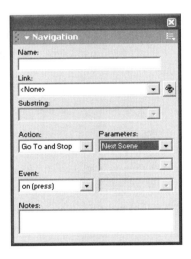

NOTE *The options in the Parameter pop-up menu for controlling the action of the button are Next Scene, Previous Scene, Next Frame, Previous Frame, and the actual page number.*

5) Close the master page edit window.

Your button now appears on both pages of your document.

POWER TIP *Master pages are stored in the Library panel. You can add, edit, rename, or remove a master page from the Library panel.*

ADDING A SECOND MASTER PAGE

You've seen how easily you can create and edit a master page. You can add as many master pages as you need in a document. Each time you add a new page, you then choose which master page you want the new page to use. You can also add pages that don't use any master page within that same document.

In this task, you will add another master page for your slide show.

1) Use the Page pop-up menu on the Status toolbar (Windows) or the document window (Mac OS) to go to page 2.

Page 2 currently uses the master page you created earlier. You want to add a new master page and apply it to this page instead. You start by removing the master page that controls page 2.

2) On the Document panel, from the Master Page pop-up menu, choose None.

Once you remove the master page, your page should be blank, but it should retain the size of the master page.

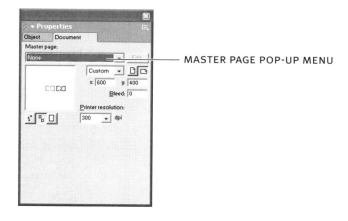 MASTER PAGE POP-UP MENU

3) Choose File > Import and locate the medium_camera.fh11 file in the Media folder within the Lesson09 folder. Place the file on the page.

The camera graphic has a gray rectangle that you will use to place some pictures. The camera was created for you to save some time, but you may want to draw it yourself.

KNOBS ON CABLE RELEASE

NOTE *Although it may look complex, the camera is simply a series of rectangles filled with solid colors or gradients.*

4) From the Document panel Options menu, choose Convert to Master Page.

Although nothing visually changes on your page, the camera graphic is now on the new master page, named Master Page-02.

In the next step, you will add actions to the master page to go to the next and previous pages.

5) On the Document panel, click the Edit button to edit the second master page. Select the camera and ungroup it.

The camera was grouped to make importing it easier for you. You want to use the knobs on the cable release as Next and Previous buttons so you need the objects ungrouped.

6) Select the left knob on the cable release attached to the camera and from the Action pop-up menu on the Navigation panel, choose Go To and Stop. From the Event pop-up menu, choose On (Press) and from the Parameter pop-up menu, choose Previous Scene.

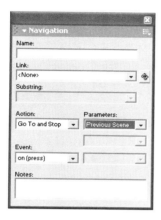

7) Repeat step 6 for the right knob, but choose Next Scene as its parameter.

8) Close the master page edit window, save your file, and test your movie.

The Next button on page 1 takes you to page 2. When you are on page 2, the Previous button on the cable release takes you back to page 1.

ADDING A PATH GUIDE TO THE MASTER PAGE

In the next task, you will add some graphics to new pages you create from a master page. All the graphics are the same dimension and you want to place each graphic in the same position on each page. You could place the first graphic, jot down the X and Y position of the graphic, and use the Object panel to position each imported graphic. Instead, you will add a guide to the master page, and use the guide to position each graphic. When you used guides before, you used ruler guides. You pulled the guides from the Page Ruler or used the Edit Guide command to add horizontal or vertical guides. In this task, you will draw an object, and then turn that object into a path guide.

1) On the Document panel, click the Edit button to edit the second master page. Draw a rectangle 287 pixels wide by 219 pixels high and place it within the gray rectangle on the camera.

The graphics you will add are this size, and you want the rectangle the same size. Your rectangle should have a stroke, but no fill.

RECTANGLE

2) Select both the gray rectangle and the rectangle you just created and align them to their centers.

Hint: remember you can use the Align panel and double-click the center panel to quickly align objects to their centers.

3) Press Tab to deselect everything, and then select the rectangle you just added.

In the next step, you will convert the new rectangle to a path guide.

4) On the Layers panel, click Guides and then move the Guides layer above the Foreground layer.

Your rectangle is converted to a path guide. You should see the outline color of the rectangle change to the guides color.

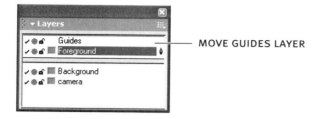 MOVE GUIDES LAYER

5) Close the master page edit window.

Your path guide appears on the page. Any new page you add that uses that master page also displays the path guide. If you want to remove the guide, drag it off the master page.

In the next task, you will use the path guide to position graphics as you import them into new pages.

USING MACROMEDIA FIREWORKS TO EDIT GRAPHICS

You want to import some pictures for your slide show. As you've seen, FreeHand can import many file formats. The format of the imported graphics you use depends on the final destination of your document. For example, in Lesson 7, "Page Layout and Printing," you imported a TIFF file. In this lesson, you are creating a slide show that will be exported as a Flash movie (a SWF file). For this purpose, you should use JPEG images optimized for the web. FreeHand is not designed to edit images, but **Macromedia Fireworks** is perfect for this task. The FreeHand application provides a quick link to Fireworks.

If you purchased FreeHand as part of the Studio MX package, you also have Fireworks. If you don't have Fireworks, you can use the images provided for you that have already been optimized and skip the optimization step, or you can use the trial version of the software included on the CD.

1) Choose File > Import and locate the climber.psd file in the Media folder within the Lesson09 folder. Place the image within the path guide on page 2.
This file is in Photoshop native (PSD) format. You will use Fireworks to optimize it in the next step.

NOTE *If you don't have Fireworks on your machine, use the climber.jpg file located in the JPEGS folder instead of climber.psd and skip this section.*

2) On the Object panel, click the Link to Fireworks button.

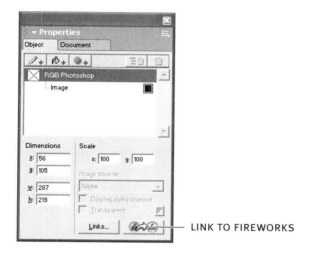

LINK TO FIREWORKS

FreeHand opens Fireworks on your machine and presents you with a dialog box asking if there is a source image for your file.

3) Click No.

The PSD file is the original source file. If you had imported the JPEG file instead of the PSD file, you could click Yes and then locate the original PSD file to optimize it.

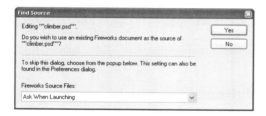

The Fireworks editing window opens.

4) Click the 2-Up tab.

The left pane displays your original image; the right pane displays the optimized image. Note the file size at the bottom of each pane. Fireworks picked a default GIF setting for your image, which you want to change.

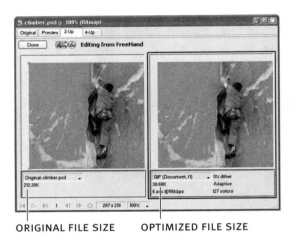

ORIGINAL FILE SIZE   OPTIMIZED FILE SIZE

5) Select the right pane. Then from the Settings pop-up menu on the Optimize panel, choose JPEG-Better Quality.

If you don't see the Optimize panel, choose Window > Optimize. Compare the two images. Visually, they should look the same, but the file size of the JPEG image is much smaller.

SETTINGS POP-UP MENU

6) Click the Done button.

Your file is optimized and saved. The PSD image in your document is replaced with the optimized version.

7) Save your file.

ON YOUR OWN

Using the second master page, add three more pages to your slide show. Use the remaining pictures (downhill2.psd, downhill8.psd, and freeride1.psd) in the Media folder for the pictures on the page. Use the path guide to place each of the images; then test your movie.

EDITING MACROMEDIA FLASH FROM FREEHAND

Once you have several slides in your presentation, you show your creation to a co-worker. Your co-worker suggests that you fade in the images as each new page opens. You like the idea, and your co-worker volunteers to use Flash to create a movie of an image for you to try in your presentation. In this task, you will import the Flash movie and then use the FreeHand to Flash link to make changes to the movie. This section is only a quick introduction to Flash. There are numerous books on Flash if you want more detailed information on using that application.

If you don't have Macromedia Flash, you can use the trial version of the software included on the CD that accompanies this book.

1) Delete the climber image on page 2.

The movie clip you import in the next step should be placed in exactly the same location as this image.

2) Choose File > Import and locate the pic1.swf file in the Media folder within the Lesson09 folder. Place the file on the page using the path guide.

The movie clip appears to be blank because to create an image that fades in, the first frame of the movie must be set to 0 percent opacity. Each frame of the movie then increases in opacity until the movie reaches the last frame, which is set to 100 percent opacity.

3) Save your file and test the movie.

When you go to page 2, you see the image quickly fade in, but the fading continually loops. In the next step, you will edit the movie clip in Flash to slow the fade and add a stop action at the end of the fade.

4) Select the movie clip on the page and then click the Flash link button on the Object panel. Select the pic1.fla file in the Media folder when asked to locate the Flash file.

You need to edit the original Flash file for the movie clip.

FreeHand opens Flash in a special editing mode. Notice the Done button at the top left of the Flash timeline.

DONE BUTTON ———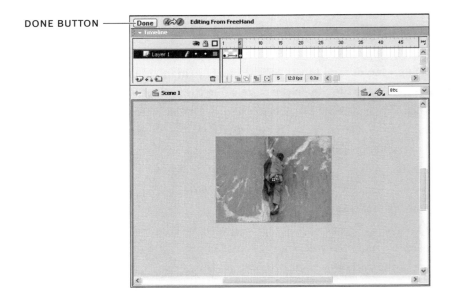

In the Flash timeline, you see **keyframes** (the circles) at frames 1 and 5. This movie takes five frames to complete. If you click the last frame, you see the final image on the stage. If you click the first frame, you see a blank image. Between the two keyframes, you see a right-pointing arrow. This arrow indicates that a **motion tween** was applied between the two frames. A motion tween in Flash is like a blend in FreeHand. If you release the blend to layers, each layer in FreeHand represents a frame in the Flash movie.

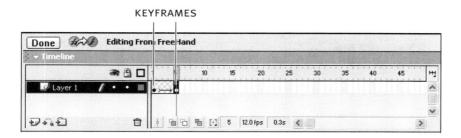

Your first task is to increase the time of the movie to slow the fade action.

5) Select the keyframe in frame 5 and drag it to frame 10.

When you release the mouse button, the arrow representing the motion tween expands across the added frames.

NOTE *The frame is black when the keyframe is selected.*

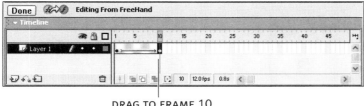

DRAG TO FRAME 10

Next you need to add an action to stop the movie once it completes the fade-in action.

6) Right-click (Windows) or Control-click (Mac OS) the last keyframe. From the context menu, choose Actions.

You can also select the last keyframe and then choose Window > Actions.

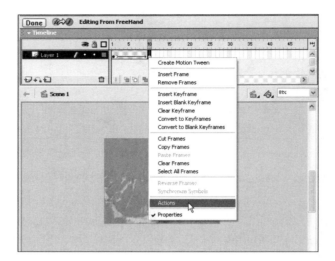

7) Double-click the Stop action under Movie Control. Then close the Actions panel.

A Stop action is added to the last keyframe of your movie. This causes the movie to stop when it gets to this frame.

NOTE *If you don't see the Stop action on the Actions panel, click Actions and then click Movie Control. These items open or close (like folders) to display their contents.*

STOP ACTION

8) Click Done.

Your Flash file is saved, and the movie clip is exported and updated in your FreeHand file.

9) Save your file and test your movie.

Now the image fades in nicely and remains in place when the fade-in is complete.

USING MACROMEDIA FLASH TO CREATE NEW MOVIES

You decide you like the fading action and want to change the other images in your presentation to fade in as well. Instead of creating a new Flash movie for each image, you can use the Swap feature in Flash to replace the images in the first and last frames. The motion tween and Stop action remain, and you then just need to save the file with a new name. To do this, you need to open the movie in Flash—you can't use the FreeHand to Flash link as you did in the preceding task.

1) In Flash, open the pic1.fla file in the Media folder within the Lesson09 folder.
You want to locate the file you updated in the last task, not the original file from the CD.

2) Select frame 1 and then click the image on the stage.
The image in frame 1 appears blank, but you'll see a blue outline of the image on the stage. Click within the blue outline.

In Flash, the stage is the area where you place all of your elements for your movie. In FreeHand, only objects with the page area are included in the final output of the document. In Flash, only objects within the stage area appear in the final movie.

STAGE AREA —

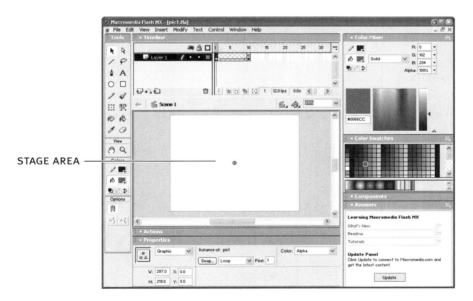

323

3) On the Properties panel, click Swap. From the Swap Symbol dialog box, select pic2 and then click OK.

In Flash, you can animate only symbols. As in FreeHand, symbols are stored in a library. The four images you are using in this lesson were converted to symbols for you and saved in this document.

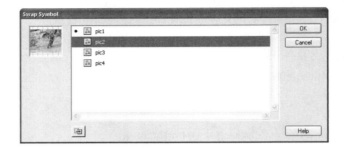

4) Select frame 10 and then repeat steps 2 and 3.

The first and last frames are replaced with the new image.

5) Choose File > Save As and rename this file *pic2.fla*.

Once you replace the images in the movie, you need to rename the file.

6) Press Ctrl+Enter (Windows) or Command+Return (Mac OS) to test the movie in Flash.

The test movie shortcut is the same as in FreeHand. When you test the movie in Flash, a SWF file is created for you. You can use that file in your FreeHand document.

ON YOUR OWN

Repeat the process to create new Flash movies for pic3 and pic4. Then replace the images in your FreeHand document with the new movie clips you just created and test your completed slide show.

WHAT YOU HAVE LEARNED

In this lesson, you have:

- Assigned a keyboard shortcut to improve your productivity (pages 280–282)

- Created a drawing for animation (pages 283–286)

- Created a blend for the animation drawing (pages 287–289)

- Released a blend to layers (pages 289–294)

- Set the export options and exported a file as a SWF movie (pages 294–297)

- Joined a blend to a path (pages 297–300)

- Animated text (page 301)

- Created a master page to use as a background for several pages (pages 302–306)

- Used the Action tool to add interactivity to a button (pages 306–308)

- Used the Navigation panel to change the actions of a button (pages 308–309)

- Edited a master page (pages 309–313)

- Changed a path to a guide (pages 315–315)

- Used Macromedia Fireworks to optimize graphics in your FreeHand document (pages 316–318)

- Linked to a Macromedia Flash movie from FreeHand and then edited the movie in Flash (pages 319–322)

- Used Macromedia Flash to create movies for your FreeHand document (pages 323–324)

creating
web pages

LESSON 10

As you've seen as you've worked through the lessons in this book, FreeHand is a premiere drawing program. With the continuing expansion of the Internet, people increasingly want to create web sites as well as print materials, and the drawing capabilities of FreeHand are as suitable for web pages as for printed documents. Although it was not designed as a complete web-production tool or as a replacement for applications such as Macromedia Dreamweaver or Macromedia Flash, FreeHand can play an important part in web-site creation.

Typically, in creating a web site, a designer draws a site diagram and then creates a sketch or digital composite (a comp) that shows more detail of a sample page of the site. Using the Connector tool in FreeHand, you can easily draw a site diagram. Then you can use FreeHand to design a page, or pages, of the site. Once you create your site design and pages, you can export the pages as a PDF file. You can even export the pages in HTML format and display them in a browser for the approval process.

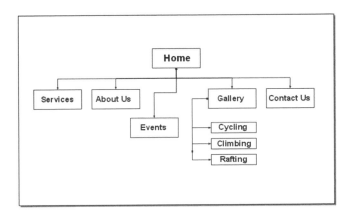

You can use the Connector tool to quickly draw the connecting lines between the boxes in this site map.

In this lesson, you will draw a site map and then create pages for a site. You will use the Navigation panel to add links to buttons and add an e-mail link to some text. Then you will export your pages as an HTML file.

WHAT YOU WILL LEARN

In this lesson, you will:

- Use the Connector tool
- Change the style of the Connector tool
- Add a note to a PDF file from FreeHand
- Use FreeHand's Paste Contents (Windows) or Paste Inside (Mac OS) feature
- Add URL links
- Export pages as HTML files

APPROXIMATE TIME

This lesson takes approximately 1 hour to complete.

LESSON FILES

Media Files:

Lesson10\Media\about_us.rtf
Lesson10\Media\contact_us.rtf
Lesson10\Media\home_page_text.rtf
Lesson10\Media\air.jpg
Lesson10\Media\climbing3.jpg
Lesson10\Media\downhill1.jpg
Lesson10\Media\racer.jpg
Lesson10\Media\racer2.jpg
Lesson10\Media\rider3.jpg
Lesson10\Media\riding1.jpg
Lesson10\Media\trackrace.jpg

Starting Files:

Lesson10\Start\site_concept_start.fh11

Completed Projects:

Lesson10\Completed\site_concept.fh11
Lesson10\Completed\site_map.fh11
Lesson10\Completed\site_map.pdf
Lesson10\Completed
*   FreeHand HTML Output*

USING THE CONNECTOR TOOL

The **Connector tool** creates connector lines that dynamically link objects together. Connector lines adjust themselves when you move the connected objects. You can use the tool to create organization charts, labels for diagrams, and site maps, as you will do in this task. Once you create the connector lines, you can use the Object panel to modify the stroke properties of the lines.

1) Create a new file and name it *site_map.fh11*. Change the page orientation to Landscape and then save the file in your Projects folder.

You will draw several rectangles to represent each page of the site and then use the Connector tool to draw lines that represent the links between the pages.

2) Draw a rectangle at the top of the page to represent the home page of your site.

Although the size of the rectangle is not critical, you want it large enough to contain some descriptive text. For example, draw your rectangle 120 pixels by 50 pixels.

You will use the Align panel in the next step to center the rectangle horizontally on the page.

3) On the Align panel, select Align to Page, choose No Change from the horizontal alignment pop-up menu, and choose Align Center from the vertical alignment pop-up menu; then click Apply (Windows) or Align (Mac OS).

Your rectangle is centered horizontally on the page.

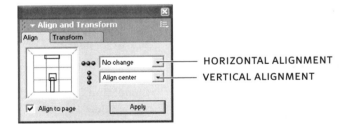

HORIZONTAL ALIGNMENT

VERTICAL ALIGNMENT

4) Draw another rectangle about the same size as the first one. Place this rectangle below the first and on the left side of the page.

This rectangle represents a page of the site that the home page links to.

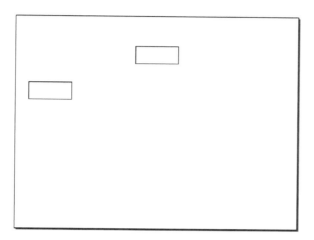

5) Use the Alt-drag or Option-drag method to create a copy of this rectangle and move the copy to the right side of the page. Hold down Shift as you drag to constrain the movement to a straight line.

Ultimately, you want five rectangles, all the same size and equally distant from one another, spaced across the page. You could have moved the copy of the rectangle slightly apart from the original rectangle and then used the Duplicate command to make the other three copies, spacing them similarly. If you use this method, it is difficult to determine how far to drag the copies to space them equally. In the next step, you will use the Blend tool to create and position the additional copies. The Blend tool calculates the distance between two objects and mathematically determines for you the spacing between any number of items that you want to place between the two objects.

6) Select the Blend tool and drag from the first rectangle to the second rectangle.

The **Blend tool** lets you easily create blends from one object to another by dragging the blend line from one object to another. Notice that you did not need to select either of the objects you wanted to blend together; you just need to drag from the boundary of one rectangle to the boundary of the other. When you drag from the first object, you see the blend line, which you then use to connect to the other object.

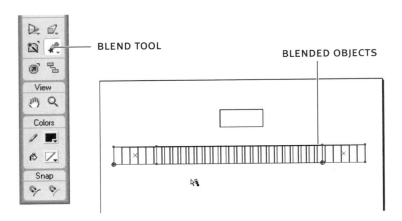

BLEND TOOL

BLENDED OBJECTS

> **N O T E** *You could also have selected both objects and used the Blend command as you've done in previous lessons.*

7) On the Object panel, change the number of steps in the blend to 3.

You now have five equally spaced rectangles across the page.

> **N O T E** *You already have two objects on the page. The number of steps in the blend, plus the two original objects, gives you a total of five objects.*

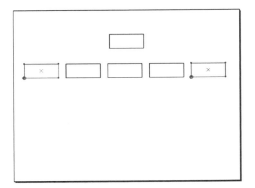

8) Choose Modify > Ungroup. Then select the middle rectangle and choose Modify > Ungroup again.

Objects in blends are grouped by default. When you ungroup the blend, the objects created from the blend are still grouped, so you need to ungroup those objects as well. In the next step, you will use the Connector tool to draw lines between the rectangles. You can't use the Connector tool between objects in a blend.

9) Use the Text tool and type *Home* as the label for the top rectangle. Move the text block to the center of the top rectangle. Add text blocks within the rectangles on the bottom row using the following labels: *Services, About Us, Events, Gallery*, and *Contact Us*. Group each rectangle with its text block.

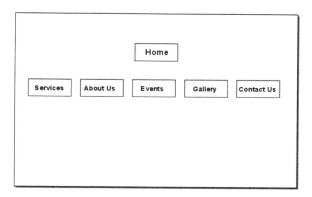

10) Choose the Connector tool on the Tools panel and drag from the bottom of the Home rectangle to the top of the Services rectangle.

The pointer of the Connector tool contains a plus sign and a connector arrow. Position the plus sign on the bottom line of the first rectangle. Release the mouse button when you see the connecting line. Notice that you did not need to select the top rectangle to use the tool.

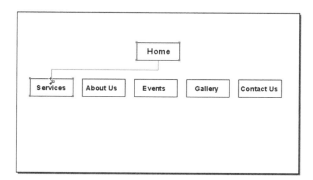

331

The Connector tool displays an arrow at the end of the line and a circle at the start of the line. You can use the Object panel to change the stroke properties of each line. Use the defaults for now. In the next task, you will change the connector style, and that will change all the connector lines on the page.

11) Repeat step 10 for the remaining four rectangles.

As you connect each rectangle to the Home rectangle, FreeHand merges the connecting lines, resulting in one line that branches to the five rectangles.

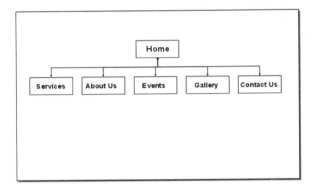

12) Drag one of the bottom rectangles down and to the left.

Notice that the connector line moves and changes shape as you move one of the connected objects.

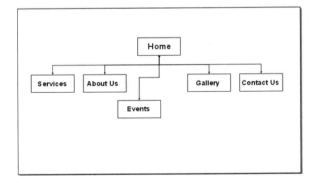

13) Draw a smaller rectangle below the Gallery rectangle. Make two copies of this rectangle and move them below the first rectangle. Label these rectangles *Cycling*, *Rock Climbing*, **and** *Rafting*.

You can use the Alt-drag or Option-drag method to create the two copies of the rectangle. These rectangles represent pages linked from the Gallery page.

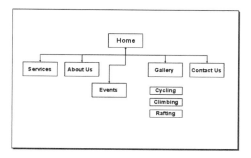

14) With the Connector tool, drag from the left side of the Gallery rectangle to the left side of each of the smaller rectangles.

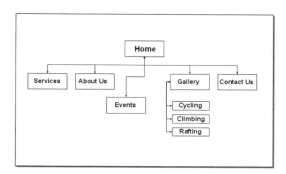

The length of the connector lines from the rectangles is set by FreeHand, but you will adjust it in the next step.

15) With the Connector tool, select one of the connector lines and then drag the handle on the connector line to the left, away from the rectangle. Repeat this step for the other lines.

When you are over the handle on the line, the pointer changes to a left-and-right pointing arrow, indicating that you can now drag the line.

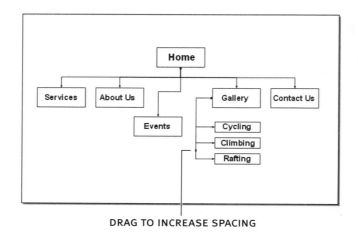

DRAG TO INCREASE SPACING

NOTE *You can reshape the connector line only by dragging a handle with the Connector tool. If you use the Pointer tool, you'll move the connector line along with the rectangle instead of reshaping the connector line.*

16) Save your file.

REDEFINING THE CONNECTOR STYLE

As you've seen, the default style for a connector line is a line with a filled circle at the start of the line and an arrow at the end of the line. You can change the look of a connector line by changing the stroke properties on the Object panel. In the previous task, you drew several connector lines. To manually change each one of the lines would take some time. An easier approach, as you will see in this task, is to edit the style that controls the look of the lines. In Lesson 3, "Colors, Gradients, and Styles," you used the Styles panel to create and save a graphic style. In this lesson, you will redefine an existing style.

1) Select one of the connector lines. On the Object panel, select the Stroke property.

You see all of the attributes for the line: the size and the color, plus options for arrowheads.

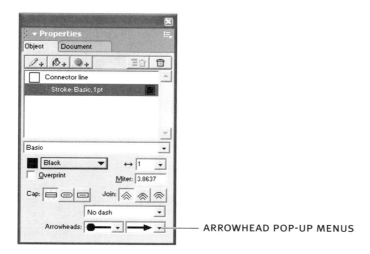

ARROWHEAD POP-UP MENUS

2) From the left Arrowheads pop-up menu, choose None.

The left pop-up menu controls the start of the line; the right pop-up menu controls the end of the line. Changing the option to None removes the circle from the start of the line for the selected stroke.

> **NOTE** *Many of your connector lines are overlapping so you may not be able to tell whether you've removed the circle. However, when you remove the circle, you may also see the line you've removed it from move slightly. When you redefine the style, all of the lines will be the same again, but now without the circle.*

3) With the connector line still selected, choose Redefine from the Styles panel Options menu. In the Redefine Style dialog box, make sure that the Normal Connector style is selected. Then click OK.

All of the connector lines in your document are updated with the new line style, and any new connector lines you draw in this document will use the new style.

NOTE *The Style panel displays a plus sign before a style name to indicate that the style for the selected item has been modified.*

POWER TIP *The start and end of the connector lines are determined by the order in which you connect the objects. If you want to reverse a connector line, you can select the line and then choose Modify > Alter Path > Reverse Direction.*

4) Save your file.

Your site map is complete. In the next task, you will use the Navigation panel to add a note to the page and then export the page as a PDF file. The note you add will be converted to a note comment in the PDF file.

ADDING A PDF NOTE

In Lesson 7, "Page Layout and Printing," you saw how easily you can export your pages as PDF documents. In that lesson, your goal was to create a document that you could send to a service bureau for printing or to a colleague for printing from another machine. In this lesson, you've created a web-site map and want to send it to a client for comments or approval. Both you and your client have Adobe Acrobat (the application, not the free Acrobat Reader), and you want to use that program to attach comments to the PDF file as you collaborate on the site design.

NOTE *You will be able to see the PDF notes in Acrobat Reader if you don't have Adobe Acrobat. If you have Adobe Acrobat, you will be able to add or edit the notes.*

Once you export your page as a PDF document, you can open the file in Adobe Acrobat and add your notes. But you can also add notes in FreeHand, before you export the page, as you will do in this task.

1) Type a title for the page. For example, type *Action Photos Site Map*. Select the text block.

Notes are added to objects on the page. You'll use the title text block as the object for the note.

2) Choose Window › Navigation to open the Navigation panel. Type a message in the Notes text box. For example, type *Joe, what do you think of this concept for the site?*

The text you type in the Notes text box appears as a note in the PDF.

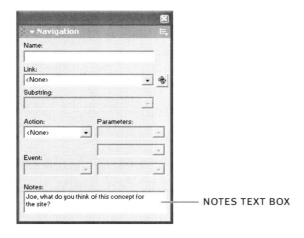 NOTES TEXT BOX

3) Type your name in the Name text box.

When you add notes in Acrobat, the user name is added to the note to identify the author of the note. In FreeHand, you need to add your name in the Name text box to activate this feature in the PDF file.

4) Choose File > Export. From the Save as Type (Windows) or Format (Mac OS) pop-up menu, choose PDF and then click Setup.

You need to specify your export settings.

5) In the PDF Export dialog box, select Export Notes and then click OK. Navigate to the Projects folder and then click Save (Windows) or Export (Mac OS).

FreeHand creates the PDF file.

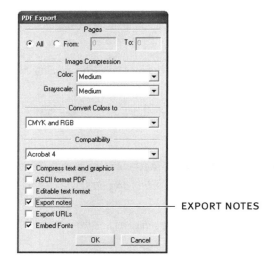

EXPORT NOTES

6) Open the PDF file in either Acrobat Reader or Adobe Acrobat. Double-click the note icon near the title.

When you open the note, you see your name in the note title and the message you entered in the Notes text box. If you are using Acrobat Reader, you can move the icon on the page, but you can't make changes to the message in the note. If you are using Adobe Acrobat, you can move the icon on the page, and you can edit the note text.

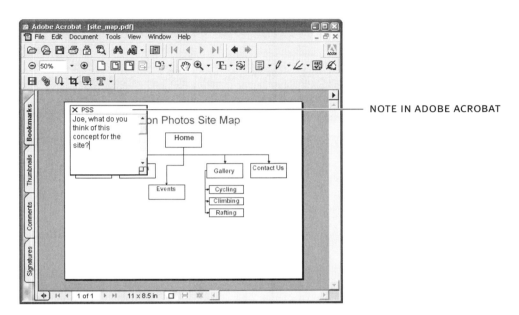

NOTE IN ADOBE ACROBAT

POWER TIP *If you return to your FreeHand document and make other changes to the document file, you can choose File > Export Again to bypass the Export dialog box. FreeHand uses the settings from the last export operation.*

7) Close the PDF file and then save and close your site_map.fh11 file.

PASTING AN IMAGE IN A PATH

You can use the **Paste Contents** or **Paste Inside** feature of FreeHand to fill a closed path with another vector or bitmap graphic. Only the part of the object located inside the closed path is displayed; the part of the graphic that extends outside the path is not displayed or printed. Pasting inside a path is also referred to as creating a **clipping path**.

In this task, you will import some graphics and then paste them inside existing rectangles on the page.

1) Open the site_concept_start.fh11 file in the Start folder. Choose File > Save As, rename the file *site_concept.fh11,* and save the file in the Projects folder.
The document contains buttons and some text. On the right of the page is a filmstrip graphic. You will use the paste inside feature to add images within the rectangle on the filmstrip.

2) Import the file air.jpg file from the Media folder within the Lesson10 folder and place it over the top rectangle at the right side of the page.
You want the image directly over the rectangle. After you paste the image within the path of the rectangle, you will still be able to move it if you want to change its position.

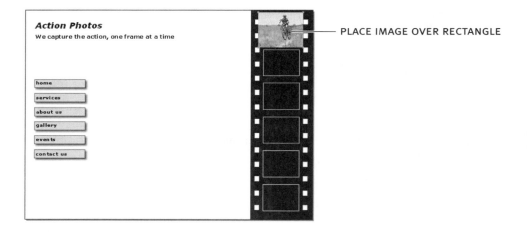

PLACE IMAGE OVER RECTANGLE

3) With the air.jpg image still selected, choose Edit > Cut. Then select the top rectangle and choose Edit > Paste Contents (Windows) or Edit > Paste Inside (Mac OS).

The image appears within the boundaries of the rectangle.

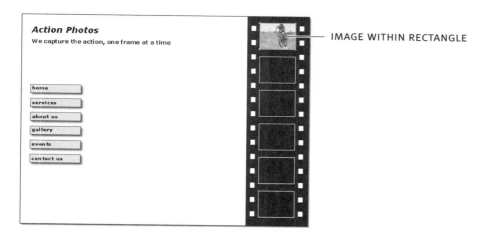

IMAGE WITHIN RECTANGLE

4) On the Object panel, select the Contents property.

The contents handle (a small blue star) appears on the image.

CONTENTS HANDLE

5) Drag the contents handle to reposition the image within the rectangle.

If you drag the image and not the contents handle, you move the rectangle, not the image within the rectangle.

N O T E *The Contents property on the Object panel must be selected for the contents handle to appear.*

6) Using the images in the Media folder, repeat steps 2 through 5 to paste images inside the remaining rectangles.

The Media folder contains several images for you to use. Choose any of the images you want to use on your page. In the next step, you will replace one of the images.

7) Select one of the rectangles with an image and then choose Edit > Cut Contents.

The image is removed from the contents of the rectangle and placed on the page.

8) Delete the image and import a new image. Paste the new image inside the empty rectangle.

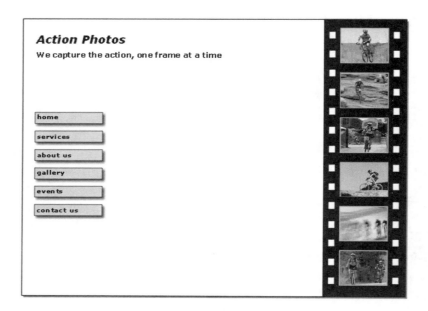

9) Select all of the objects in the filmstrip and group them.

In a later task, you will export your file as an HTML document. FreeHand exports grouped items as a single graphic when exporting as HTML.

10) Save your file.

342

ADDING URL LINKS

You've completed the web page design. Now you want to add links to the buttons. You add links to objects on a page using the Navigation panel. Not only can you add links to navigate to other pages in the document, you can also add links to external web sites and even links to send an e-mail message. Of course, you will need Internet access to check your links. Once you add the links to the buttons, you will export the pages as an HTML file.

First, you need to add another page to your document so you can test the links you add to the buttons. The new page will use the same buttons and filmstrip graphic.

1) From the Document panel Options menu, choose Duplicate.

A new page is added to your document containing all of the objects of the first page.

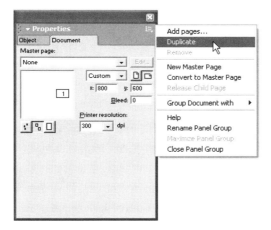

2) From the Media folder, import the home_page_text.rtf file and place the text on the first page. Import the about_us.rtf and contact_us.rtf files and place the text on the second page.

You'll use the first page as the home page of your site; the second page will be the About Us page.

3) On the first page, select the Home button, and on the Navigation panel, choose Page 1 from the Link pop-up menu. Next, on the first page, select the About Us button; then choose Page 2 from the Link pop-up menu on the Navigation panel. Repeat this process to add the links to the buttons on the second page as well.

HTML links to the specified pages will be added to these button graphics when you export your document as HTML.

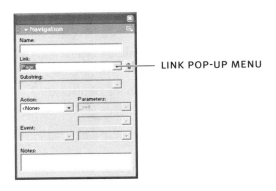

— LINK POP-UP MENU

In the next step, you will add an e-mail link to the e-mail address on page 2.

4) Select the text on page 2 that contains the e-mail address. On the Navigation panel, in the Link text box, type *mailto:info@actionphotos-online.com*.

Note that the entry in this example is not a valid e-mail address; you may want to use your e-mail address instead. Be sure to include the mailto: prefix. This is the HTML format for adding e-mail links to pages and must be entered before the e-mail address.

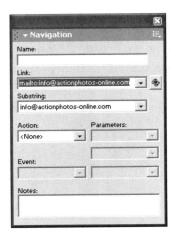

5) Save your file.

EXPORTING AS HTML

Although it is not designed to compete with Dreamweaver, FreeHand does a good job of creating HTML pages, but it does have limitations. For example, in the last task you added links to buttons using the Navigation panel. When you check your links in the browser, you'll see that the buttons work as expected, but FreeHand offers no way for you to provide alternate text for a link—that is, text that appears when the user rolls over a button or image. As you build your pages in FreeHand, remember that you are using Freehand as a design tool for your web pages. Once the approval process is complete, you can take the FreeHand HTML files into Dreamweaver for fine-tuning.

1) Choose File > Publish as HTML. In the HTML Output dialog box, click Setup.

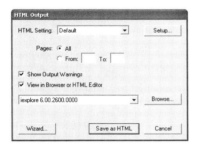

In the HTML Setup dialog box, you specify the method for creating the HTML pages from your document. The default settings create a folder on your desktop. This folder is titled FreeHand HTML Output. All of the HTML pages and the exported images are placed within that folder.

2) From the Vector Art pop-up menu, choose GIF. Click OK.

The FreeHand default file format for exporting vector art is SWF. You've added links to the buttons on the page and want the button links to work in all browsers, so you want your buttons exported as GIF files. If you export your buttons as SWF files, your users will need the Flash plug-in to view your buttons.

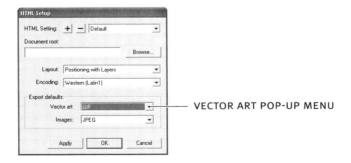

VECTOR ART POP-UP MENU

345

3) In the HTML Output dialog box, select View in Browser or HTML Editor. Choose your browser from the browser pop-up menu.

If your browser does not appear in the pop-up menu, click Browse and locate your browser.

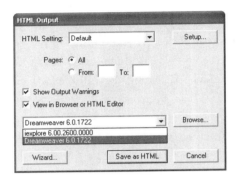

NOTE *If you have Macromedia Dreamweaver installed, you can select it from the pop-up menu instead of a browser. When FreeHand completes exporting your file, it will open Dreamweaver for you.*

4) Click Save as HTML.

FreeHand exports your files and saves them in the specified folder. Your home page opens in the browser (or HTML editor) you selected in step 3.

If FreeHand encounters problems when exporting your files, it displays the HTML Output Warnings dialog box listing all of the errors.

TIP *If you make changes to your FreeHand document and export it again as HTML, you may need to refresh your browser or reload the file in your browser to update the images.*

WHAT YOU HAVE LEARNED

In this lesson, you have:

- Used the Connector tool to show links in a site map (pages 328–334)

- Changed the end style of the connector line (pages 334–336)

- Added a note to a PDF file from FreeHand (pages 337–339)

- Used Paste Contents or Paste Inside to display images inside path objects (pages 340–342)

- Added URL links to buttons (pages 343–344)

- Exported your pages as an HTML file (pages 345–346)

index

trail option (releasing to layers), 291
Transform command (Window menu), 160
transparency lens, 163
Trash icon, 20

U

Ungroup command (Modify menu), 69
ungrouped ellipse, 69
Union command, 126
Units menu, 13
URL links, web pages, 343–344

V

Vector effects, 195
Vertical orientation (text), 173
view magnification, changing, 24–25
View menu
  Fit to Page command, 11
  Guides command
    Edit, 135
    Show, 14
    Snap to Guides, 137
  Page Rulers command (Show), 12
  Snap to Object command, 21
  Text Rulers command, 52

W

web pages
  adding PDF notes, 337–339
  Connector tool, 328–334
  defining connector style, 334–336
  exporting as HTML, 345–346
  pasting image in path, 340–342
  URL links, 343–344
web-ready colors (color cubes), 303
web-safe colors, 80
websites
  Kelleigh, Ian, 283
  PANTONE, 129

Window menu
  Align command, 9, 112
  Color Mixer command, 81
  Library command, 244
  Movie command
    Settings, 291
    Test, 292
  Navigation command, 308
  Object command, 18, 36
  Styles command, 91
  Swatches command, 82
  Toolbars command
    Envelope, 190
    Info, 15
    Status, 13
    Text, 60
    Xtras Tools, 79
  Tools command, 8
  Transform command, 160
Wireframe setting, extrude control, 185

X

Xtras menu
  Animate command (Release to Layers), 293
  Create command (Blend), 254
  Distort command (Add Points), 284
  Path Operations command (Insert Path), 303

Z

zero points, 204–205
zoom
  changing view, 24–25
  magnification
    glass, special effects, 160–167
    lens, 163
Zoom tool, 25

WWW.PEACHPIT.COM

Quality How-to Computer Books

Visit Peachpit Press on the Web at www.peachpit.com

- Check out new feature articles each Monday: excerpts, interviews, tips, and plenty of how-tos

- Find any Peachpit book by title, series, author, or topic on the Books page

- See what our authors are up to on the News page: signings, chats, appearances, and more

- Meet the Peachpit staff and authors in the About section: bios, profiles, and candid shots

- Use Resources to reach our academic, sales, customer service, and tech support areas and find out how to become a Peachpit author

Peachpit.com is also the place to:

- Chat with our authors online
- Take advantage of special Web-only offers
- Get the latest info on new books

Sidebar navigation:
About
News
Books
Features
Resources
Order
Find
Welcome!

Macromedia Tech Support: http://www.macromedia.com/support

LICENSING AGREEMENT

The information in this book is for informational use only and is subject to change without notice. Macromedia, Inc., and Macromedia Press assume no responsibility for errors or inaccuracies that may appear in this book. The software described in the book is furnished under license and may be used or copied only in accordance with terms of the license.

The software files on the CD-ROM included here are copyrighted by Macromedia, Inc. You have the non-exclusive right to use these programs and files. You may use them on one computer at a time. You may not transfer the files from one computer to another over a network. You may transfer the files onto a single hard disk so long as you can prove ownership of the original CD-ROM.

You may not reverse engineer, decompile, or disassemble the software. You may not modify or translate the software or distribute copies of the software without the written consent of Macromedia, Inc.

Opening the disc package means you accept the licensing agreement. For installation instructions, see the ReadMe file on the CD-ROM.